THE NEW
PARADIGM
IN BUSINESS

Beverlee Aaron

A NEW CONSCIOUSNESS READER

This *New Consciousness Reader* is part of a new series of original and classic writing by renowned experts on leading-edge concepts in personal development, psychology, spiritual growth, and healing.

Other books in this series include:

THE NEW PARADIGM IN BUSINESS

Emerging Strategies for Leadership and Organizational Change

EDITED BY

MICHAEL RAY
AND **ALAN RINZLER**

for the World Business Academy

JEREMY P. TARCHER / PERIGEE

To all of those who are dedicated to developing and implementing the emerging paradigm in their lives and in business.

Jeremy P. Tarcher/Perigee Books
are published by
The Putnam Publishing Group
200 Madison Avenue
New York, NY 10016

Jeremy P. Tarcher, Inc.
5858 Wilshire Blvd., Suite 200
Los Angeles, CA 90036

Published simultaneously in Canada

Library of Congress Cataloging-in-Publication Data

The new paradigm in business : emerging strategies for leadership and
    organizational change / edited by Michael Ray and Alan Rinzler for
    the World Business Academy.
        p.   cm.
    ISBN 0-87477-726-7 (pbk. : acid-free paper)
    1. Industrial management.   2. Industrial management—Case studies.
I. Ray, Michael L.   II. Rinzler, Alan.   III. World Business Academy.
HD31.N4542   1993   92-26205 CIP
658.4—dc20

Design by Irving Perkins Associates
Printed in the United States of America

1   2   3   4   5   6   7   8   9   10

This book is printed on acid-free paper.

ACKNOWLEDGMENTS

Putting together an anthology is like completing a jigsaw puzzle in which every part must make a beautiful picture in itself while still contributing to a fine overall image of what is usually a constantly changing field. Each piece is made by a different artist and the editors somehow have to make certain that while individual expression is maintained, the total package is one that is consistent and gives the best view of the field possible.

Since both of us have been involved a number of times in this process in the past, we know that the only thing that makes it possible is help. The most important comes from the contributors themselves, and we certainly want to thank most profusely those for this book. They were generous, patient, creative, and gave us the best that is available for understanding and living in the transition that is occuring in business today.

The original idea for this book came from many sources, but particularly from conversations between Rinaldo Brutoco and Jeremy Tarcher. Perhaps the greatest single aid for getting it done came in the person of John Renesch, the managing director of the World Business Academy. His counsel, urging, suggestions, wisdom, and assistance carried us along at many points, even after he left his post at the WBA to head New Leaders Press. For all this he has our gratitude.

We also want to thank our editor at Tarcher, Rick Benzel, for both his patience and his lack of patience with us as we worked with this book. Without his outbursts as well as his editing, we would have had much less to be proud of here. Marjorie Kelly at *Business Ethics* exemplified the highest values and the humanity of the emerging paradigm in her work with us. Sylvia Lorton at Stanford University gave us key assistance at critical times. And we both thank our families, particularly our spouses, for putting up with this effort and giving us inspiration.

The members and fellows of the World Business Academy, many of whom are directly represented in these pages, deserve our thanks also for sponsoring this book and continuing to support the explorations and changes that must occur in these times. Perhaps the best way we can thank them is to suggest that readers not already involved do so by calling the Academy offices at 415/342-2387 or by contacting Michael Ray at Stanford University.

Finally, our hearts go out to all those who in his or her own way are dedicated to developing and implementing the emerging paradigm in business. It is to them that we dedicate this book.

CONTENTS

FOREWORD: SCULPTING A NEW BUSINESS PARADIGM

When asked how he could so miraculously carve warm, emotion-laden human forms from cold, lifeless marble, Michelangelo Buonarroti responded that he never carved anything *in* marble. Rather, he revealed, his technique was to merely "chip away" the excess marble from the form already within the marble, so it could be freed. His task was to liberate the form *from* the marble, not to carve his abstract concepts into it. This book has the same goal: liberating from the marble slab of current business practices those forms that will empower human society and create a sustainable global economy.

The post–World War II, hierarchical model of the business enterprise, as previously taught and practiced for decades at business schools throughout the world, has, in part, been successful in creating the explosion of material wealth of the industrialized world throughout the past fifty years. Whether the system was ideal for its time, or even desirable, is a matter of some debate, which need not be examined here. What is indisputable is that, for whatever good or bad that system has wrought, it is no longer possible to continue in the same way. In fact, it would be literally suicidal to continue employing the same business model, as can clearly be discerned by the fact that our current application of that model is destroying the planet. Due to industrial and technological developments, we find food not fit to eat, water not fit to drink, air not fit to breathe, and, now, we can't even safely walk in the sunshine. Historically, business has been blamed for these challenges. The point of this book is not to blame but to look forward, to look for answers.

At the World Business Academy, we believe that of all social institutions only *business* has the power to facilitate the solutions to these and other challenges with which we are now confronted. It is also our belief that the ability of business to resolve these perilous challenges translates into a *responsibility* for business people to act as trustees for human society.

As noted in the Academy's Premises, business is the engine of modern societies and will play a dominant role in shaping the future. Although many people may question the historical dedication of business to serve the common good, very few would challenge the enormous energy and power that business institutions wield globally. We are aware that business executives already comprise an informal worldwide economic network; that the challenges and rewards of business have attracted some of the most competent and innovative people alive; that business organizations are highly adaptable and flexible; and that the long-term success of business ultimately depends upon the effective use of resources for the benefit of the societies that business serves, in order for those societies to continue to flourish and utilize the goods and services business has to offer. Clearly, business has the capacity to play an innovative leadership role in creating a positive, sustainable future.

Most individuals in the industrial world spend their time inside business organizations. Business is the place where most of us have our greatest daily contact with other human beings. When our schools fail to educate our children properly for the work force, business must do the training—a multibillion-dollar annual expense in the United States alone. It is also in business that most of us expend our creative energy and where we form the relationships that most influence our daily conduct. It would be folly to fail to see the role business can, and must, play in the development of human beings to their fullest expression. In fact, the Academy's vision is that many leaders soon will come to see the primary role of business settings as incubators of the human spirit, rather than factories for the production of mere material goods and services.

Why should business, with all its enormous capabilities, choose human development over the short-term pursuit of profit? One reason was given by the eighteenth-century essayist Edmund Burke when he wrote, "All that is necessary for evil to triumph is that good men (and women) shall do nothing."

Another is even more fundamental to the very nature of business. Since the first grain merchant provided a valuable service by exchanging an excess of grain grown in one region for products that could be returned to the grain farmer who supplied them, business has been a discipline of service. Those companies prosper most, and are more clearly aligned with the fundamental role of business, that choose to serve society, rather than abuse it. And, at this time in human history, the global family can be better served by business than by any other institution of human society.

Western Society has progressed considerably since the phrase was first coined—"The business of business is business." If that ever was true, it is clearly no longer true today. The business of business is to be responsible for the whole of creation, for the well-being of the earth and all its creatures. The Academy members believe that as business people we have the capability and duty to assure the global community's safe transition to the next stage of history.

How will that be achieved? Will we replace the conventional wisdom of yesterday with some equally conventional, new theory that we will uniformly apply to all enterprises? Is there some all-encompassing formula that, once discovered, will relieve us of the task of further explorations into the unknown? Regrettably, the answer to those questions is a resounding "no." Not only are the business nostrums of the past inapplicable to our present state, but the concept of universally applicable "business solutions" is equally antiquated.

The raw resources of business await the hand of the sculptor to "chip away" excess materialistic practices to enable the authentic spirit of business to emerge, the spirit of service that nurtures and empowers human society rather than enslaves it. Business leaders can replace simplistic goals, which are viewed as "pragmatic," with corporate and individual vision; rigidity with flexible business cultures; management hierarchies with individual empowerment; logic-driven analysis with a new blend of analysis and attuned intuition; competition with cooperation and co-creation; aggressive values with harmony, trust, honesty and compassion; and short-term focus with the "seventh generation" test of America's Iroquois Indians.

We as business leaders can rediscover the value of wholeness. We can learn to be guided by our inner wisdom. We can operate from a broad awareness of enlightened self-interest.

These are the goals of the World Business Academy. As originally conceived and currently operated, the Academy is a forum for ideas and theories pertinent to the dawning business paradigm. It is a forum where ideas about the evolving "best practices" for business can be shared and examined among a peer group of corporate practitioners and academic catalysts. The ongoing dialogue has developed into numerous conferences around the world, an expanding network of Academy chapters reaching five continents, and the quarterly publication of a journal of leading-edge articles, called *Perspectives*. It also has culminated in this volume, our first book, articulating a few of the options growing from within the new business paradigm, emerging in business enterprises of all sizes, in all countries of the world, and in the consciousness of individuals at all levels within organizations.

We trust that the provocative perceptions that follow will impel you to determine which practices in your organization are "excessive," environmentally or personally, or incongruent with your values. We also hope the articles will challenge you to identify those business practices that honor your core value systems. We encourage your personal evaluation of how these ideas might foster your effectiveness in offering the goods or services you supply to the marketplace and in building a sense of community, a reciprocal relationship among your colleagues, your customers and others. Whether or not you subsequently choose to join the Academy to participate directly in our dialogue, we would sincerely appreciate your feedback on how these concepts fare in the crucible of your own workplace experience.

In the Academy, we are humbled by the knowledge that we are faced with many good questions and are merely groping our way together toward the solutions that are beginning to take shape. It is our objective for these solutions, these new forms of business organization, to be chiseled as uniquely and skillfully as each of Michelangelo's human forms released from the unsculpted marble.

Writing as one member of the Academy, I believe we human beings are positioned at the threshold of the period of greatest abundance the world has ever known. The principal question for business to ask is: How can we get from this world, where we are constantly surging up against our limits, a world of "less," to the world of "more" that awaits us? Even more significant to consider, the abundance we are about to co-create is more than mere material wealth, which itself will mushroom to heights beyond our dreams; the abundance that awaits us will substantially influence *every* aspect of human awareness. I personally believe we are entering an era of reintegration of *what* we do in the marketplace with *who* we are as spiritually developing human beings. The human spirit is what remains when the excess is chipped away.

As we approach the millennium, the necessity for the transformation of our goals and values intensifies. I believe that the metamorphosis need not be a struggle, but an adventure, a passion, a mission, a work of art. You, together with everyone else engaged in enlightened commerce, are the sculptors. We hope that the individual tools we are sharing in this book will prove helpful as you embrace the opportunity to free the spirited form that lies within.

Rinaldo S. Brutoco
Founder
World Business Academy

THE NEW
PARADIGM
IN BUSINESS

INTRODUCTION: WHAT IS THE NEW PARADIGM IN BUSINESS?

If you sense that a profound change is happening in the business world, but you're not quite sure what it is; if you've noticed that old visions and strategies don't seem to work anymore; if you feel deeply that you need to learn new ways to lead, to express and maintain values, be creative, and foster community—you are not alone. Throughout the world, people in business—including owners, managers, and employees—are changing the way they think and work. They are engaged in a transformation that some have said is as great as any in history. This shift is leading to the new paradigm in business. But what is this new paradigm exactly and why is it happening? And why does it sometimes seem so difficult to achieve?

"BROTHER, CAN YOU PARADIGM?"

In this book we use the word "paradigm" in a precise way. Look in any dictionary and you'll find a definition such as "a pattern, example, or model." But with the publication of Thomas Kuhn's book, *The Structure of Scientific Revolutions*, the word paradigm came to mean the fundamental assumptions about the nature of the world, particularly in the sciences. In fact, Kuhn said that a field wasn't a science unless it had a paradigm. Furthermore, a scientific revolution occurs when there is a paradigm shift—when the old set of assumptions no longer holds true, and a small band of scientists develops a new paradigm that everyone recognizes and applies, until yet another change seems necessary again.

The last great paradigm shift was the Copernican or scientific revolution in which Copernicus overturned the Ptolemaic paradigm that the earth was the center of the known universe. This change had enormous effects on science, and on all the reigning institutions of the day, especially the church, as it eventually relinquished its leading role in society to science.

Of course, it took well over a century for Copernicus's ideas to have an effect, even in science. Copernicus probably formulated his ideas in 1530, and they weren't published until 1543 when he was on his

I

deathbed. Eventually they led to Kepler's laws (the first two were published in 1609), Galileo's ideas about the solar system, which resulted in his trial for heresy in 1633, Newton's laws (including the discovery of gravitation), which he developed between 1664 and 1666, and the scientific revolution that resulted in the dominant paradigm today, not only in science but also in every aspect of our culture and everyday life.

The scientific paradigm is based on "objective" knowledge developed from such methods as experimentation and controlled observation. All truth, according to this paradigm, exists outside of the human individual. The phrase, "I'll believe it when I see it," is a common one in our culture, whether used by scientists or not. We have depended on outer knowledge or experts for truth, no matter how much we may feel otherwise. This dependence on outer knowledge and senses is the societally approved basis for our behavior and opinions, whether we are engaged in science or not.

But at the beginning of this century, science itself began to change, primarily with quantum mechanics in physics. Instead of Newton's depiction of the universe as a large number of discrete objects working like some giant clockwork or machine, physicists such as Einstein and Bohr, who examined what happens at the speed of light and searched for the smallest particles, began to discover that, as the ancient sages told us, the world is virtually nothing but energy, one whole with an infinite number of intimately connected, always varying parts, rather than discrete permanent entities.

As the twentieth century developed, discovery after discovery in physics depicted a far different world than the one most of us assume as we go through our everyday lives. Quantum physics led to a system that reveals Newton's predictions to be only approximations, holding true only in such large-scale events as the movements of planets. In the world of the very small or the very fast, Newtonian mechanics are totally wrong.

The world of mechanistic science consists of large, solid objects with empty space between them. The world of the new science is made up of vibrations and energy waves. What appears to be solid matter is actually the mutual vibration of particles so small and relatively so far apart that they dwarf astronomers' pronouncements of the distances between planets and galaxies. The revolutionary implication of Einstein's simple equation, $E = mc^2$, is that there is no true distinction between energy and matter.

Throughout this century, the changes in physics were paralleled by similar discoveries in other sciences. In chemistry at the end of the nineteenth century the discoveries of electrons and radioactivity actually moved the field closer to physics. Theorists began to apply the work of physicists on atomic structure to the study of molecular structure. This type of work was typified by the discovery of polymers—natural (silk, cellulose, natural rubbers, and proteins) and synthetic (plastics) compounds of high molecular weight. Polymers represent a turning point in chemistry because they are made up of millions of repeated linked units, each a simple, light molecule. Their often nonlinear combinations supported the idea of connections, and they became a model for a whole systems view.

Later, Belgian physical chemist Ilya Prigogine announced his theory of dissipative structures, for which he won the 1977 Nobel prize in chemistry. He used the polymer process of crystallization as one illustration to negate Newton's second law of thermodynamics. Newton posited that everything in the world is in a process of entropy or breakdown; Prigogine showed that the universe is in a constant process of creation rather than breakdown. Just as in polymers, where molecules cooperate in vast patterns in reaction to new situations, Prigogine posited and found many situations in which the creative response of the universe was apparent. Some of these even mirrored the social systems that people must face in a time of transition, when chaos and disorder eventually lead to higher levels of order.

While the scientific paradigm of objectivity had led society to trust only objective evidence and to see the world as solid discrete objects, the findings and theories of the current sciences were suggesting something else. In biology the rise of hybrids and the development of the new field of genetics in 1900 showed connections that had never been considered before, while at the same time raising the possibility of the scientific paradigm gone awry. In ecology scientists discovered that it is impossible to deal with environmental problems one at a time and moved to a whole systems view with success.

In psychology the shift early in the twentieth century had to do with a recognition of the unconscious. Even though the field has tried to apply the outer view of the scientific paradigm, the consideration of the unconscious—in combination with the findings of other sciences of the ephemerality of a deceptively solid material world—revealed the role of individual consciousness.

One view of the paradigm that seems to be emerging is that consciousness is causal, that the inner experiences of individuals, including intuition, emotions, creativity, and spirit, are vastly more important than the world of the senses alone. In fact, even the messages we get from our senses about reality are ultimately affected by our inner consciousness. As the ancient sages put it, "The world is as you see it." The scientific discoveries, coupled with the experience and yearnings of many of us, have moved us to a view of the world that is characterized by wholeness and connection and of the primacy of inner wisdom and inner authority. The everyday statement of this has moved from "I'll believe it when I see it" to "I'll see it when I believe it."

These developments have persisted throughout the century so that the present shift is characterized as comparable to the Copernican one. George Gilder, in his book *Microcosm: The Quantum Revolution in Economics and Technology*, calls all this "a Copernican break in modern history." He goes on to say: "In the early 16th century, Copernicus displaced the earth from the center of the universe. Early this century, quantum physics displaced the human senses as the central test of reality."

The question is, Now that human senses have been replaced, what is the central test of reality? Again, inner experience or consciousness is the answer that appears from a very powerful minority within every science, at especially the highest levels. For instance, in his "Search of Beliefs to Live by Consistent with Science," the Nobel laureate and neuroscientist Roger Sperry says that he has come to reject the view "that science has absolutely no need for recourse to conscious mental or spiritual forces." He stresses his belief that "the fate of the biosphere will depend on human value priorities."

In business this emphasis on human consciousness in the new paradigm elevates the importance of people and includes our subjective experience in decision-making. Leaders of the new paradigm will honor our inner wisdom or authority, rather than outer impersonal forces alone. They will value each person and, as one executive has expressed it, "do business as if people mattered." Later in this book, Robert Haas, CEO of Levi Strauss and Company, comments: "The most visible differences between the corporation of the future and its present-day counterpart will not be the products they make or the equipment they use—but who will be working, why they will be working, and what work will mean to them."

THE OLD AND THE NEW

So one answer to the question, "What is the new paradigm in business?" is that it is doing business from our most profound inner awareness and in connection with the consciousness of others and the earth. Simply put, this means that we each acknowledge that we have an inner wisdom and authority and that others have this too. And as physicists, systems theorists, ecologists, biologists, chemists, and virtually all scientists operating from the new paradigm tell us, there is a wholeness and connectedness between all living things. Everything and everyone is connected in some way to everything else. In business this means that the watchwords for this period are connection, creativity, compassion, and intuition. It is a time of having the freedom to use our highest resources while taking responsibility for ourselves, for others, and for the environment in which we live.

The new paradigm becomes clearer especially when it is contrasted with the old paradigm in which much of everyday business is conducted. The old, or scientific, paradigm is best typified by Newton's mechanistic, clockwork view. Even though science has rejected this view as unrealistic in many ways, our culture and our business strategies are still largely based on this idea, to our great detriment. We set up clockworks of organizations that function by rigid hierarchies, with people seen as replaceable components who work on the basis of orders from above. Those orders come from managers who have been taught that individual values and intuition are to be scorned, that rationality based on data is the only way to make decisions, that management is defined as "getting things done through people," as if people are the parts that get in the way, rather than the contributors to success who simultaneously grow from their contribution.

With this old paradigm view, we reject our own feelings, insights, and intuition as improper sources of information. By doing this, the old paradigm approach throws out the basis of all advances in business: the entrepreneurial spirit, the drive to go beyond or against "the facts" on faith, and a passion to make a contribution in a particular way.

We know this old paradigm style because we are living in it. It is the accounting or survey research form of business that doesn't accept what people know in their hearts. But whatever our role in life, we are beginning to realize that we need to listen to our own creative impulses, to our own inner knowledge. This is where the emerging paradigm, based on the centrality and causality of consciousness, begins. The fundamental assumption of the new paradigm is that our inner knowledge directs the way the world is going to look and the way we respond to it. We are beginning to realize that if we don't believe in something, it doesn't exist—no matter how much data is thrown in front of us.

George Gilder characterized this shift in this way: "The central event of the 20th century is the overthrow of matter. In technology, economics, and the politics of nations, wealth in the form of physical resources is steadily declining in value and significance. The powers of mind are everywhere ascendant over the brute force of things."

In the new paradigm, the key challenge is therefore to apply inner knowledge, intuition, compassion, and spirit to prosper in a period of constant and discontinuous change. But the ways in which this is done can be different for each individual, organization, and time period.

This situational specificity is one reason that the new paradigm can't really be defined in a final way. Even the title of this book is not meant to imply that there is one best way of doing business or one new paradigm for the current world. Rather, we need to view the world and act in a way that is appropriate for the situation in which we find ourselves. We need to acknowledge and act as if there is a process going on, rather than a static Newtonian ideal that either exists or doesn't exist. We need to consider changing our fundamental assumptions, our paradigm, in order to operate within the emerging climate, so that we can survive and contribute to its success.

WHY WE MUST CHANGE

Business as an institution operates more efficiently in change than any other social institution. In fact, in some ways it might be said that change created business expressly for this time of discontinuous transition. Ed Zschau, former U.S. congressman and Censtor Corporation CEO, explains the preeminence of business in society quite simply: "Politicians can be successful, get re-elected, just talking about the problems. In business, you have to have results."

Business brings people together to meet the tests, relate to each other, nurture the environment, be flexible, creative, and caring for the whole. The founding president of the World Business Academy, Rinaldo Brutoco, points out, "Because business is fully internationalized, it is the only institution with the resources and structure to serve as a catalyst for the broader planetary evolution that is underway."

Of course, business itself will have to change if it is going to meet this challenge. For instance, systems theorist George Land tells us that the concept of management itself—with its emphasis on treating people like machines, on using the environment as if it were inexhaustible, on short-term financial goals to the exclusion of long-term consequences—is obsolete in the new paradigm. Yet business for the most part has not made the transformation to a new form of management that is appropriate for our present and future needs.

One reason for this lag is that fear can drive us to operate efficiently in the old ways of business in order to maintain or recapture control. The change, or more properly, transition—a discontinuous, qualitative shift rather than merely a quantitative one—can be so frightening that we go back to what is comfortable or what has worked in the past, even though this approach to business is no longer appropriate. Business people and management scientists have developed great innovations for doing business—from community building to empowerment to self-directed teams to total quality management (TQM) to visioning. But at the slightest sign of difficulty, executives often start circling the wagons and attempt to use the new paradigm approaches in old-fashioned ways.

A recent speaker in the New Paradigm Business course at Stanford University, which I teach, told the class that if people were applying TQM techniques in the seventies, they were pioneers; if they were doing it in the eighties, it was a good idea; but if they are doing it in the nineties, it is corporate suicide. His reasoning was that the recent applications of such techniques have been used to manipulate people as objects in the context of management fear, so that some corporations have regressed to paying only lip service to empowerment, to starting cost (people) cutting to look good in the short term, and to totalitarian controls that breed secrecy, stress, and ultimately the breakdown of individuals and organizations.

Walter Kiechel III, in a *Fortune* magazine article called "When Management Regresses," wrote about a consultant who "compares giant companies that refuse to change, and that indeed grow more repressive in the face of tough times, to the former communist regimes of the Soviet Union and Eastern Europe. They were topdown, bureaucratic, and hard on dissent. Now they're gone."

CHARACTERISTICS OF THE NEW PARADIGM PROCESS

This book presents an alternative to this destructive cycle in business and society. The new paradigm offers a way of doing business based on the constants of change, good questioning, and the inner and outer power of consciousness. The overarching objectives of new paradigm business are essentially the awakening and personal development of everyone associated with it and the corresponding service to the surrounding community. People practicing business in this way base their actions on the guiding principles of wholeness and connectedness in a systems theory sense. They operate from inner wisdom and make decisions by consensus, instead of submitting to some arbitrary outside control.

You've probably seen lists of characteristics (e.g., lack of hierarchy, importance of vision and alignment, emphasis on empowerment and values) of what might be called new paradigm business, the learning organization, the creative workplace, or transformational business. However, such lists can only indicate what might be true for a narrow range of organizations. New paradigm business is not a static template of criteria that an organization either has or doesn't have. It is a process that is in a constant state of development. For instance, it is generally thought that a sure indication of a new paradigm business is a relative lack of hierarchy. But there are instances in which a sense of community and cooperation have been developed so that a clear hierarchy can have a better fit with the needs of the organization. When there is cooperation, community, and compassion within an organization, a hierarchy becomes an efficiency system, rather than a power system. The hierarchy actually can facilitate business from inner wisdom and authority. People can take responsibility when they are personally empowered and when the hierarchy lets them know everyone's responsibilities.

Instead of reciting a list of new paradigm business characteristics here that may not be appropriate for you, we would like to suggest that you try using your own inner creative resources to discover what you probably already know about this kind of business from your own experience. As Rochelle Myers says, "There is something within you that knows much more than you know."

Please take some time right now to contemplate two specific situations that we'll describe below. These can be situations that you experienced in the past or that may be part of your business climate in the present. You might even put this book aside as you do this. Try contemplating each situation with your eyes closed, and then jot down the characteristics you come up with after each question about characteristics.

First, consider a group situation you have experienced in which you couldn't really operate from your fullest capacities, a situation that was not successful from an external standpoint and in which people were not growing. What were the characteristics of that situation or group? Please jot them down.

When you've finished contemplating and writing down the characteristics of that unsuccessful situation, turn your attention to a group or organizational situation in which you were able to grow and prosper, in which you could operate from your fullest capacities, a situation that would be considered to be successful from an external standpoint and in which people were growing and making contributions. What were the characteristics of that organization and situation? Please jot them down.

If you took the time to write out the characteristics from the two situations that you have experienced, or even if you just thought about them, you should now have lists reflecting what people often refer to as old paradigm and new paradigm business, respectively. If you compare the two, you'll see that in the first situation there is probably control and regulation, while in the second there is leadership with openness, a move from management direction to employee empowerment. Instead of being treated like children, individuals are treated like adults and equal partners, as a community or a group of all leaders.

The old situation is typified by fear stemming from short-term goals, while the newer way is based on corporate and individual vision. The old way is a rigid hierarchical culture, while the new model moves toward flexibility. In the new way there is a market orientation and a people orientation. Rather than being concerned with ingroup politics based on satisfying stockholders, the new way has an external focus that takes all stakeholders (employees, customers, suppliers, surrounding community and environment, as well as stockholders) into account. Instead of just competition, the new way includes cooperation, co-creation (in which relationships within and outside of the organization are not just cooperative but also creative), and the contribution of everyone. Instead of aggressive warlike values, the new way is based firmly on values such as openness, integrity, trust, equality, mutual respect, dignity, harmony, and compassion.

This is just a sample of the emerging direction in business. You can probably add a number of other characteristics from your own experience. But the important point is that you've already experienced something like new paradigm business in your own career. The question now is how this kind of experience can be expanded and sustained.

In order to do this, we need to be disciplined, to hold scrupulously to higher values, to operate with creativity, compassion, and community, and to become leaders who see the greater good for each other as the motivating force for what we do. In the present world situation we must ask, as Catherine Ingram did in her book *In the Footsteps of Gandhi*, "How should one lead his life in a world of seemingly intolerable suffering?" Or as Winston Churchill put it, "We make a living by what we get. We make a life by what we give." These are the directions for an individual career and for business in general that are necessary in this time of change.

THE FORMAT OF THIS BOOK

In this book the path toward this new paradigm in business is explored in five sections. In "The Roots of Present Change" you will read the fascinating story of how the world is changing and how that shift affects business and demands leadership from business. "The Beginning of New Leadership" reveals the personal changes that we must go through in order to lead our organizations through this transition and how some breakthrough organizations are exploding our very concept of leadership. Once you have an idea of what the new type of business might be, the section entitled "Organizational Transformation" begins to answer the inevitable question, "How do we get there from here?" Cutting-edge approaches in a number of companies provide guidelines.

Of course, a new paradigm in business doesn't merely move toward personal development for everyone connected with it. It also provides the corresponding service to the surrounding community. In the section entitled "Social and Environmental Responsibility" you will see how business can take responsibility for the welfare of society, as the leading institution in any era should do. And in the final section, "Visions of the Future," seven well-known authors show what business and the world can be if we follow the new directions of the paradigm shift.

We have collected in this book the best thinking about the new paradigm, as well as indications of the best practice of it. In his writing about the new paradigm in science, Kuhn said that we could detect the existence and nature of a paradigm by the "exemplars" of it. In this book you will find vignettes about people and organizations that are actually putting new paradigm business into practice. These are our exemplars of the new paradigm in action in business.

This book is sponsored by the World Business Academy, an international body of business leaders, entrepreneurs, and scholars engaged in an interactive dialogue to identify, analyze, and publicize insights about the ways that business institutions and the people within them can best contribute to the creation of a positive global future. Nearly thirty of the authors or subjects of the articles in this anthology are members or fellows of the Academy. Because Academy members believe that business best serves itself and the world when it operates from integrity and an understanding of its interconnectedness with all of life, the publication of this book is important to them. And we greatly appreciate their support and contributions.

—MICHAEL RAY

Part I

THE ROOTS OF
PRESENT CHANGE

Industrial society is in its death throes.

TAICHI SAKAIYA, FORMER MEMBER
OF JAPAN'S MITI
The Knowledge-Value Revolution

The fate of the biosphere will depend on human value priorities, which will depend upon assumptions about human life and its meaning.

NOBEL LAUREATE ROGER W. SPERRY

The pressure of the facts is that we must either change or disappear. To meet priorities that require immediate action and begin managing change without losing time, a true transformation of mind sets and behavior is imperative.

THE CLUB OF ROME
The First Global Revolution

I feel that all mankind is entering a new age, and that the world is beginning to obey new laws and logic, to which we have yet to adjust ourselves.

MIKHAIL GORBACHEV

INTRODUCTION

What is the social, political, and economic context of the change in paradigm? How did we get to our current situation of turmoil? How can we participate and even support the paradigm shift?

One of the fascinating aspects of the current transition is that most people tend not to ask questions like these. For a variety of reasons, primarily psychological, we find it painful to consider the difficulties of a world in transition, and this seems to mean that often the whole subject is avoided. Without knowing the context in which we do business, however, we are doomed to repeat history's errors. And in a time of radical paradigm shift, this is dangerous indeed.

In science a paradigm shift occurs when there are anomalies, when research results don't fit the fundamental assumptions of the discipline. This certainly has been the cause of the paradigm shift that has been going on in science in this century. As physicists continued the age-old search for the smallest particle, investigated the implications of velocity beyond the speed of light, and discovered a previously unseen order in a seemingly chaotic world, the old Newtonian laws had to be largely discarded as fundamental assumptions.

But the larger societal paradigm shift that grows from the scientific anomalies occurs because the old ways are just not working anymore in the social and economic spheres. Despite the fact that the scientific revolution has led to technologies that have bettered the lives of a certain proportion of the world's people, they also have led to terrible side effects. Three to four hundred species become extinct every day; the destruction of the rain forests is proceeding at a rate that is unthinkable; the ozone layer is disappearing at a rate greater than the worst predictions; world hunger is so great that thousands die of starvation every day; population growth is out of control and moving beyond the ability of the planet to support it. Despite all of these dire results of our materialist, growth-oriented paradigm, people in underdeveloped countries around the world say they want the same kind of culture. So the destructive forces feed on themselves. As African scholar and educator Motombe Mpana puts it, "The American Dream has become the world's nightmare."

Mpana is joined by business people, scholars, and experts from around the world in his assessment of a need for a change in our fundamental assumptions. France's Jacques Attali writes of "a world that has embraced a common ideology of consumerism but is bitterly divided between rich and poor, threatened by a warming and polluted atmosphere, girdled by a dense network of airport metropolises for travel, and wired for instant worldwide communication."

Many people emphatically feel that *we* have to change in order to get through the world's inevitable change. As polio vaccine discoverer Jonas Salk puts it, "Survival of the world as we know it is not possible. The world will have to be transformed and evolve for continual survival."

And there is no doubt that a major transformation is occurring. Futurist Willis Harman says: "The latter third of this century is a period of fundamental transformation of the modern world, the extent and meaning of which we are only beginning to grasp. . . . The role of business in that transformation is absolutely crucial."

Philosopher and religious studies scholar Huston Smith observes: "Quietly, irrevocably, something enormous has happened to Western man. His outlook on life and the world has changed so radically that in the perspective of history the twentieth century is likely to rank—with the fourth century, which witnessed the triumph of Christianity, and the seventeenth, which signalled the dawn of modern science—as one of the very few that have instigated genuinely new epochs in human thought. In this change, which is still in process, we of the current generation are playing a crucial but as yet not widely recognized part."

From around the world, among members of many disciplines, there is agreement. The Club of Rome says, "We are . . . in the early stages of the formation of a new type of world society which will be as different from today's as was that of the world ushered in by the Industrial Revolution from the society of the long agrarian period that preceded it." Attali says that this shift could be "far more profound than the harnessing of steam and electricity in the nineteenth century, and perhaps more akin in impact to the discovery of fire by primitive tribes."

Czechoslovakian President Vaclav Havel, speaking to the World Economic Forum, concentrated on what he called the end of the modern era, which has been dominated by the belief that "the world—and Being as such—is a wholly knowable system governed by a finite number of universal laws that man grasps and rationally directs for his own benefit." The old paradigm (although he didn't use those words), said Havel, represented "a cult of depersonalized objectivity." In the new era, he said, "a politician must become a person again. He must trust not only an objective interpretation of reality but also his own soul."

In this section the authors discuss how our fundamental assumptions have led to this worldwide transition and how our ways of thinking about and practicing business must change also. The old industrial-scientific paradigm is dying, and a new one is yet to be fully born. In that light, there are some emerging answers to the key questions about the social context within which business is operating. But perhaps the most important contribution that the authors make is to stimulate us to continue to pay attention to the world's difficulties, no matter how painful that might be, to "maintain the gaze," as Joanna Macy puts it, and to keep asking questions about how business and business people fit into this massive societal transformation.

1

THE BREAKDOWN OF THE OLD PARADIGM

by Willis Harman and John Hormann

To understand the emerging paradigm in business, we must first analyze the manifest problems and dilemmas of contemporary economic, corporate, and social policies, appreciate the ways in which they seem so intractable, and search for their origins in the development and basic characteristics of modern society. In other words, where are we now and how did we get here?

In this essay the authors present a comprehensive and insightful view of the old Western industrial–era paradigm, including conventional beliefs about the scientific method, unlimited material progress, industrialization, and other short-term pragmatic values. They examine our underlying pathogenic assumptions about nationalism, government by interest group, and the predominance of a world view based on manipulative economic "rationality" and acquisitive materialism.

Willis Harman has for many years been the dean of new paradigm thinking and a powerful creative force in its dissemination. After a distinguished career as a professor at the University of Florida and Stanford University, he was on the staff of the Stanford Research Institute (now SRI International) and is now president of the Institute of Noetic Sciences. One of the founders of the World Business Academy and a former regent of the University of California, he is also the author of numerous books, including An Incomplete Guide to the Future *(1979) and* Global Mind Change *(1988). His co-author, John Hormann, has worked for over twenty-five years for IBM in various international management positions.*

The central theme throughout the discussion of this essay can be summarized in one telling observation: *Present economic, corporate, and social policies are, by and large, inconsistent with viable long-term global development, and are being everywhere made without a picture of a viable global future in mind, or an understanding of the global system change required to bring about such a future.* This is the predicament of the contemporary world.

CONTRIBUTING FACTORS FROM THE PAST

To really understand this predicament, it is necessary to inquire into its origins. When seeking an explanation as to why the world is in its present state, it makes a great difference what time interval is used for viewing. If one thinks of trends that have been evident in Western Europe and North America since around the end of World War II (about half a century), certain things stand out. If instead the focus is on the period since the Middle Ages (roughly, three and a half centuries), other factors emerge as critically important. (These are discussed immediately below.) Again, if one looks with a time span of millennia rather than centuries, then the factors that stand out are things like the agricultural revolution, the rise of cities, and, particularly, the emergence of patriarchal society with values and assumptions that have dominated Western society for the past five thousand years, until challenged by the recent emergence of the women's movement. All of these factors contribute to the ultimate explanation of how we got to our present situation, and of the whole-system change required to reach satisfactory resolution of our manifold problems and dilemmas.

Thus, while some of the factors that contribute to the present state of the world arise out of changes that have taken place over the last half century, the problem cannot be seen adequately without bringing in at least two longer-term factors: (a) the full import of the "modernization" trend that set in with the ending of the Middle Ages in Western Europe; and (b) the influence of patriarchal society.

The "Modernization" Revolution of the Seventeenth Century

The seventeenth-century developments in Western Europe not only marked the ending of the Middle Ages there, they ultimately had an impact on practically every area of the globe.

It is not too great a simplification to say that the fundamental thing that happened in this century was that the prevailing "picture of reality" changed from a medieval one to one we would recognize as at least proto-modern. In medieval reality the Earth was the center of the cosmos—the seat of change, decay, and Christian redemption. Above it circled the luminous heavenly bodies, themselves pure and unchanging, but moved by divine spirits and signaling and influencing human events by their locations and aspects. The universe was alive and imbued with purpose. All creatures were seen to be part of a Great Chain of Being, with man between the angels and the lower animals. Events were explained by divine purpose or by their function in a meaningful world.

An educated man in 1600 would still have perceived the medieval cosmos; by 1700 his counterpart would literally have perceived a different reality. Where the universe of stars and planets had been alive, it was now essentially dead: initially constructed and set in motion by the Creator, with subsequent events accounted for by mechanical forces and lawful behaviors. The Earth was known to be but one of many planets circling around one of many stars, moving through and separated by unimaginable distances. The natural resources and the diverse creatures of the Earth were put here for man's use. On the one hand, man and the planet Earth were removed from their special position at the center of creation; on the other hand, man's destiny was beginning to be seen as unlimited material and moral advance. The concept of material progress, in particular, was coming increasingly strongly into focus.

The seventeenth century was the time of Galileo and Newton; we usually think of it as the era of the scientific revolution. But other important things were going on as well. This period encompassed the latter part of the Reformation and the rise of Puritanism in England. It saw the first of the liberal-democratic revolutions that were to remake most of the governments of the world. And it saw the rise of capitalist philosophy and institutions. It was a time of tremendous controversies in religion, philosophy, and social theory, which set the tenor of the modern mind. It was a great historical watershed. Prior to this were half a dozen centuries of the period we call broadly the Middle Ages. After the impact of the Copernican revolution in the early decades of the seventeenth century, the course was irrevocably set for what we now call the modern era.

Among the persistent themes of the modern, Western industrial–era paradigm are:

• The *scientific method* as the supreme mode of inquiry. The search for scientific knowledge has come to be predominantly utilitarian: Its guiding values are prediction and control and ability to manipulate the physical environment. Although it was not so initially, the ultimate goal of most present-day science is technological advance.

• *Unlimited material progress* as the inherent goal. The paradigm implies belief in man's expanding control over nature; and in his unlimited ability to understand the universe from the data provided by the physical senses. Acquisitive materialism is a central operative value.

• *Industrialization* of the production of goods and services, achieved by subdividing work into increasingly elemental (and less intrinsically meaningful) increments, and replacing human labor by machines. The goals of industrialization are increasing labor productivity and wealth, presumably leading to a higher material standard of living for all.

• *Pragmatic values* predominate, with individuals free to seek their own self-interest in the marketplace. Hence the future is not defined by tradition nor achieved through organized plan, but rather it happens as a consequence of relatively autonomous units in the system pursuing their own practical ends.

One of the features of this paradigm is the increasing monetization of society. More and more of human activities take place within the mainstream economy, and are valued in economic terms. Increasingly a person defines himself or herself by relationship to the economy, either by job, spouse's job, or job-in-training. Gradually, the economic and financial institutions came to be the paramount institutions. Economic production became (except in time of war) the central concern of society, and economic growth the primary measure by which societies judge their progress.

In *The Transformations of Man* (1956) Lewis Mumford vividly summarizes the vast change that was involved in shifting from the old feudal paradigm of the Middle Ages to the new, industrial-era paradigm: "Within the span of a few centuries the focus of interest shifted from the inner world to the outer world. . . . All but one of the [seven deadly] sins, sloth, was transformed into a virtue. Greed, avarice, envy, gluttony, luxury, and pride were the driving forces of the new economy. . . . Unbounded power was harnessed to equally unbounded appetites."

By the latter part of the twentieth century the technological power of the industrialized societies was awesome, and its benefits were impressive. Equally impressive is a fundamental observation whose implications we are only now beginning to grasp: *Most of today's critical societal and global problems have come about, directly or indirectly, because of the successes of the Western industrial paradigm.*

THE UNDERLYING PATHOGENIC ASSUMPTIONS

Let us now try to identify the underlying assumptions which are at the root of the malfunctioning of modern society, and hence will be at the heart of the necessary system change. We observed above that modern society is beset with innumerable specific problems and symptoms of malfunctioning. At this level social critics deplore, and politicians promise, but nothing much happens. If symptoms are relieved, they reappear in another form, or the problem "solution" brings "unintended consequences" that often turn out to be at least as bad as the original problems.

If we think in more whole-system terms, we can identify intermediate-level problems that are of a more systemic nature. That is to say, they are described as undesirable characteristics of the overall systems, and their solution is imagined in terms of whole-system change. Many times these are not the problems of any one nation or region, but situations where the welfare of the whole of humanity is involved.

Needless to say, there is more than one way to analyze the dilemmas of modern societies, but the following four intermediate-level problems stand out:

INTERMEDIATE PROBLEMS AND ATTEMPTED "SOLUTIONS"

1. Tendency of World Economy to Create Scarcity of Fresh Air and Water, Arable Land, and Spirit-Renewing Wilderness; Environmental Deterioration; Ecological Crises; Toxic Substance Concentrations; Man-made Climate Change

Nations have not done well at managing their own "commons"—the land, air, water, and space that must be commonly used. The imperative is to move rapidly to some management of the "global commons." "Global commons" means primarily the four environments which are so recognized by international law and custom: the oceans (including the ocean floor); outer space; atmosphere, weather and climate; and the continent of Antarctica. To these must be added the situations where actions within one nation affect the fresh-water rivers and aquifers of another. The most powerful nations have been among the more reluctant to pool sovereignty to accomplish this management.

The usual approach to environmental problems is to try to ameliorate the symptoms directly, and at the same time adjust the legislative and economic incentive structures to foster desirable changes—reduced energy use and substitution of renewable energy sources;

reusable containers and other ways to decrease the amount of solid waste created; biodegradability of non-eliminable waste; reduced pollution and impact on ecological systems; decelerated logging of tropical rainforests; etc. Direct legislation may be used to prohibit CFCs, strictly limit toxic waste, and so forth.

One often suggested measure is better economic and social indicators and a more adequate accounting system. The costs and benefits associated with the social and ecological consequences of economic activity are not commensurate with each other, or with money. Nevertheless, there are numerous ways in which a better job could be done of incorporating the costs of "externalities" such as acid rain, soil erosion, solid waste production and deforestation into a systematic framework that could lead to more enlightened decision making. In the U.S., for example, environmental impact statements (EIS) now required of various projects, to make publicly available information with regard to anticipated impacts of a decision, make no attempt to express these impacts in some common currency; they simply display them to encourage more awareness about overall consequences of deciding to go ahead. Even so, the EIS proves to be a significant achievement toward facilitating citizen participation in the political process.

However, the intrinsic characteristics of the world economy are such that *all of the above tends to be a desperate catch-up attempt*. The problems continue to worsen at a greater rate than the ameliorative measures patch up the effects. Beyond all of these measures, reassessment of the fundamental characteristics of the global economy is necessary. Resistance to this re-examination is extremely strong.

2. Tendency of World Economy to Create Marginal People and Marginal Cultures; Chronic Poverty, Hunger and Maldevelopment

Here the major attempts of the past have been to ameliorate crises as humane considerations dictate. Recently there have been increasing attempts to help individuals and communities help themselves feel more empowered, become more self-sufficient, regenerate group pride, and embark on a development path appropriate to their unique cultural roots.

Nonetheless, there is a natural tendency in any social system for power to accumulate. Those who have political or economic power are in a good position to gain still more power; those with less power tend to be in a progressively poorer position. Within any society there are some institutionalized mechanisms for limiting this tendency. (Obvious examples are recognized civil rights, the graduated income tax, free legal services for the poor.) But there are at the international level only very primitive and ineffective mechanisms. Thus, for example, the degrees of wealth and income disparities that exist between nations are far greater than would be tolerated even within countries having the most notoriously authoritarian and unjust regimes.

It appears to be difficult for the materially rich countries to move beyond the idea that their affluence is a function of their own merit, and to recognize that the conflict-producing tensions in the world will require what Harlan Cleveland has called a "fairness revolution." Some way must be found, in other words, to limit the natural tendency for power to accumulate at the global level, and to empower the poorest of the poor to assure themselves of those human rights without which existence can hardly be termed human living.

3. Crisis of Control

Perhaps the ultimate challenge facing humankind today can be summed up in a single question: *We humans have developed consummate technological capability to do almost anything we can imagine wanting to do; can we now develop corresponding ability to choose wisely which things should be done?*

How can we avoid choosing short-term objectives that induce clearly undesirable long-term consequences, such as resumed nuclear arms race, or gross environmental destruction? How can we exercise needed societal control over technology without sacrificing individual liberty?

Industrial society now has the power:

- To change the characteristics of our physical environment, including climate, as well as the plant and animal population of the biosphere.
- To modify the physical characteristics of individual human bodies and the evolutionary development of the human race, by means of biological and genetic engineering.
- To drastically alter social and psychological environments, including people's mental and emotional characteristics.
- To annihilate large segments of the human race and devastate large areas of the Earth.
- To change significantly, in many other ways, the kind of world that is passed on to future generations.

These powers are so awesome that they clearly must be directed and channeled. And yet it is not clear how this control can be exerted without impinging on fundamental characteristics of our free enterprise system and our democratic society. Nor is it clear how to counteract the built-in bias toward favoring short-term benefits so that more consideration is given to long-term consequences of technological choices.

4. Crisis of Meaning and Values

It has been said in many ways by many people; surveys show it, and people know it: Modern industrial society knows how to do almost anything that can be imagined, and is totally confused about what is worth doing. In contrast to U.S. or European society of a couple of generations ago, the collective today is deeply perplexed and uncertain about meanings and goals. What is modern society about? Technological advance? Material standard of living as measured by the GNP? Keeping what we have regardless of the welfare of those living in other parts of the planet? Contemporary problems with drugs, gambling, inner-city crime, and the homeless are directly related to this confusion.

The intermediate-level solution that seems to be universally proposed for this crisis is education. Why can't we educate people to find meaning in their lives, and a sound basis for personal and social values? Certainly much can be done, in terms of increasing people's self-awareness and sense of their own power, by ways which are exemplified in numerous weekend workshop and seminar situations. The matter is made more difficult by the fact that the prevailing scientific picture of reality tends to be antithetical to personal discoveries that imply ultimate meanings or eternal values.

But it is not enough for people to find individual meaning when they are surrounded by (and despite) a system which does not reflect that meaning. The prevailing meanings and values of that system must also change. A significant fraction of the world has advanced technologically to the point discussed above, where economic production of all the goods and services that society can imagine needing or desiring (or that the resources and environment can stand) can be provided using only a small fraction of the population. It no longer makes sense for the "central project" of society to be economic production and consumption. What, then, is the new "central project" of advanced societies, and what does this imply for global society as a whole?

We repeat again our main theme in delineating these intermediate-level problems: As basic as they may seem, the change necessary to make them resolvable lies at a still deeper level. If the above four systemic problems can be assumed to summarize the most severe challenges we face, what are the underlying assumptions that will need to change as a part of whole-system change? Perhaps we can identify a few of the most important:

DEEPER-LEVEL ASSUMPTIONS

1. Predominance of Economic Institutions and Economic Rationality

Modern society is characterized by the predominance of economic institutions and economic rationality. For us who have grown up taking this for granted, it may be difficult to imagine that things might be otherwise. Other long-lived societies in history have had as their paramount institutions those that dealt with knowledge, meaning, humane or spiritual goals; no other society has been so focused around economic production and consumption. No other society has attempted to guide a society with decisions shaped primarily by economic considerations. No other society has taken as its highest value acquisitive materialism.

In the first place, there is no reason whatever to assume that economic rationality will lead to decisions that are wise from human, ecological, compassionate, and spiritual standpoints. As a matter of experience, it doesn't. Whereas the Iroquois tradition was to make decisions having in mind the welfare of those who will live seven generations hence, contemporary decisions—profoundly affecting future generations and people around the globe—are guided by next quarter's financial bottom line, or the way the next electorate will perceive the state of the economy.

Furthermore, the economic and technological values that dominate modern society are really pseudo-values. They only seem like values because of a confusion of means—technology and economic institutions—with ends. And that confusion arises when true ends, which are always transcendental, become obscured through the power given to a materialistic worldview.

2. Nationalism and the Concept of "National Security"

The rise of the nation-state from the seventeenth century onward brought order out of chaos in many parts of the world. The industrializing nation-state was an extremely effective kind of organization for its own purposes, and few could look ahead to realize that there was an intrinsic contradiction in the long term. The advance of technology inevitably made the world smaller and the problems more global. At the same time, it was clear that certain types of problems involving the well-being of individuals and families could best be handled at the community level. Thus the nation-state became too small for the global problems and too large for the local ones.

That could be handled in various ways. However, the really serious aspect of the nation-state was its tendency to seek its security through building and maintaining military strength. Each nation was autonomous and resisted any thought of worldwide collaboration to maintain order on the planet. World War I brought the shocking realization that continuance of this state of affairs was going to be terribly costly. And with World War II, the point was emphasized still more strongly by introduction of mass obliteration of civilian populations through saturation bombing and nuclear weapons. Thus it should have become apparent that, from World War II on, *national and global security, in any meaningful sense of the term, can no longer be attained through military strength*. Mikhail Gorbachev so wrote in *Perestroika* in 1987. However, the history of politics over the past four decades has been largely a history of attempts to evade and deny that fact.

Something over a half century ago it was commonplace to hear talk of some future world government. Since then, people have become extremely wary of concentrations of power, because they tend to attract corruptible individuals. It seems that national and global security will have to be sought elsewhere than either military strength or world government. As of the beginning of the new decade little progress has been made, and highly armed nations have made the world, despite recent progress, remarkably a perilous place.

3. Government by Interest Group

In the absence of a compelling sense of national or supranational purpose to which all subscribe, politics becomes largely a matter of competing groups, each vying for its own self-interests. That the result lacks the coherent sense of purpose necessary to solve the world's vexing problems should not be surprising.

The United States had, through most of its history, a strong sense of national purpose and overarching goals; the 1988 presidential campaign and succeeding events furnish ample evidence that whatever of this remains is very weak indeed. In the developing European Community one sees the beginning, perhaps, of overarching goals that go beyond economic and political power. Surely the shift from separate and competing nations to a sense of common European destiny is in itself a revolutionary step.

If fragmentation and lack of overarching goals is characteristic of present-day United States and European society, the same is all the more true at the global level. Although the United Nations has development and environment programs, there is no agreement on what development is good for people and for the planet, and no agreement on what system change will be required to halt the disastrous environmental and climate-change consequences of the world economy's carrying on "business as usual." Although the nations of the world have agreed in principle to the U.N.'s Universal Declaration of Human Rights, the guaranteeing of which could suffice as a worthy overarching global goal, there is no agreement on what to do when the normal practices of nations and the world economy systematically infringe upon those rights.

4. Predominance of Materialistic Picture of Reality

It is apparent that a good formula for disaster is to attempt to make decisions affecting the future of a person, a society, or the planet, based on a perception of reality that isn't true. Many persons in recent years have been shocked at realizing that is precisely what modern society has been attempting to do.

The development of modern science was one of the great evolutionary leaps in the history of human societies. It was the democratization of knowledge, as well as the evolution of a set of highly effective techniques for gaining new knowledge of a certain sort. The scientific spirit was a new spirit of open inquiry, and public validation of knowledge. No longer was knowledge to be the property of a priesthood or power elite; anyone interested was invited to perform the experiments, and validate knowledge for himself or herself.

For a long time few noticed that the new scientific knowledge had a bias, which over several centuries began to have serious consequences. The bias was simply that it focused on the world of outer experience and neglected the world of *inner* experience. Closely related to that was the fact that it explained phenomena in terms of physical causation, neglecting that in our experience we find that there is also *volitional* causality; that is, human decisions causing things to happen. There were good reasons for that bias at the time empirical science was first being developed; it was highly advantageous in terms of a strong and effective science.

Nevertheless, one of the consequences of such a science—which seemed to be making an increasingly strong case for a materialistic worldview and random evolution of life forms, including us—was the erosion of the religious base underlying the values of Western civilization. As that base became weaker, particularly among those with the most education, the values became weaker. Manipulative rationality and acquisitive materialism became the hallmarks of "advanced" societies. But they are inadequate values, and the materialistic worldview is an inadequate worldview on which to make the kinds of decisions the future requires.

The predominance of a materialistic worldview and the accompanying weakness of value and meaning commitments has led to what is probably the deepest-level problem of all—alienation. We are alienated from nature, of which we are a part and upon which we utterly depend. As a result, we foul our own nest and threaten the Earth's life-support systems necessary for our prospering and, in the end, for our survival. We are alienated from our work, since that has in so many cases become devoid of meaning. We are alienated from each other, since the sense of joint commitment to any transcendent goals is so weak. And, being deeply confused about our own being, we are alienated from ourselves.

That is not a pessimistic observation. It is simply an indication of where we must start, as we seek to find our way out of the present predicament.

2

THE TRANSFORMATION OF VALUES AND VOCATION

by Marilyn Ferguson

One of the most significant characteristics of the new paradigm is the struggle of individuals to find higher purpose and meaning in work. The result has been the gradual emergence of new values reflecting authentic needs and desires for work as a vehicle of transformation.

These new attitudes toward work, career choice, and consumption are replacing the old, external philosophies imposed by economic materialism. These new values are beginning to create a social and business ethic characterized in the SRI report Changing Image of Man *as concern for the quality of life, appropriate technology, entrepreneurship, decentralization, ecology and spirituality.*

No one has written about this gradual transformation with more persuasive optimism than Marilyn Ferguson. She is the author of The Aquarian Conspiracy *and publisher of* Brain/Mind Bulletin (*formerly* New Sense), *the widely read report on brain research and consciousness.*

If there is power in the transformative experience, it must inevitably shake our values and, therefore, the total economy—the marketplace, the factory, corporations, the professions, small business, social welfare. And it must redefine what we mean by words like "rich" and "poor"; it must make us rethink what we owe each other, what is possible, what is appropriate. Sooner or later, the new paradigm changes the individual's relationship to work; part-time transformation is inherently impossible.

Making a life, not just a living, is essential to one seeking wholeness. Our hunger turns out to be for something different, not something more. Buying, selling, owning, saving, sharing, keeping, investing, giving—these are outward expressions of inward needs. When those needs change, as in personal transformation, economic patterns change. For example, spending is an opiate to many people, a balm to disappointments, frustrations, emptiness. If the individual transforms that inner distress, there is less need for drugs and distractions. Inner listening makes clearer to us what we really want, as distinct from what we have been talked into, and it might not have a price tag. We may also discover that "ownership" is in some sense an illusion, that holding on to things can keep us from freely enjoying them. Greater awareness may give us new appreciation for simple things. And quality becomes important—the much-talked-about "quality of life." If work becomes rewarding, not just obligatory, that also reorders values and priorities.

We will look at the evidence for a new paradigm, based on *values*, which transcends the old paradigm of economics, with its emphasis on growth, control, manipulation. The shift to the values paradigm is reflected in changing patterns of work, career choice, consumption . . . evolving lifestyles that take advantage of synergy, sharing, barter, cooperation, and creativity . . . the transformation of the workplace, in business, industry, professions, the arts . . . innovations in management and worker participation, including the decentralization of power . . . the rise of a new breed of entrepreneurs . . . the search for "appropriate technology" . . . the call for an economics congruent with nature rather than the mechanistic views that have propelled us into our present crises.

CRISIS AND DENIAL

We have proved that you can't eat yourself slim. Trying to consume our way to prosperity, we have been exhausting our resources. High production costs, scarcities, inflation, and severe unemployment have become our regular diet.

Because the economy is such a political issue it is propagandized, rationalized, lied about. Because our beliefs about the economy affect it, as in the "confidence index," business and government try to buffer the reaction of investors and consumers to unnerving economic news.

And because divergent viewpoints are loudly argued, you can choose whom to believe:

Nuclear power is essential/deadly.

Solar energy will be cheap/impractical.

Fossil fuel is plentiful/exhausted.

We should consume/conserve.

Full employment is feasible/impossible.

Automation/environmentalism do/do not undermine jobs and growth.

There are illusions of rescue by technology, by the reshuffling of moneys and resources. But our temporary easing of this chronic illness—scarcities, dislocated markets, unemployment, obsolescence—is as dangerous as the medical treatment of symptoms when the cause of disease is unknown. Our intervention in the body economic, like intervention by drugs and surgery, often leads to severe side effects requiring further and deeper intervention.

The crisis is evident in the chronic nature of unemployment and underemployment: the technological obsolescence that has overtaken millions of specialized skilled workers, increasing numbers of the highly educated vying for too few white-collar jobs, increasing numbers of teenagers and women trying to enter the work force.

A United States Department of Labor study found "true unemployment"—including those working but with earnings below the poverty level—more than *40 percent*. Fewer jobs, more applicants. Proportionately fewer interesting jobs. Technological ingenuity that doubles the productivity of worker A so that B can be laid off so that A can grumble about paying taxes to help support a demoralized B. Affirmative-action programs that often just redistribute the unfairness and bitterness to a different group.

Labor and management savage each other periodically, like crazy Siamese twins who don't know that their lifeblood is the same.

The indices of our economy are often misleading. For example, the Gross National Product figures include the expenditures for treating disease, repairing wrecked automobiles, and eliminating factory pollution; that is, we are measuring activity, not true production. It is increasingly evident that our efforts to control, explain, and understand the economy are wholly inadequate.

The unexamined assumption of the old paradigm—dominant since the days of John Locke—is that human beings are most deeply motivated by economic concerns. Yet, beyond a certain level of material sufficiency, other strong needs clearly take precedence: the desire to be healthy, to be loved, to feel competent, to participate fully in society, to have meaningful employment. And even if Locke were right about our economic motives, we would have to change: Our civilization cannot go on escalating its manufacture and consumption of non-renewable resources.

Assessing the New York City financial crisis in the mid-seventies, Julius Stulman of the World Institute said that our greatest mistake is that we continue to relate everything to the past, "the steps we have laboriously climbed for six thousand years—brick by brick, hand over fist, in singular, linear fashion. However necessary those steps may have been to our evolution, that stage has ended. *We cannot cope until we think differently.*"

Our best hope now is to pay attention, to recognize the ways in which our lives and livelihood have been influenced, even run, by outmoded structures. Our ideas about work, money, and management grew out of an old stable social order irrelevant to present flux and were based on a view of humankind and nature long since transcended in science. The real world turns on different principles than those imposed by our partial economic philosophies.

THE EMERGENT PARADIGM: VALUES, NOT ECONOMICS

The economic systems of the modern world take sides in the old argument: individual versus society. When we are polarized, we are arguing about the wrong issue. Rather than debating whether capitalism is right in its emphasis on opportunities for the individual or socialism in its concern for the collective, we should reframe the question: Is a materialistic society suited to human needs? Both capitalism and socialism, as we know them, pivot on material values. They are inadequate philosophies for a transformed society.

The failures of our economic philosophies, like the failures of our political reforms, can be attributed to their emphasis on the external. Inner values, like inner reform, precede outward change. In synthesis may be our salvation—the path between right and left Aldous Huxley called "decentralism and cooperative enterprise, an economic and political system most natural to spirituality."

Just as health is vastly more than medicine, just as learning transcends education, so a system of values is the context for the workings of any economy. Whatever our priorities—self-aggrandizement, efficiency, status, health, security, recreation, human relationships, competition, cooperation, craftsmanship, material goods—they are reflected in the workings of the economy. A society that prizes external symbols will want showy automobiles, whatever the cost. A family that values education may make considerable sacrifices to pay tuition for a private school. One who values adventure may give up a financially secure job to sail around the world.

Most importantly, when people become autonomous, their values become *internal*. Their purchases and their choice of work begin to reflect their own authentic needs and desires rather than the values imposed by advertisers, family, peers, media.

Louis Mobley, former director of executive training for IBM, suggested that the turn inward marks a cultural reversal. Having concluded an era in which we looked only outward and denied our inner realities, we are now making value judgments. "And that's why the answers escape economists." The 1978 Nobel laureate in economics, Herbert Simon, criticizes the classic "rational" assumptions of economists and their consequent failure to deal with changing values and expectations.

Societies, as Ilya Prigogine pointed out, are the strangest and most unstable of dissipative structures. The complexity of our modern pluralistic society and the increasingly autonomous values of its people have created vast economic uncertainty. Now we need an approach to the economy comparable to the wise uncertainty of the physicist.

The two paradigms might be summarized as follows:

ASSUMPTIONS OF THE OLD PARADIGM OF ECONOMICS	ASSUMPTIONS OF THE NEW PARADIGM OF VALUES
Promotes consumption at all costs, via planned obsolescence, advertising pressure, creation of artificial "needs."	Appropriate consumption. Conserving, keeping, recycling, quality, craftsmanship, innovation, invention to serve authentic needs.
People to fit jobs. Rigidity. Conformity.	Jobs to fit people. Flexibility. Creativity. Form and flow.
Imposed goals, top-down decision-making. Hierarchy, bureaucracy.	Autonomy encouraged. Self-actualization. Worker participation, democratization. Shared goals, consensus.
Fragmentation, compartmentalization in work and roles. Emphasis on specialized tasks. Sharply defined job descriptions.	Cross-fertilization by specialists seeing wider relevance of their field of expertise. Choice and change in job roles encouraged.
Identification with job, organization, profession.	Identity transcends job description.
Clockwork model of economy, based on Newtonian physics.	Recognition of uncertainty in economics.

Aggression, competition. "Business is business."	Cooperation. Human values transcend "winning."
Work and play separate. Work as means to an end.	Blurring of work and play. Work rewarding in itself.
Manipulation and dominance of nature.	Cooperation with nature; taoistic, organic view of work and wealth.
Struggle for stability, station, security.	Sense of change, becoming. Willingness to risk. Entrepreneurial attitude.
Quantitative: quotas, status symbols, level of income, profits, "raises," Gross National Product, tangible assets.	Qualitative as well as quantitative. Sense of achievement, mutual effort for mutual enrichment. Values intangible assets (creativity, fulfillment) as well as tangible.
Strictly economic motives, material values. Progress judged by product, content.	Spiritual values transcend material gain; material sufficiency. Process as important as product. Context of work as important as content—not just what you do but *how* you do it.
Polarized: labor versus management, consumer versus manufacturer, etc.	Transcends polarities. Shared goals, values.
Short-sighted: exploitation of limited resources.	Ecologically sensitive to ultimate costs. Stewardship.
"Rational," trusting only data.	Rational and intuitive. Data, logic augmented by hunches, feelings, insights, nonlinear (holistic) sense of pattern.
Emphasis on short-term solutions.	Recognition that long-range efficiency must take into account harmonious work environment, employee health, customer relations.
Centralized operations.	Decentralized operations wherever possible. Human scale.

Runaway, unbridled technology. Subservience to technology.	Appropriate technology. Technology as tool, not tyrant.
Allopathic treatment of "symptoms" in economy.	Attempt to understand the whole, locate deep underlying causes of disharmony, disequilibrium. Preventive "medicine," anticipation of dislocations, scarcities.

EXEMPLAR:
Semco

In Brazil, Ricardo Semler runs Semco, an equipment manufacturing company, in a way that illustrates new paradigm business. Virtually everyone sets their own hours. There is no dress code. Some people with particularly valuable skills make higher salaries than their bosses without having to be in the management track. There is no hierarchy to speak of, other than titles of counselors, partners, and associates who do the research, design, sales, and manufacturing work.

Employees also make many of the important corporate decisions. For instance, workers, not real estate agents, found three prospective factory sites for one division of Semco. Then everyone from that division got into buses to visit the sites. The employees voted for one building that management didn't really want because it was across the street from a plant with one of the worst labor records in Brazil. But after the plant was purchased, the workers' creativity flourished as they designed the factory for a flexible manufacturing system and had one of Brazil's top artists paint the factory inside and out, including the machinery. As Semler says, "That plant really belongs to its employees. I feel like a guest every time I walk in." But he doesn't mind because its productivity per employee jumped from $14,200 to $37,500 four years after moving into the new site.

At Semco employees are treated like adults rather than adolescents. More than 150 of the management people set their own salaries. Semco encourages employees to rotate jobs every three to five years. When supervisory people are hired, they are interviewed and evaluated by their future subordinates. There is an openness of information that includes providing classes so that each worker can learn how to understand financial data. Then monthly balance sheets, profit and loss analysis, and a cash flow statement are provided to each division. This information offers a context for creativity for everyone.

Semco's combination of democracy, profit sharing administered by the employees, and open information has created one of Brazil's fastest-growing companies. It was voted the best company in which to work, and it has a profit margin of 10 percent.

3

REDEFINITIONS OF CORPORATE WEALTH

by Herman Bryant Maynard, Jr.,
and Susan E. Mehrtens

The old paradigm always has measured wealth strictly as financial assets derived from productivity and profit. This kind of thinking has focused on short-term exploitation and competition, the traditional balance sheet and financial statement, and a quick return for stockholders.

The new paradigm is beginning to explore a different concept of wealth, based on intellectual capital and social accounting. Its proponents also are developing a sense of value based on a corporation's contribution to global responsibility, the health of the planet, and the personal fulfillment of its employees, in addition to the financial rewards of its stakeholders.

This "fourth wave" accounting of corporate wealth is presented here by one of the pioneering activists of new paradigm thinking. Herman B. Maynard is a member of the Board of Governors of the World Business Academy and an active participant in the organizational transformation movement. He is co-author of The Fourth Wave: Business in the Twenty-first Century. *His experience includes twenty-two years with Du Pont in professional and line management positions, including all phases of the business.*

Susan Mehrtens is head of The Potlatch Group, Inc., a research organization specializing in business trends related to the new paradigm shift. Besides co-authoring The Fourth Wave *with Maynard, Mehrtens has written a history of humanism, texts on environmental studies, and several business histories.*

The need to redefine corporate wealth is a consequence of the corporation's moving out of its current parochial view of itself and its role in the world into a larger role. In developing new ways to define its wealth, the corporation articulates its choice to pursue goals in addition to making money. By moving in this direction in the near future the corporation will be taking a proactive response to current trends relating to the issue of wealth.

Some of these trends have been exhibited around the world. For example, we have seen respiritualization as a global phenomenon, with a concomitant shift away from materialism and greater attention given to intangibles. Greed has become less acceptable and personal gratification is seen less in terms of the acquisition of things. Society is beginning to put a premium on environmental health as the basis for personal well-being. Corporate concern for community relations—"acting locally"—suggests the corporation finds a certain value in the goodwill and vitality of the local communities where it has its plants. This is coming to be a new form of "wealth."

Other trends have also emerged. The very old trend of criticizing capitalism bears on this issue of new and old definitions of wealth. For more than 150 years, capitalism has been the subject of critiques for its tendencies to exploit natural resources and human beings and for fostering the concentration of capital in the hands of a few. Concentration of wealth certainly has been a trend of recent decades in America: at the moment, it is estimated that one percent of the U.S. population holds 50 percent of all the privately held corporate stock. More and more, we hear that this situation is not sustainable. Redistribution is inevitable out of concern for economic justice, a concern that is likely to grow as the shift in consciousness occurs.

We see hints of this growing concern in the spreading realization among Americans that they are, in effect, the owners of corporate America. This is not yet direct ownership, but by virtue of the widespread involvement of many workers in company or group pension plans, individual American workers are the owners of our major corporations, simply because the large pension systems—such as TIAA/Cref and the California State Employees Association—hold so much of the corporate stock of the nation. What this trend will lead to over time remains to be seen, but it could be the basis for a redefinition of corporate ownership in the third wave phase of our transition.

Another trend widely noted in contemporary business literature is the redefining of "business." Once seen as a way to make a living or a way to get rich, business is rather seen today as a vehicle through which individuals can realize their personal vision, serve others and the planet, and make a difference in the world. People increasingly are saying they don't want to work just to make money; they want to create value. And they want to create this value in an environment that meets their needs and gives them something to feel proud of. This means that it matters how the corporation acts. Its workers want its values to be such that they can identify with it and share its commitments.

Part of the trend of redefining business involves the search for new parameters to replace those now seen as no longer appropriate. Twenty years ago, as Milton Friedman noted, business's responsibility was solely to its stockholders, and financial performance was the only criterion of evaluation. At the moment, the more progressive business analysts realize that the "rules of finance," while necessary, are no longer sufficient because they are inadequate as a means of determining the well-being of either individuals or society as a whole. Business is being called to assume responsibility for the whole, and its taking on of such a role is forcing a redefinition of wealth and the development of new parameters to monitor it.

SOCIAL ACCOUNTING

The concept of the "living economy" suggested by advocates of the New International Economic Order (NIEO) and The Other Economic Summit (TOES) may be a possible replacement for the outmoded parameters. In this vision, economic equity would be improved; capital ownership would be universalized; the "conserver economy" would be the norm; the informal economy, currently hidden, would become visible; and locally based economic activity would be "human-scale." New forms of accounting, "social accounting," would allow the evaluation of business activity.

The concept of "social accounting" arose in the 1960s, one of many manifestations of the generalized questioning of conventions that characterized that decade. This led in the economic realm to the development of concepts like Net National Welfare, Social and Demographic Statistics, and the Adjusted National Product. Actually implemented in the 1970s by the Norwegian government, these new forms of monitoring business activity seek to calculate into the performance of business the social costs to society of various economic activities. A whole series of intangibles are factored in, such as the costs of environmental protection and clean-up, costs for R & D, costs of urbanization (travel accidents, rent, security, transport of goods), costs of industrialization (crime, defense spending), costs of unhealthy lifestyles spawned by industrialism (smoking, substance abuse, industrial diseases and accidents).

Also included here are new forms of capital accounting at the macroeconomic level. This "resource accounting" strives to describe such things as the state of the resource base, the depreciation of natural assets, the depreciation of manufactured assets (the infrastructure), and the maintenance or deterioration of human health. It also capitalizes natural resources, no longer willing to regard them as the "commons" to be trashed. To prevent this trashing, the advocates of social accounting suggest the internalizing of what are now "externalities" of production, so that the costs of clean-up for polluting the air or water or for the disruption of natural ecosystems (such as in open pit mining in arid regions) would be borne by the company that creates the pollution.

Besides the trend to find new forms of accounting, there is also a trend to identify new resources in business. This trend is the result of several other trends, most notably the concern to compete effectively against the Japanese. Many regard creativity and innovation as keys to such successful competition. Many articles, books, and monographs have argued America's need to become more entrepreneurial. Within the corporation, this is taking the form on the personal level of workers trying to become more "intrapreneurial," that is, more creative and productive within the corporate mandate. At the same time, many analysts point out the demographics we are facing, which will give us a serious labor shortage in the decades ahead and make all workers that much more valuable, whether they are intrapreneurial or not.

PEOPLE AS WEALTH

The more prescient business leaders thus see the need to redefine the corporation's wealth base not in its physical assets, such as plants and equipment, but in its only source for long-term health and competitiveness: its workers. Walter Wriston, in a recent issue of *Fortune*, for example, stressed the need to focus on "intellectual capital" in a business environment where ideas are "currency," information and customers are money, and vision is valued. John Sculley of Apple Computers echoes Wriston in his statement that the major investment of his corporation is in its people. The idea behind this redefinition of wealth from plants to people is that the workers bring certain economic value to the company; their knowledge, resourcefulness, and creativity translate directly into earnings. The investment of the corporation, in other words, is as much in men and women as it is in machines.

SECOND WAVE ACCOUNTING

What is American business doing these days in response to these trends? Not much. We remain very much in the second wave, where wealth is defined as physical assets and is evaluated in terms of the traditional balance sheet. Our focus is still short-term (beating the Japanese), and our walk is still out of sync with our talk: long on talk of creativity and innovation, but very short on concrete support and encouragement to those workers who manifest these qualities.

This discrepancy is due to the fact that the biggest drivers of corporate business today are product quality (in an attempt to catch up to the Japanese, who are far ahead of us here), and lowering costs (via "back to basics"). Such concerns when driven top-down are basically antithetical to creativity, because they tend to lock people into fear, which closes down their creative potential. Consequently, they are rooted in the conventional, leaving little room or appreciation for the iconoclast.

When faced with the arguments for "social accounting," most corporate executives today respond negatively, regarding the advocates for the New International Economic Order as just another activist group, if not actual troublemakers. The pleas of such groups fall on deaf ears, and few within the financial branches of American corporations are developing new internal accounting methods to address NIEO demands.

The notion of intellectual capital is recognized and valued in the contemporary corporation in the form of stories and vignettes, passed around via word of mouth, press releases, videotapes, public TV programs and other such means, which describe the corporation's positive actions on behalf of the environment and the local community. All of this "story-telling" permits a qualitative assessment of the business, without, as yet, a translation into actual accounting procedures.

Fundamentally, corporate performance in our second wave mode is still seen in terms of finances, expressed in the financial statement and balance sheet—financial return made for the stockholders. Activities such as environmentalism where practiced are done so with the belief that such things will eventually impact positively on the bottom line and provide a suitable return on investment.

Good deeds are done by the major American corporations today out of self-serving interest. Progressive second wave businesses care for the environment as a way to bolster the public's perception of their activity and to promote the desirability of their products. Greater attention and benefits are given to employees to make them happier, with the ultimate goal of boosting their productivity to produce better business performance. All these decisions about how to treat people, the environment, and the customers are fundamentally financially (and management) driven. Only as we begin to shift from third wave into fourth wave does our perspective rise above self-serving motives.

THIRD WAVE TRANSITION

Third wave business begins to share responsibility with its employees, the community, and other constituencies. It does so while still retaining the self-serving attitude characteristic of the second wave: Its good works are done out of self-interest.

With this approach, it is not surprising that the early third-wave corporation is likely to regard social-accounting procedures as much the same sort of hassle they currently represent to second wave business. They make things more complicated. There are more constituencies to serve and a wide range of data to collect (data that are often difficult to interpret and fit into quantifiable form). These data are intended to describe and evaluate how value is being created for the different stakeholder groups connected with the corporation, with the ultimate intent being self-interest: to get these groups to act more favorably to the corporation.

While its goal is self-serving, the third wave corporation will play a vital function related to the nature of third wave as a transition phase. In terms of redefining the wealth of corporations, this will be the time when the new parameters represented by social accounting and NIEO principles become incorporated into the thinking and procedures of our businesses. The third wave will be a bridging time, a time when business conduct and record-keeping will bridge the gap between the straight financial accounting methods in use today and the markedly different ideas of wealth and accounting expected for businesses in the fourth wave.

FOURTH WAVE ACCOUNTING

By the time of the fourth wave, business will have emerged as the leader of society, accepting responsibility for the whole. It will, in short, have taken on a much wider agenda for itself, and this will require a redefinition of corporate wealth.

From our vantage point, with our second wave mentality, it is very hard for us to imagine the mind-set of the fourth wave. By that time, the consciousness shift we see underway now will have completely reformed both business and its basic concerns. People living in the fourth wave will consider a host of questions we would never think to apply to business now: How is the corporation handling its global responsibility? or, What is the corporation doing to improve the health of the planet? There is no way that current definitions of wealth will be adequate then to evaluate corporate performance or to express the value that business then will be creating, given its global mandate and leadership role.

Social accounting in the fourth wave will become the principal form of accounting used by corporations for the simple reason that the distinction between corporate activity and social activity will fall away: "Corporate" will be "social," when the ownership and purview of the corporation will have expanded beyond the narrow realm of stockholders and manufacturing. The value created by the activity of corporations will have many more forms than dollars or other currencies, because the corporation will be recognized as having an impact extending beyond its tangible business-related interactions.

This extension of corporate activity is likely to have several consequences. First, the people (both inside and outside the corporation) will demand a say in how the corporation conducts itself; that is, they will begin to assert their rights as stakeholders in the corporate enterprise. Secondly, the whole idea of "ownership" will change, capitalism as we know it having disappeared and been replaced by more positive images of humankind and a more communitarian form of ownership. No longer will other people seem threatening, competing, violent, or potentially dangerous, making necessary the privatizing of property. In the fourth wave view, human beings will be creatures of trust, caring, altruism, and cooperation, ready and able to share freely in the abundance of the Earth.

Fourth wave corporate wealth will be seen as peace, service, personal fulfillment, planetary and personal health, justice, and sharing, in addition to financial rewards for stakeholders. Given the very different sense of values in fourth wave thinking, security will no longer be seen as lodged solely in the accumulation of money, but rather in personal inner trust and the certainty of the cooperation and mutual aid of one's fellows. At this point, extreme personal wealth will be seen as an anachronism, leading to a more equitable distribution of wealth.

The democratizing of wealth will be matched by democratizing tendencies in the political and corporate realms. As we noted in earlier sections, political power will devolve to lower levels, to human-scale local democratic entities, just as corporate governance comes to be rooted in the clusters that carry out the business of the corporation, choosing their managers by democratic process. Throughout both society and the corporation, there will be a concern for minimal regulation and maximum freedom. And this has strong implications for the leadership of the corporation as it deals with the biopolitics of the fourth wave is the subject of the next section.

4

ESCAPING THE CAREER CULTURE

by Susan Albert

One of the major problems facing old paradigm business today is the alienation of its work force. Many employees are finding it impossible to reconcile the demands of a career with their needs as individuals and members of a family.

In the following essay, Susan Albert discusses the dilemma facing workers, particularly women, who are no longer willing to become workaholics and sacrifice their relationships, their children, and their health on the altar of financial gain, status, and steady progress up the career ladder. She documents a new paradigm alternative: a less institutional, more human concept of work that is more autonomous, creative, and personally fulfilling.

Susan Wittig Albert has taught at the University of Texas, Tulane, and Southwest Texas State University, where she was also Vice-President for Academic Affairs. A prolific writer of fiction and nonfiction, her previous books include Steps to Structure *and* The Participating Reader, *as well as a new detective series. The following article is adapted from her book* Work of Her Own.

The American dream is built on a successful career. In this culture, every successful person has a career. Americans define themselves in terms of their careers—what they do, how long they have done it, what level of career advancement they have achieved. In fact, what I call the *career culture* has come to dominate more and more of American life.

This culture, oriented around careers and the organizations in which careers are shaped, is the framework for millions of Americans' dreams of social and economic empowerment, of personal prosperity, of individual accomplishment. The career culture not only controls people's decisions about how and where to work, but also where and how to live, spend money and leisure time, when to marry and bear children and how to raise and educate them. It identifies people, classifies them, and differentiates them from one another, in both obvious and subtle ways.

The idea of a career is a relatively new phenomenon, a product of a highly specialized industrial technology that requires specialists to keep it operating. For most people, commitment to a career is a lifetime commitment. A man (until the 1960s, people who entered careers were nearly all male) educated himself specifically for a particular career. He spent his work life in a single company or in two or three companies in a single industry, gaining successive promotions from one rung of the career ladder to another.

Today, however, men no longer have a monopoly on careers. Since the 1960s, increasing numbers of women have sought and achieved positions traditionally held by males. Further, one-career lives are no longer the norm. Because of the rapid displacement of old technologies by new ones and because of the dramatic ups and downs of the economic climate, both women and men are opting to change careers, to step off one career ladder and onto another. And in a very recent phenomenon, they are also opting to "down-shift" their career commitment—reduce the amount of time or effort they give to getting ahead in their careers—or to step out of the career culture altogether.

I stepped out. In 1985, after a successful fifteen-year career in higher education, I left my $70,000-a-year vice-presidency, moved to the country, and became a freelance writer and part-time teacher. My new work is enjoyable work, and it pays me what I need to live contentedly. But it is *not* a career. It does not involve consecutive progressive advancement within an organization that confers rank, title, and salary upon me. I do not expect to move up to the higher echelons of anything, except in the sense of choosing more personally challenging projects. As a *career-leaver*, I work on the margin of the career culture, with all the risks and challenges—and uncertainty—that being a marginal person involves. I traded *institutionalized* work—work defined and controlled by a business or corporation—for self-generated work: work that I create and carry out according to my desires and needs. The work I do now is truly work of my own.

As I began to talk with other women about this experience, I discovered that I was not alone in abandoning a career to create my own work. After two decades of effort to establish themselves in the American workplace, growing numbers of women are now jumping *off* the career ladder. The popular media documents this developing trend. According to *The New York Times* (February 8, 1990), the 1990s promise to be the "Flee Decade," with increasing numbers of people saying no to demands for more hours on the job, more single-minded focus, more commitment. A marketing research firm estimates that in 1992, 31 million Americans started working at home for the first time, up from 2.4 million in 1987. *Entrepreneurial Women*, a magazine targeted at women who own their own businesses, estimates that nearly 2 million women started new at-home businesses in 1990.

Many of these women, the magazine says, are "refugees from the rat race." Growing numbers of well-established, high-achieving women are deciding that while work itself remains central to their lives, they are no longer willing to commit themselves to the exclusive and unthinking pursuit of career success. Increasingly, they are insisting on a new work ethic, one that does not require them to spend the most productive years of their lives working sixty- and seventy-hour weeks, leaving no room in their lives for anything but the career chase. Many women no longer believe that their high salaries, public authority, power as policymakers, and social status are worth the cost to their own personal lives. They are willing to sacrifice their gains in the career culture—recognition and prestige, title, salary, future security—for the opportunity to do work that *they* create.

As a participant in and witness to this new phenomenon, I began to search out other participants. In this search, I interviewed or corresponded with over a hundred women career-leavers, all of whom left successful positions in established careers to create work of their own. That new work is as diverse as the women's interests and backgrounds. In their former lives, they were geologists, CPA's, college and university professors, botanists, sales managers, systems analysts, teachers, public relations executives, nurses, bank executives, public and private sector senior managers. Some were making $100,000 a year and up. Now they own bookstores, run farms, operate child-care and elder-care centers, manage spiritual organizations. They have their own at-home consulting practices; they do freelance writing, speaking, and teaching; provide physical and massage therapy; and offer accounting services—from the place where they live. They have become full-time artists and full-time mothers. They have down-scaled their own and their families' economic needs (always with great effort and sometimes with great pain) so that they can support themselves by working as they choose. And they choose to work in a way and at a pace that permits them to do *other* enriching work for themselves and others: they participate in community child-care programs, run for town and country office, volunteer at local hospitals or in their children's schools, take classes and read books on self-development and personal growth, open to their own deep spirituality. They are doing what they love and living what they believe.

For these women, the process of leaving their successful careers was an extraordinarily difficult one, for they had committed enormous amounts of time, effort, and emotional energy to gaining a secure place in a man's world. Many of them had compelling personal reasons for committing what some career-oriented feminists have called the "suicidal act" of abandoning a successful career. But all of them are deeply critical of the career culture and the belief that the career should be the crowning achievement of their lives. Their actions constitute a radical critique of the career culture and of institutionalized work. This critique is a feminist critique, but it goes far beyond that usually offered by career-committed feminists. Let me make a distinction between the two by first describing the important points on which they agree.

Women are late entrants into the career culture, career "outsiders" who have only in the last few decades been admitted to careers shaped and directed by men. Most women agree that even though they make up an increasingly large percentage of the work force, they are still not "insiders." Not only does the male-dominated culture of the workplace generally bar them from advancement above the "glass ceiling," but from full and equal participation at the levels they have managed to reach. They often work with the debilitating sense that they are illegitimate members of the corporate family, second-rate and second-class. They speak of constantly working "in spite of"—in spite of the lack of full acceptance and earned recognition; in spite of sexual harassment; in spite of salary discrimination; in spite of having to work harder than their male colleagues to find a corporate place and stay there, let alone advance. They speak of having to work in a hostile environment in which their need to lead full, rich lives *outside* the corporation is consistently denied.

These criticisms of the workplace are raised both by career-committed feminists and by women career-leavers. Career-committed feminists, however, argue that the problem is one of "critical mass."

"As a woman, you can make a difference," the message goes. "Work hard, climb the ladder, and get to the place where you can reform the system from the inside, where you can make it safe and comfortable for other women." This message is delivered through innumerable magazines and books that offer advice on how a smart, tough woman can gain entrance to a career and climb the ladder in record time—at the same time managing to marry a husband, care for a home, and raise children in her spare time.

Most women career-leavers, on the other hand, have come to believe from their experience that they are not likely to make a significant difference by staying in the career culture—or, at least, that the difference they *can* make is not worth the personal price they have to pay to make it. "I can earn plenty of money," one former executive said, "and I can have plenty of power, as long as my employer wants to give me that power. But it's naive to believe that the patriarchal system will ever give me the power to change the patriarchal system!" (The term "patriarchal" suggests the extent to which any individual or organization is shaped and directed by males and informed by male habits, beliefs, and values.)

Women leave their careers, at least in part, *because* they are pessimistic about the possibility of "feminizing" business and industry, except through some very limited and superficial changes in personnel policies. More flex-time may be offered. Leave for child care, elder care, and family crisis may become available as employers compete for employees in a declining labor pool. "But those are gimmicks," a former bank executive told me. "The *real* changes go far beyond personnel policies. The *real* changes are absolutely fundamental to the system. To make those changes, the system is essentially going to have to remake itself."

What are the *real* changes this woman and others are talking about, and how can they be achieved? In order to answer this question, it is helpful to know something about the kind of human achievement and human interaction that occur within work organizations and in the career culture as a whole.

In America today, the highest level of personal growth is allegedly achieved at what Harvard psychologist Robert Kegan in *The Evolving Self* calls the "institutional level" of psychological growth and development. This phase of adult maturation, which we might call the "institutional self," emphasizes the traditional masculine values of independence, autonomy, and competition. The institutional self is autonomous, individual, independent, highly competitive, and free from the limits and constraints of personal relationships. As most people recognize, a careerist who is fully committed to moving upward in a demanding career does not have the time, the energy, or the inclination to be equally committed to a relationship.

A recent study found that only a third of executive women have children by the age of forty. In 1985, 75 percent of the women students surveyed at a leading business school reported that they viewed children as a "roadblock" in their careers. Furthermore, the career culture's reward system works in favor of affiliations with institutions rather than with people. A personal relationship does not "pay off" in terms of financial rewards, prestige, and power, as does an institutional relationship.

And therein lies an interesting irony, for in the place of an intimate relationship to a person, careerists substitute an intimate relationship to an institution. Careerists no longer have careers, they *are* their careers. Their personal identities become institutional identities. Their sense of power, self-worth, and personal authority is entirely derived from the institutions with which they are affiliated. In that sense, then, careerists only appear to be independent and autonomous: in fact, they are entirely dependent for their continued self-definition and their personal power upon the institutions from which they derive their careers.

In the career culture, there is neither true personal autonomy nor true personal independence. Nor can there be, for most organizations (and this includes such hallowed institutions as government, religion, and education) rigidly defend themselves against all forms of significant change, from within and without. In that context, *real* personal autonomy and truly self-derived power cannot be tolerated.

What is the effect of all this on people? In his book *Modern Madness: The Emotional Fallout of Success*, Douglas LaBier describes the "negative adaptations" and internal conflicts that women and men develop as they attempt to cope with the career culture. Adaptation to the organization, he writes, may ultimately create deep feelings of "rage, depression, anxiety, and escapism . . . the emotional effects of too much compromising and trading-off to get ahead." In this hazardous environment, we find such psychological afflictions as workaholism—which can be seen as one's frenzied commitment to maintaining the viability of the career, and through the career the viability of the self—and sexual harassment—which can be seen as inflicting one's sense of powerlessness and vulnerability upon one who is even *more* powerless, *more* vulnerable. Attempting to meet the continually escalating demands of the career culture can produce what some psychologists call "co-dependency," learned coping behaviors like denial and repression that people use to lessen the negative psychological impact of a dysfunctional situation. But co-dependency is an illness in and of itself, psychologists tell us. Often the only treatment is to remove oneself, if possible, from the dysfunctional situation.

The popular media these days are full of descriptions of the psychological stress and physical illnesses that people suffer in their efforts to develop careers. But as psychologist Carol Gilligan suggests in *In a*

Different Voice, women and men bring profoundly different psychological orientations to the workplace. Men are trained to compete, women to cooperate; men are encouraged to be aggressively self-sufficient, women to develop strong connections to others. It is reasonable to expect that the career culture will affect them differently. What is the effect of the career culture on women?

The beliefs and behaviors required of those in the career culture are male beliefs and values. To succeed, women must adapt to organizations in ways that often violate their basic sense of being female. A former advertising executive said, "Talk about me changing my company? That's a laugh. The higher I got in the hierarchy, the more my company changed *me*. I hated the person I was becoming—competitive, angry, always ready to defend my territory. And it was true of other women I knew. The higher they got, the more they acted out the corporate BS."

But something other than fear of losing themselves was involved in these women's decision to leave the career culture. Most had come to the point where, even though they still had to earn a living, they no longer needed to view their careers as the central, pivotal experience that organized the totality of their lives. Robert Kegan speaks of this personal evolution when he describes the next level of adult growth and development *beyond* the institutional level. He calls this the "inter-individual" stage and defines it as a phase of psychological growth where the self accepts both its own personal authority *and* its responsibility for other selves within a community of involvement. We might call this the *self-in-community*, for while the self is for itself, it is also for others. It is independent and whole, but it is *not* separate or alienated. It is cooperative, not competitive.

5

COMPETITION, COOPERATION AND CO-CREATION: INSIGHTS FROM THE WORLD BUSINESS ACADEMY

by Cynthia Joba, Herman Bryant Maynard, Jr., and Michael Ray

Questions about the appropriate form of relating in the current and future business climate led the World Business Academy to hold two retreats on the relationship modes of competition, cooperation and co-creation. Although competition is something of a sacred cow within business, it has taken tremendous criticism from outside of business, especially from the preponderance of research that indicates the efficacy of cooperation. Co-creation and the creativity it implies also seem to be much needed in this time of transition.

The two three-day retreats examined such questions as: What does co-creation look like? What is the changing role of competition and cooperation in the new framework that is emerging? How does this change show up in our daily business and personal lives? What are the implications for our companies, our countries, our world?

The following report is based on discussions led by retreat facilitators Cynthia Joba and Herman Maynard, and in sessions of Michael Ray's New Paradigm Business course at Stanford University.

Cynthia Joba is a cultural anthropologist with extensive corporate business experience and former executive director of the World Business Academy.

The ways that we choose to relate—to ourselves, to each other, between businesses, between economies, to other species, to the earth itself—drive the outcomes we get more than perhaps any other fundamental assumption. In fact, our very survival may depend on our ability to shift into new ways of relating.

There is mounting evidence that reliance solely on competition as a mode of relationship is destructive. But there is also good evidence that dependence on any one form of relationship can be dysfunctional too. What is the basis on which we should relate to each other given the conditions of world transformation in which we find ourselves?

Business dependence on competition provides one of the best examples of a dominant paradigm. Competition has so infused the economic philosophy of the developed world that we consider only various forms of competition rather than other alternatives. Economists and policymakers, for instance, look at whether competition is true, monopolistic, pure, oligopolistic, but not whether there are any alternatives to competition itself. From the very earliest years in school through the highest levels of education, we are urged to compete, not to "cheat" by cooperating with others, not to taste the benefits of the co-creation that can come from working in teams.

Yet, research in almost every human science field since the late 1800s has indicated that cooperation is a superior form of relationship in nature and organizations, psychologically, physiologically, and economically. The paradigm emerging in science even goes further to indicate that the universe itself is creative, so that the notion of co-creation becomes another candidate for the way we do business and relate to one another.

Our focus of the World Business Academy retreats and Stanford New Paradigm Business class sessions was not to determine which of the three modes—competition, cooperation or co-creation—was best, but rather to dialogue about the fundamental assumptions underlying them, their value and benefits, and how they relate to each other. These are three modes of relationship that we can choose; each may be appropriate given certain circumstances. We searched for the basis on which we can make this choice in specific situations. We explored the needs of people, businesses and the global environment that might move us toward a greater emphasis on one or the other.

By definition, these modes of relating all emphasize doing something *together*. The word "together" invokes the concepts of wholeness and interconnectedness that systems thinking and the new science have contributed to the emerging paradigm.

The Latin roots of the words themselves indicate that competition is *striving* together, coooperation is *working* together, and co-creation is *creating* together. That commonality in definition says something about the potential value of each of these modes, depending on what we are doing and what needs to be done. As engineer and organization theorist

Don Yates puts it, "It is possible to look at them in terms of energy or in a force field sense. Competition is forces opposing; cooperation is forces in parallel; co-creation is forces fusing."

The question becomes, then, what does each person or business need at this particular time: striving, working or creating in opposition, parallel or fusion? There is no single answer. The best way to understand the factors affecting the best mode of relating is to first consider each individually in some depth.

COMPETITION: STRIVING TOGETHER

If you look at a dictionary, you'll find two sorts of definitions of striving. One says that striving is to make great effort to do one's best, a matter of moving toward excellence. When athletes, engineers, politicians and business people talk about the benefits of competition, they are referring to this definition of striving. It's the other definition of striving—to be in opposition to or in conflict with—that underlies the negative effects that have been observed with competition.

But even when competition is considered in terms of opposition or conflict, there is the possibility of some benefit. Friction typically creates an energy soak. But friction can create a spark or fire; that is, competition can be a catalyst, it can motivate people to higher and higher achievement. In the context of John Kennedy's vision of getting to the moon within a decade, scientists, engineers and businesses competed. Although some companies lost certain contracts, the level of excellence was pushed to the point that the vision was realized in amazing ways. To some extent, everybody won in that situation.

There are many examples within industries of competitors pushing each other to unexpected heights. In fact, stories are told of cooperation and co-creation occurring with benefit within a setting of competition. The space race certainly was one of competition between the U.S. and U.S.S.R. at one point. The amazing increases in the power of computers is another example.

Are there really winners or losers in some situations of competition within a larger vision? Some corporate veterans in the WBA report that some of the best outcomes were contracts that they lost, because each loss caused them to find better ways of working. It heightened their attention, led to cooperative efforts within their companies, and also led to creative efforts beyond expectation.

So where do the negative effects of competition come in? Author Alfie Kohn, who has studied over 400 research reports on competition and cooperation, says that competition causes anxiety, is inefficient, undermines intrinsic motivation, destroys self-esteem, and poisons relationships. His position is that competition "is destructive and counterproductive not merely in excess; it is destructive not merely because we are doing it the wrong way; it is destructive by its very nature."

Our discussion of this radical point concentrated on the conditions under which this may be true and those in which it may be false. When there is a larger vision and an expanding perspective or market, there is the opportunity for the positive benefits already mentioned. But when the situation is seen in a limited context, in the belief system of separation between people, or in the business sense of maintaining the status quo, competition is done within a zero-sum game with winners and losers, and all the negative effects accrue.

Our perspective drives the result. A perspective combining competition with the other two modes seems to be most powerful. Since competition is goal-oriented and linear in nature, for instance, the more process-oriented cooperative mode provides a balance that is important, particularly for those working within organizations.

COOPERATION: WORKING TOGETHER

Cooperation is working together within a boundary with outcomes that are defined as attractive to both or all the parties involved. Competition between companies can create strong cooperation within each organization. For instance, the Total Quality Management movement within the U.S.—which was initially generated by strong industrial competition from Japan—has been further fueled by competition between industries and companies, which has led to a high level of cooperation within companies. Self-directed, cooperative teamwork has led to higher production with higher quality.

One reviewer of the evidence on cooperation, Perry W. Buffington, says that the research "demonstrates that cooperation surely brings out the 'best' in us. This finding has been held in virtually every occupation, skill, or behavior tested. For instance, scientists who consider themselves cooperative tend to have more published articles than their competitive colleagues. Cooperative business people have higher salaries. From elementary grades to college, cooperative students have higher grade point averages. Personnel directors who work together have fewer job vacancies to fill. And, not surprisingly, cooperation increases creativity."

But the experience of many of our business participants, both in the retreats and the classes, was that the situation isn't really that simple. Cooperation in a group business situation can lead to a sort of codependence in which people support each other's worst tendencies. It can create a pseudo-community in which people are playing as if they are getting along. The requisite conflict, the spark or fire, may be missing. There may be a lack of reality check, which leads to groupthink. Single individuals can dominate the discussion, so that there is no real participation and input from everyone. People can sugarcoat, rather than say things directly. Just as competition often focuses too much on goals, cooperation can focus too much on process and relationships without anything getting done.

Participants gave positive examples that involved cooperation within competition. The California wine industry operates with an extraordinary climate of cooperation, with growers helping each other get started, sharing the lessons of mistakes, giving details of breakthroughs. This kind of cooperation led to the California industry catching up and in some ways surpassing the French industry in competition. One of the class members pointed out that this kind of cooperation within competition is found in many agricultural fields at the micro level between farms and at the macro level in industry cooperatives.

One industrial marketing specialist who participated in the retreats told of a situation in which the management had changed at the site of the largest customer. Up to that point the marketing company had 95 percent of the customer's business. The new management said the company had to make an outstanding price bid in order to retain 80 percent of its business. Instead of participating in a bidding war, however, the marketer and his team developed a partnership proposal in which they would provide new services to their customer.

A year later in a contract negotiation, the key customer executive said that he realized that the marketer's company should have 100 percent of the business in order to serve him properly. The marketer said he realized that his company would need to become the research and development arm of the client company. They decided that they would work out the specific price over a six-month period. At one point the customer pointed out that the marketer's competition was offering a 10 percent lower price. The marketer's team showed him how their service could reduce costs even more than that for the customer. Price became secondary and was determined as they moved ahead; it became a fairness issue that they worked on together.

This story generated a great deal of discussion about the nature of competition and cooperation. Was this simply some kind of collusion to control the market? Or did this signify a new way of doing business that could improve the quality of business in the industry? What about the other competitors for the customer's business? Since he was the largest customer in the industry, weren't other companies hurt by the competitive effects of the cooperation? Or would this kind of cooperation lead to improving their way of doing business to more productive forms of relationship and business for everyone? And what about the creativity that might have been generated in this situation?

CO-CREATION: CREATING TOGETHER

There is a fine line between cooperation and co-creation. Cooperation can generate some form of creativity. But it appears that in cooperation creativity is within rigid boundaries, while with co-creation the boundaries are open. As Don Yates pointed out, cooperation is forces operating in parallel; co-creation is forces fusing. Another way of saying this is that co-creation is synergistic: the whole is greater than the sum of the parts, $1+1=3$.

Co-creation combines the best of competition and cooperation with a balance between goal and process orientation. In some sense, co-creation seems to be the necessary mode of relating in the emerging paradigm, and actually represents what it is, just as competition seems to be the fundamental assumption of the old paradigm.

While everyone could talk about situations in which they had worked with others to create something new and valuable outside of previous boundaries, few of these personal stories came from corporate situations. Some spoke of their experience that in engineering situations there was this form of co-creation, but often when the engineers interacted with the business people in the companies, they found that those people tended to be rules-oriented and biased against a co-creative form of relationship. Start-up companies, especially in high-tech fields (that naturally involve engineers) tended to have the potential for co-creation. And it happened in the creation of advertising to the point that multiple people often take credit for a particularily successful piece of advertising.

The benefits of co-creation seem to outweigh the disadvantages (which include the need for compromise and surrender and the possibility of a kind of codependency). The appeal of co-creation is so strong that it was necessary to control our discussion to cover competition and cooperation first, so that these modes got covered adequately.

There was a feeling that co-creation was the form of relationship that was desperately needed in the business transition that is occurring.

How can co-creation be fostered in organizations? Some suggested that there had to be a true commitment to it in the organizational unit. In fact, others told of tragic circumstances in which management appeared to be giving support for creativity and co-creation but were insincere. When co-creation occurred there, the ideas were devalued as impractical and off the company mission. After a time, the process completely fell apart because it had no real support.

Commitment to co-creation has to be implemented in terms of physical space and materials that facilitate the co-creation process. Everyone needs to begin to notice co-creation when it happens. It needs to be publicized. Just as it is difficult to notice our own creativity, it is difficult to pay attention to co-creation when it happens. On a personal basis we need to be unattached, free of the outcome. In co-creation one has to allow oneself to be vulnerable. In contrast to what is taught in the standard educational system, we have to recognize that it isn't a failure to need help from others.

WHAT IS NEEDED NOW

It is clear that just as we weren't able to move without preparation to a total concentration on co-creation, the world is not ready for an immediate move to that seemingly preferred mode of relationship. There are strong questions as to whether it would be functional for any individual or organization to move totally to any one of the modes.

A new sort of synthesis seems to be occurring between ancient philosophical traditions and the new science. The ideas of wholeness and connectedness argue against considering any of these ways of relating in terms of difference, comparison or opposition. No one mode can be considered in isolation from the others. Development of the use of these three approaches must take place within each of us. We will want to be conscious of the choices we are making organizationally and individually. We need to continue to ask these questions.

EXEMPLAR:
The Calvert Fund

In the current climate of jolting change, business people will look for any new source of ideas. Take the case of Wayne Silby, founder of the Calvert Group, one of the first and largest socially responsible investment funds. Silby shuns competition in favor of cooperation in his work.

An example of this principle came when there was a dramatic change in the banking industry. The early growth of Calvert and many similar funds was due to the fact that they could offer 13 or 14 percent returns, while their major competitors, the banks, could offer only about 5. When legislation was about to be enacted that would allow the banks to offer money-market deposit accounts, the basis of Calvert's competitive advantage appeared to be on the verge of being destroyed.

Silby already had been designated Calvert's corporate daydreamer. Even before the legislative threat, he and his associates had conducted brainstorming sessions, with the participants lying on their backs in order to produce a more meditative state. But since his company had grown to almost two billion dollars in assets, and the bank's money-market deposit accounts might severely cut into that base, Silby decided to take more extreme measures than simply lying on the floor. Specifically, he meditated in a flotation tank (also known as a sensory deprivation tank or an isolation tank), which is sound-proof, lightproof, and buoyant.

He explains, "To get new ideas you need to have a space where your mind chatter and judgments in your mind about who you are and what you are doing are turned down. And you can get in touch with a deeper part of yourself that can start revealing patterns that are pretty awesome."

The solution he came up with in the isolation tank was a financial instrument that allowed Calvert to cooperate rather than compete with banks. It worked by funneling Calvert customer money into the twelve to fifteen bank market-rate deposit accounts with the highest returns. This gave Calvert an extra fee from the banks for servicing accounts, provided FDIC insurance for the investments, and allowed its customers to conveniently bypass the upper limits on bank market-rate deposit accounts and invest almost any amount in them, because Calvert could spread the money around the banks with the highest returns. And it led the Calvert instrument to produce a higher yield than 98 percent of the individual bank accounts, resulting in some $800 million in maintained and increased business.

6

LABOR AS TRASH

by Michael Phillips

Is it ethical to fire twenty machinists and sheet metal workers who do good, consistent work, saving $700,000—instead of one vice-president with a $400,000 salary and $300,000 of expenses who made a major mistake in marketing? This and other questions are raised in the following essay about the justice of old paradigm tactics for cost-cutting in the face of declining profits.

More appropriate alternatives to wholesale layoffs are also presented in this timely essay by the well-known business philosopher and iconoclast Michael Phillips. He is the author of The Seven Laws of Money, Simple Living Investments, *and (with Salli Rasberry)* Honest Business.

One overcast afternoon shortly after my eighteenth birthday, working my first job in Seattle's UCC electronics firm, I was directed to join a personnel manager, to stay around the plant and talk to the night shift. At the appointed time, he told two hundred female assembly line workers they were being laid off, effective immediately. There was panic, many tears and loud crying. In retrospect I see that I was there being groomed for management.

It has long been an axiom of American business that when sales or profits decline, the first element of cost that should be reduced is labor. "Labor" usually means the lowest paid employees. In instances where drastic cutbacks occur, such as Chrysler, white collar middle management is reduced too.

The American explanation is that in addition to reducing costs rapidly, there is a side benefit of making the remaining workers work harder.

In the original firing and three others I saw subsequently in other firms, that theory was not substantiated. Emotional depression was very common among the remaining workers, deep suspicion of the company was pervasive, but most importantly the reaction was to *appear* to work hard while decreasing quality. Auto workers under such circumstances are noted for leaving off critical bolts and dropping them inside some other vital mechanism. I always saw a drop in quality for long periods after firings.

FOREIGN PRACTICES

Two foreign practices are occasionally cited in public discussion of this monstrosity as an alternative approach to "cost saving" layoffs.

One is the type of government intervention that has occurred in Europe where companies in financially troubled industries have been forced to remain open or to sell their factories to workers.

The other is the Japanese practice of lifetime employment where companies drastically reduce dividends, and borrow money to avoid firing workers. The high productivity and quality of Japanese factories has been linked to their generous treatment of workers.

So far American corporate response has been to say that Europeans and Japanese are different and that it wouldn't work here; furthermore, the free market has such great philosophical validity that it must be preserved regardless of the minor flaws. In some rare cases American companies have opened joint factory ventures with Japanese to test whether humane labor treatment will work here. So far the practice is not spreading rapidly.

Regardless, the basic axiom is fully intact. Every company in the U.S. from yuppie electronics firms in Silicon Valley to U.S. Steel believes it has an absolute right to fire employees, limited only by Federal laws governing sex, race and age discrimination and union rules, in the rare instances where they exist, governing seniority.

NEW FORCES IN THE U.S.

There are two emerging forces in our own society that are bringing this lay-off practice into question. One is the environmental movement; the other is shareholder activism.

For fifteen years we have been learning that trash is not something to be thrown away and forgotten. Concepts of ecology have taught us that some trash is dangerous (toxic or radioactive) and must be dealt with carefully, while other trash is valuable and worth more when recycled than having to re-create it from scratch, such as aluminum.

We treat labor as trash, to be fired and forgotten. The time is coming when we may learn the same lessons about labor that we have learned about trash. Labor costs that are *reduced* are actually people. They can be traumatized by firing and the social costs in terms of health treatment can be high for the society as a whole. The costs of abused children, crime and poor education among families that have to keep moving are also great and unmeasured. Similarly we are firing trained people with skills and former loyalties who were especially useful to their employer; the costs of training new people is high and often ignored in the panic of cutting costs.

The free market doesn't seem responsive to this social cost, which is why government action is favored in Europe. The typical argument here in favor of passing these social costs on to the society and not worrying about the retraining costs is that the business's first responsibility is to the shareholder and higher earnings.

But surprisingly, there is a second force that is bringing this practice into question—shareholder concern. The emerging observation about our sanctified freedom to fire labor is that *top management* may have made the mistakes which led to the sales or profit decline that necessitates firing.

MANAGEMENT IS NOT BLAMELESS

Shareholders are seeing that the captain runs his ship aground, throws part of the crew overboard and gets new crew in the next port. The owners of the ship get stuck with the same careless, possibly incompetent captain.

We can expect lawsuits in the future from shareholders who question the priority of firing. Twenty machinists and sheet metal workers who do good, consistent work are fired, saving $700,000 instead of firing one vice-president with a $400,000 salary and $300,000 of expenses who made a major mistake in marketing.

One reason such suits have not appeared on a large scale is that identifying clear-cut mistakes in business is often difficult to do, and pinpointing specific responsibility for mistakes is even more difficult. From the shareholders' point of view, it is becoming more important, and the valuable lessons we need to learn from mistakes are not learned when the kneejerk solution is to fire low level workers.

ALTERNATIVES

There are a number of approaches that are appearing on the horizon; many are borrowed from practices already in effect in Europe.

1. The use of outside people on the corporate board of directors to specifically examine cost cutting procedures when downturns in sales

or profits occur—prior to firing labor. (Most major U.S. companies have boards of directors dominated by their own management directly or indirectly.)

2. To establish cost reduction procedures well in advance of business downturns so that panic is replaced by careful long-term planning. This kind of planning seldom results in firing low level workers.

3. To have labor active in management and board decisions, particularly cost cutting and labor saving. This has worked especially well where changes in work rules and workers' suggestions have resulted in lower costs and higher productivity.

4. The conscious and planned corporate use of independent subcontractors. This approach was developed in Sweden and is fostered by a number of large Swedish companies. They create small companies made up of clusters of their existing employees to primarily supply themselves. In downturns these subcontractors move to greater reliance on other businesses to fill the slack. Nobody gets fired, the subcontractors scramble harder to find other work.

5. Company-wide pay cuts to preserve jobs, particularly management cuts.

The companies that learn these lessons may well be protected from the emerging generation of aggressive shareholders. For the companies that don't . . .

REFERENCES

Shoten Yamamoto, *Japanese Business Philosophy*, PHP, a book on the evolution of the Japanese business ethic. Resembles Bob Bellah's *Tokugawa Religions* which sought Max Weber's equivalent of the Protestant Ethic in Japanese history. Shoten Yamamoto describes a wonderful tradition in Japan, the *opposite* of the Swedish fostering of independent small companies for low level workers, where Japanese companies (since the 1600's) have rewarded *successful* executives who couldn't rise higher in a company (because of the limited number of slots at the top) with their own independent company. The net effect was to create families of businesses which in this century have become corporate giants. Mitsubishi has followed this practice of generating offspring businesses for centuries.

Noteworthy too is that Shoten Yamamoto is recognized as a great Japanese thinker, known behind the scenes as the man who wrote *The Japanese and the Jews* in 1971, under a pseudonym that showed the Japanese how very much like the Jews they are in intelligence, business skills, social attitudes and how the world reacts to them in very similar ways.

Part II

THE BEGINNING OF
NEW LEADERSHIP

The first responsibility of a leader is to define reality. The last is to say thank you. In between, the leader is a servant.

> MAX DE PREE
> *Leadership Is an Art*

One can paraphrase Gertrude Stein by saying, "a leader is a follower is a leader."

> *Administrative Science Quarterly*

True leaders inspire people to do great things and, when the work is done, their people proudly say, "We did this ourselves."

> LAO-TZU
> *Tao Te Ching*

Genuine leadership involves getting all the wisdom that is available in a group, and helping that group come to a better decision than any one of its members would have been able to achieve himself. The servant leader is the person who gets the unsuspected best out of his group of people.

> J. IRWIN MILLER

INTRODUCTION

It takes a particular sort of leadership to catalyze the kind of creativity that is needed in business today. During a time of scientific revolution or paradigm shift there are two kinds of scientists: the journeyworker doing traditional science and being affected by the transition, and the discoverer or leader of the new paradigm—the Newton, Einstein, Bohr, or Prigogine.

Just so in business: there is the worker who is feeling the shift and contributing to it and there is the leader who recognizes the new needs and has the vision to activate the shift to a new way of doing business. However, in the case of the present transition, the form of leadership itself is changing. Instead of being just a person at the top of the organization, leadership is becoming a context in which all participants are leaders and in which the staff of leadership can be taken by each individual at the appropriate time. In the paradigm that is emerging, there seems to be a need for both strong leadership and for participation by all in a leadership mode.

The key seems to be in the attitude that permeates the organization. What is required is a leadership that operates from compassion and community. Perhaps a story can convey what this means.

In Scott Peck's book *The Different Drum*, he tells a story called "The Rabbi's Gift." In it, the abbot of a dying Christian order with only five monks, all over seventy years old, pays a call to an old rabbi visiting in the forest near the order's decaying house. They commiserate with one another over the lack of religious fervor left in the world. They embrace, and as the abbot is about to leave, the rabbi says, "I have no advice to give. The only thing I can tell you is that the Messiah is one of you."

This was the rabbi's gift. Once the abbot reported this to the other four aged monks, they began to treat themselves and each other as if each was the Messiah. People who happened to be hiking near the monastery were attracted by the extraordinary love and respect there. More and more people came to play and pray. Young men began to talk to the monks. A steady stream of them asked to join the order, and it began to flourish once again.

The creativity practiced by these monks was no longer problem-solving. They forgot about their problem of the decaying monastic order and went on with their work—but they did it with extraordinary compassion. In this situation each one of them served as a leader at various times as they went about their work with the attitude of respect and compassion.

The story of "The Rabbi's Gift" is being lived out in the leadership of corporate America, albeit in different ways. Take the case of Jack Welch, CEO of General Electric. When he assumed the head of the company in 1981, he took the mandate to make changes in the structure of GE that had been planned some fourteen years earlier but not implemented. As he has worked to make this change, his emphasis on people and empowerment at GE is almost an icon for the paradigm shift in business. His initial cost-cutting and housecleaning earned him the nickname "Neutron Jack" because "GE buildings remained standing but the people disappeared." However, he was moving the giant multinational from a dependence on analytic strategy formulation (old paradigm leadership) to a greater concern with employee empowerment (new paradigm leadership). In a cover story interview in *Fortune* magazine he said, "The idea of liberation and empowerment for our work force is not enlightenment—it's a competitive necessity."

That article in *Fortune* highlighted a number of GE product or service lines that were either first or second in domestic or worldwide sales during Welch's tenure there. Later in an interview in the *Harvard Business Review*, he once again illustrated the paradigm shift when he commented on the *Fortune* list: "Ten years from now, we want magazines to write about GE as a place where people have the freedom to be creative, a place that brings out the best in everybody—an open, fair place where people have a sense that what they do matters, and where that sense of accomplishment is rewarded in both the pocketbook and the soul."

This kind of goal for an organization comes from leadership *and* shapes the nature of leadership. And Jack Welch is far from being alone. There are many examples of this new type of leadership in this section and throughout this book.

In a meeting of the Presidents' Council of the World Business Academy, a group of CEOs managing businesses ranging from multibillion-dollar corporations to smaller multimillion-dollar enterprises, members talked about the barriers and solutions to new forms of leadership as they move through the present transition. They talked about such issues as the importance of love and being vulnerable, the centrality of communication, the dangers of ego, the need for integrity and service, true employee ownership, and reverence for life—all hints at the beginnings of a new kind of leadership.

7

A NEW KIND OF COMPANY WITH A NEW KIND OF THINKING

by Rolf V. Osterberg

The shift from the old paradigm to the new is slow but inevitable. But what can we expect in the future, as this enormous transformation occurs? And what will be the new role of a leadership that is also in transition?

The following essay looks ahead to consider what this transition would mean to our economic system, our companies, and ourselves. The author gives thoughtful consideration to a new generative rather than consumption-oriented economy. He presents a vision of the company as an arena for creativity and cooperation, with an organizational structure that eliminates hierarchy and establishes instead a collaborative process of problem solving, goal-setting, personal growth, and profits that are plowed back into the company.

Rolf V. Osterberg, author of Corporate Renaissance: Business as an Adventure in Human Development, *has been President of the largest film company and Executive Vice-President of the largest newspaper company in Scandinavia, as well as Chairman of the Newspapers Association.*

I am writing this in the garden of my summerhouse about one hour's drive north of Stockholm, Sweden. I look at the birds in the sky above, at the trees and flowers around me and envy them. To them there is no time—no past, no future. To them there is only now. No worries for tomorrow; no fear of what the future might bring. They express total harmony within themselves and with nature. They creatively exist in cooperation. I cannot help asking myself when will human beings reach that state? When will we see that there is no reason for fear and thus no reason for striving for power? When will we see that we are part of nature and not its master? When will we see that time is an invention and does not really exist?

However, in our minds time still exists. In that sense, and for reasons I will try to explain, I believe that when we look back from some vantage point early in the 21st century, we will regard the time from now to the end of the century as a period of rapid, radical and dramatic change—the most profound revolution ever experienced.

What is happening now is subtle and abstract. It is difficult to put into words.

Whether we are willing to accept it or not, there is currently some sort of raising of the human consciousness, the arena of human cognition and inner experience. As a result, we are leaving the old way of thinking with its over-dependence on the logical mind, which has put the planet we live on at the edge of catastrophe. A new kind of thought is awakening, characterized by a balance between thinking and feeling and a high regard for intuition. It is a thought that contains consideration and compassion, and acknowledges other dimensions than those we catch with our physical senses.

Having lived most of my adult life as a business executive, I have pondered deeply what this transition would mean to our economic system and our companies.

THE ANTI-ECONOMIC NATURE OF OUR ECONOMIC SYSTEM

The present economic system is a *consuming* system. It takes far more than it gives. It consumes/exploits human beings wherever they are in the hierarchy. It consumes/exploits, to the extreme, the resources of the planet, especially in Third World countries.

The present economy is based on fear and the backside of fear, the struggle for power. The energy (money) generated by business is to a great extent channeled to and collected by such power centers as banks, insurance companies, and other financial institutions. To a large extent it is used for speculation rather than investment. To a large extent it represents locked-in power and dead energy. It seems to me that we are maintaining a paper economy, an old system that has lost its vitality. I anticipate—and there are today many signs to support the anticipation—that the present economic system will collapse, and that on its ruins an entirely new economic system will be built.

There are signs that the new economy will be more balanced and will be based on generating rather than consuming. It will be based on the new consciousness and, particularly, on the concept that every part of creation, be it a living entity or "dead" material, is intimately related to every other part. In other words, it will be a true economical system. The units that make it up (companies) will be run accordingly.

I want now to turn to an examination of the critical issues that this poses for business leaders.

COMPANIES EXIST PRIMARILY AS AN ARENA FOR THE HUMAN CONDITION

In the old way of thinking, companies exist primarily to make profit. In the new way of thinking, companies exist primarily as structures within which people come together to create cooperatively.

Part of the new understanding of human beings is that every person bears within him/herself extraordinary resources (knowledge, wisdom, creativity, etc.) that are immense, far greater than we can imagine. The workplace is now changing to accommodate this new image.

The key to our inner resources is self-knowledge. Self-knowledge is gained by personal development—that is, by collecting experiences out of which new insight and wisdom are born. In fact, this comes close to being the meaning of life. Consequently, the raison d'être for a company is to supply an environment within which personal development of the human beings involved in the company can best take place.

Assuming all of the above, it seems to me that there are six components of awareness which are critical for today's business leader:

1) The Hierarchical System Is a Serious Block to Personal Development

The hierarchical system is built on fear and mistrust; there are no greater obstacles to personal development. All hierarchies based on power considerations must be erased. (That does not mean, of course, that for any given task there may not be followers and leaders.)

2) A New Way of Thinking Means a New Role for the Business Leader

In this new thinking, the leader is more like a coordinator than a traditional manager. In the new company the leader is not at the top of the organization; he is in its midst. He is not giving orders; he is not formulating policies; he is not controlling. He is coordinating a self-organizing, self-renewing and self-transcending system. He is coordinating a very flexible, but stable, system.

3) A Nonhierarchical System Involves a Different Process of Problem Solving

In a hierarchical system there is a strong tendency to push problems upwards to be solved at the higher levels of the organization. To "solve" someone else's problem is one of the greater disservices one can do to a fellow human. In a nonhierarchical system there is no one "above" to solve where it has arisen: "He who owns the problem *is* the solution."

4) Goal Setting Is an Impediment to Personal Development

In the old system we are typically advised to set goals (in terms of profit, production quotas, market shares, etc.) and then work to achieve the goals. But to work toward a specific goal requires walking a road which is straight and narrow. It eliminates the opportunity to take side paths, "to see what happens" and through that experience to meet new challenges creatively and collect new experiences. In the new company, goals are replaced by a commonly shared vision. That vision has no specific form; it is more a direction. Everyone in the company has his/her individual road toward that cooperative direction. The road is the goal.

5) The Profit/Energy Generated by a Company Should be Plowed Back into the Company

In the new company, the profit is a by-product to the human processes going on within the company. To tap these processes of the energy generated and divert the profits off to some outside interest tends to devitalize them and will ultimately stop them. Furthermore, it brings the interference of "outside interests" to the human processes going on within the company.

Produce what you can believe in. Look carefully on the purpose of your product and how it is produced. Not for the old reasons, but because it is a primary importance that the products are produced by people who believe in them.

HOW TO LEAD THE CHANGE

The new way of thinking presents a tremendous challenge to business in the areas of personal development and human growth. The question remains, how to make the new thinking an integral part of business life.

To my mind, we are facing one of the greatest pedagogical challenges ever. The new way of thinking will be regarded by many in the establishment as a threat to which they may respond with increased rigidity. My suggestion is, let them be. It is a waste of time and capacity to act as missionaries attempting to convince and convert. Better to find and join forces with those companies and individuals who are open to and longing for the new way. Encourage networks to be created amongst them and concentrate the efforts on these networks. These efforts may include seminars, articles, books, and so on. However, the new thought is sufficiently subtle and abstract that much of the "work" and the communication will be simply being with one another.

Another very useful work is the creation of examples and careful documentation (perhaps by videotape) of the process involved. This documentation should not be focused on figures (profitability, productivity, etc.), but on what happens to human beings during the process and what it means to them to work in "the new company." Let them show their feelings on videotape by their expression, body language, etc. This will speak much more loudly than any statistics. Every such example will be a stone thrown into the water spreading its ripples. Let us trust the ripple effect which has its own life and its own power.

Finally, let me give my personal conclusion from my reflections. What a precious gift to mankind and our planet it would be if the remarkable knowledge we have achieved should be united with wisdom. Then our planet would be the paradise it is meant to be. Business life has the opportunity to bring that gift forward.

8

LEARNING SOME BASIC TRUISMS ABOUT LEADERSHIP

by Warren Bennis

If a genuine transformation within any business is to occur, the leadership of that organization must be both willing and able to provide the energy and power to enable change. Warren Bennis often observes instead men and women suffering under the burden of a high position, still proving themselves, still suffering from battle fatigue, overworked, compulsively intervening, and becoming, ultimately, burned-out victims of the Peter Principle.

In the following article, Bennis discusses how leaders can overcome the obstacles of isolation, cynicism, routine, inertia, and turmoil. He demonstrates how they can instead fuse work and play in a way that makes people feel significant; values learning and competence, and makes work more exciting.

Warren Bennis has written fifteen books, including The Unconscious Conspiracy: Why Leaders Can't Lead *and* Leaders, *plus hundreds of articles on the dynamics of organizations. He has served on the faculty of MIT, Harvard, and Boston universities, among others. He was the President of the University of Cincinnati and has advised four U.S. Presidents. Currently he is Distinguished Professor of Business Administration at the University of Southern California.*

A moment of truth came to me toward the end of my first ten months as president of the University of Cincinnati. The clock was moving toward four in the morning, and I was still in my office, still mired in the incredible mass of paper stacked on my desk. I was bone weary and soul-weary, and I found myself muttering, "Either I can't manage this place, or it's unmanageable." I reached for my calendar and ran my eyes down each hour, half hour, quarter hour, to see where my time had gone that day, the day before, the month before.

Nobel laureate James Franck has said he always recognizes a moment of discovery by "the feeling of terror that seizes me." I felt a trace of it that morning. My discovery was this: *I had become the victim of a vast, amorphous, unwitting, unconscious conspiracy to prevent me from doing anything whatever to change the university's status quo.* Even those of my associates who fully shared my hopes to set new goals, new directions, and to work toward creative change were unconsciously often doing the most to make sure that I would never find the time to begin. I found myself thinking of a friend and former colleague who had taken over one of our top universities with goals and plans that fired up all those around him and who said when he left a few years later, "I never could get around to doing the things I wanted to do."

This discovery, or rediscovery, led me to formulate what might be called Bennis's First Law of Academic Pseudodynamics: Routine work drives out nonroutine work and smothers to death all creative planning, all fundamental change in the university—or any institution.

These were the illustrations facing me: To start, there were 150 letters in the day's mail that required a response. About 50 of them concerned our young dean of the School of Education, Hendrik Gideonse. His job was to bring about change in the teaching of teachers, in our university's relationship to the public schools and to students in the deprived and deteriorating neighborhood around us. Out of these urban schools would come the bulk of our students of the future—as good or as bad as the schools had shaped them.

But the letters were not about education. They were about a baby, the dean's ten-week-old son. Gideonse felt very strongly about certain basic values. He felt especially so about sex roles, about equality for his wife, about making sure she had the time and freedom to develop her own potentials fully. So he was carrying the baby into his office two days a week in a little bassinet, which he kept on his desk while he did his work. The daily *Cincinnati Enquirer* heard about it, took a picture of Hendrik, baby, and bassinet, and played it on page one. TV splashed it across the nation. And my "in" basket began to overflow with letters that urged his arrest for child abuse or at least his immediate dismissal. My only public comment was that we were a tax-supported institution, and if Hendrik could engage in that form of applied humanism and still accomplish the things we both wanted done in education, then, like Lincoln with Grant's whiskey, I'd gladly send him several new babies for adoption.

Hendrik was, of course, simply a man a bit ahead of his time. Today, his actions would be applauded—maybe even with a Father of the Year award. Then, however, Hendrik and his baby ate up quite a bit of my time.

Also on my desk was a note from a professor, complaining that his classroom temperature was down to sixty-five degrees. Perhaps he expected me to grab a wrench and fix it. A student complained that we wouldn't give him course credit for acting as assistant to a city council member. Another was unable to get into the student health center. The teacher at my child's day school, who attended the university, was dissatisfied with her grades. A parent complained about four-letter words in a Philip Roth book being used in an English class. The track coach wanted me to come over to see for myself how bad the track was. An alumnus couldn't get the football seats he wanted. Another wanted a coach fired. A teacher had called to tell me the squash court was closed at 7 P.M. when he wanted to use it.

Perhaps 20 percent of my time that year had been taken up by a problem at the general hospital, which was city-owned but administered by the university and served as the teaching hospital of the university medical school. Some terminal-cancer patients, with their consent, had been subjected to whole-body radiation as possibly beneficial therapy. Since the Pentagon saw this as a convenient way to gather data that might help protect civilian populations in nuclear warfare, it provided a series of subsidies for the work.

When this story broke and was pursued in such a way as to call up comparisons with the Nazis' experiments on human guinea pigs, it became almost impossible for me or anybody else to separate the essential facts from the fantasized distortions. The problem eventually subsided, after a blue-ribbon task force recommended significant changes in the experiment's design. But I invested endless time in a matter only vaguely related to the prime purposes of the university— and wound up being accused by some of interfering with academic freedom.

The radiation experiment and Hendrik's baby illustrate how the media, particularly TV, make the academic cloister a goldfish bowl. By focusing on the lurid or the superficial, they can disrupt a president's proper activities while contributing nothing to the advancement of knowledge. This leads me to Bennis's Second Law of Academic Pseudodynamics: Make whatever grand plans you will, you may be sure the unexpected or the trivial will disturb and disrupt them.

In my moment of truth, that weary 4 A.M. in my trivia-cluttered office, I began trying to straighten out in my own mind what university presidents should be doing and not doing, what their true priorities should be, how they must lead.

Lead, not manage: there is an important difference. Many an institution is very well managed and very poorly led. It may excel in the ability to handle each day all the routine inputs yet may never ask whether the routine should be done at all.

All of us find ourselves acting on routine problems because they are the easiest things to handle. We hesitate to get involved too early in the bigger ones—we collude, as it were, in the unconscious conspiracy to immerse us in routine.

My entrapment in routine made me realize another thing: People were following the old army game. They did not want to take the responsibility for or bear the consequences of decisions they properly should make. The motto was, "Let's push up the tough ones." The consequence was that everybody and anybody was dumping his "wet babies" (as the old State Department hands call them) on my desk, when I had neither the diapers nor the information to take care of them. So I decided that the president's first priority—the sine qua non of effective leadership—was to create an "executive constellation" to run the office of the president. It could be a mixed bag, some vice-presidents, some presidential assistants. The group would have to be compatible in the sense that its members could work together but neither uniform nor conformist—a group of people who knew more than the president about everything within their areas of competency and could attend to daily matters without dropping their wet babies on the president's desk.

What should the president him- or herself do? The president should be a *conceptualist*. That's something more than being just an "idea man." It means being a leader with entrepreneurial vision and the time to spend thinking about the forces that will affect the destiny of the institution. The president must educate board members so that they not only understand the necessity of distinguishing between leadership and management but also can protect the chief executive from getting enmeshed in routine machinery.

Leaders must create for their institutions clear-cut and measurable goals based on advice from all elements of the community. They must be allowed to proceed toward those goals without being crippled by bureaucratic machinery that saps their strength, energy, and initiative. They must be allowed to take risks, to embrace error, to use their creativity to the hilt and encourage those who work with them to use theirs.

These insights gave me the strength to survive my acid test: whether I, as a "leading theorist" of the principles of creative leadership, actually could prove myself a leader. However, the sum total of my experiences as president of the University of Cincinnati convinced me that most of the academic theory on leadership was useless.

After leaving the university, I spent nearly five years researching a book on leadership. I traveled around the country spending time with ninety of the most effective, successful leaders in the nation, sixty from corporations and thirty from the public sector. My goal was to find these leaders' common traits, a task that required more probing than I had expected. For a while, I sensed much more diversity than commonality among them. The group included both left-brain and right-brain thinkers; some who dressed for success and some who didn't; well-spoken, articulate leaders and laconic, inarticulate ones; some John Wayne types and some who were definitely the opposite.

I was finally able to come to some conclusions, of which perhaps the most important is the distinction between leaders and managers: Leaders are people who do the right thing; managers are people who do things right. Both roles are crucial, but they differ profoundly. I often observe people in top positions doing the wrong thing well.

This study also reinforced my earlier insight—that American organizations (and probably those in much of the rest of the industrialized world) are underled and overmanaged. They do not pay enough attention to doing the right thing, while they pay too much attention to doing things right. Part of the fault lies with our schools of management; we teach people how to be good technicians and good staff people, but we don't train people for leadership.

The group of sixty corporate leaders was not especially different from any profile of top leadership in America. The median age was fifty-six. Most were white males, with six black men and six women in the group. The only surprising finding was that all the CEOs not only were still married to their first spouses but also seemed enthusiastic about the institution of marriage. Among the CEOs were Bill Kieschnick, then chair and CEO of Arco, and the late Ray Kroc, of McDonald's.

Public-sector leaders included Harold Williams, who then chaired the Securities and Exchange Commission (SEC); Neil Armstrong, a genuine all-American hero who happened to be at the University of Cincinnati; three elected officials; two orchestra conductors; and two winning athletics coaches. I wanted conductors and coaches because I mistakenly believed that they were the last leaders with complete control over their constituents.

After several years of observation and conversation, I defined four competencies evident to some extent in every member of the group:

management of attention; management of meaning; management of trust; and management of self. The first trait apparent in these leaders is their ability to draw others to them, not just because they have a vision but because they communicate an extraordinary focus of commitment. Leaders manage attention through a compelling vision that brings others to a place they have not been before.

One of the people I most wanted to interview was one of the few I could not seem to reach—Leon Fleischer, a well-known child prodigy who grew up to become a prominent pianist, conductor, and musicologist. I happened to be in Aspen, Colorado, one summer while Fleischer was conducting the Aspen Music Festival, and I tried again to reach him, even leaving a note on his dressing-room door. Driving back through downtown Aspen, I saw two perspiring young cellists carrying their instruments, and I offered them a ride to the music tent. They hopped in the back of my jeep, and as we rode I questioned them about Fleischer. "I'll tell you why he's so great," said one. "He doesn't waste our time."

Fleischer finally agreed not only to be interviewed but to let me watch him rehearse and conduct music classes. I linked the way I saw him work with that simple sentence, "He doesn't waste our time." Every moment Fleischer was before the orchestra, he knew exactly what sound he wanted. He didn't waste time because his intentions were always evident. What united him with the other musicians was their concern with intention and outcome.

When I reflected on my own experience, it struck me that when I was most effective, it was because I knew what I wanted. When I was ineffective, it was because I was unclear about it.

So the first leadership competency is the management of attention through a set of intentions or a vision, not in a mystical or religious sense but in the sense of outcome, goal, or direction.

The second leadership competency is management of meaning. To make dreams apparent to others and to align people with them, leaders must communicate their vision. Communication and alignment work together. Consider, for example, the contrasting styles of Presidents Reagan and Carter. Ronald Reagan is called "the Great Communicator"; one of his speech writers said that Reagan can read the phone book and make it interesting. The reason is that Reagan uses metaphors with which people can identify. In his first budget message, for example, Reagan described a trillion dollars by comparing it to piling up dollar bills beside the Empire State Building. Reagan, to use one of Alexander Haig's coinages, "tangibilitated" the idea. Leaders make ideas tangible and real to others, so they can support them. For no matter how marvelous the vision, the effective leader must use a metaphor, a word or a model to make that vision clear to others.

In contrast, President Carter was boring. Carter was one of our best-informed presidents; he had more facts at his fingertips than almost any other president. But he never made the meaning come through the facts. I interviewed an assistant secretary of commerce appointed by Carter, who told me that after four years in his administration, she still did not know what Jimmy Carter stood for. She said that working for him was like looking through the wrong side of a tapestry; the scene was blurry and indistinct.

The leader's goal is not mere explanation or clarification but the creation of meaning. My favorite baseball joke is exemplary: In the ninth inning of a key playoff game, with a three-and-two count on the batter, the umpire hesitates a split second in calling the pitch. The batter whirls around angrily and says, "Well, what was it?" The umpire snarls back, "It ain't *nothing* until *I* call it!"

The third competency is management of trust. Trust is essential to all organizations. The main determinant of trust is reliability, what I call *constancy*. When I talked to the board members or staffs of these leaders, I heard certain phrases again and again: "She is all of a piece." "Whether you like it or not, you always know where he is coming from, what he stands for."

When John Paul II visited this country, he gave a press conference. One reporter asked how the pope could account for allocating funds to build a swimming pool at the papal summer palace. He responded quickly, "I like to swim. Next question." He did not rationalize about medical reasons or claim that he got the money from a special source. A recent study showed that people would much rather follow individuals they can count on, even when they disagree with their viewpoint, than people they agree with but who shift positions frequently. I cannot emphasize enough the significance of constancy and focus.

The fourth leadership competency is management of self, knowing one's skills and deploying them effectively. Management of self is critical; without it, leaders and managers can do more harm than good. Like incompetent doctors, incompetent managers can make life worse, make people sicker and less vital. There is a term—*iatrogenic*— for illnesses caused by doctors and hospitals. There should be one for illnesses caused by leaders, too. Some give themselves heart attacks and nervous breakdowns; still worse, many are "carriers," causing their employees to be ill.

Leaders know themselves; they know their strengths and nurture them. They also have a faculty I think of as the Wallenda Factor. The Flying Wallendas are perhaps the world's greatest family of aerialists and tightrope walkers. I was fascinated when, in the early 1970s, seventy-one-year-old Karl Wallenda said that for him living was walking the tightrope, and everything else was waiting. I was struck with his capacity for concentration on the intention, the task, the decision. I was even more intrigued when, several months later, Wallenda fell to his death while walking a tightrope without a safety net between two high-rise buildings in San Juan, Puerto Rico. Wallenda fell still clutching the balancing pole he had warned his family never to drop lest it hurt somebody below. Later, Wallenda's wife said that before her husband had fallen, for the first time since she had known him he had been concentrating on falling, instead of on walking the tightrope. He had personally supervised the attachment of the guide wires, which he had never done before.

Like Wallenda before his fall, the leaders in my group seemed unacquainted with the concept of failure. What you or I might call a failure, they referred to as a mistake. I began collecting synonyms for the word *failure* mentioned in the interviews, and I found more than twenty: *mistake, error, false start, bloop, flop, loss, miss, foul-up, stumble, botch, bungle* . . . but not *failure*. One CEO told me that if she had a knack for leadership, it was the capacity to make as many mistakes as she could as soon as possible, and thus get them out of the way. Another said that a mistake is simply "another way of doing things." These leaders learn from and use something that doesn't go well; it is not a failure but simply the next step.

Leadership can be felt throughout an organization. It gives pace and energy to the work and empowers the work force. Empowerment is the collective effect of leadership. In organizations with effective leaders, empowerment is most evident in four themes:

• *People feel significant.* Everyone feels that he or she makes a difference to the success of the organization. The difference may be small— prompt delivery of potato chips to a mom-and-pop grocery store or developing a tiny but essential part for an airplane. But where they are empowered, people feel that what they do has meaning and significance.

• *Learning and competence matter.* Leaders value learning and mastery, and so do people who work for leaders. Leaders make it clear that there is no failure, only mistakes that give us feedback and tell us what to do next.

• *People are part of a community.* Where there is leadership, there is a team, a family, a unity. Even people who do not especially like each other feel the sense of community. When Neil Armstrong talks about the Apollo explorations, he describes how a team carried out an almost unimaginably complex set of interdependent tasks. Until there were women astronauts, the men referred to this feeling as "brotherhood." I suggest they rename it "family."

• *Work is exciting*. Where there are leaders, work is stimulating, challenging, fascinating, and fun. An essential ingredient in organizational leadership is pulling rather than pushing people toward a goal. A "pull" style of influence attracts and energizes people to enroll in an exciting vision of the future. It motivates through identification, rather than through rewards and punishments. Leaders articulate and embody the ideals toward which the organization strives.

People cannot be expected to enroll in just any exciting vision. Some visions and concepts have more staying power and are rooted more deeply in our human needs than others. I believe the lack of two such concepts in modern organizational life is largely responsible for the alienation and lack of meaning so many experience in their work. One of these is the concept of quality. Modern industrial society has been oriented to quantity, providing more goods and services for everyone. Quantity is measured in money; we are a money-oriented society. Quality often is not measured at all but is appreciated intuitively. Our response to quality is a feeling. Feelings of quality are connected intimately with our experience of meaning, beauty, and value in our lives.

Closely linked to the concept of quality is that of dedication to, even love of, our work. This dedication is evoked by quality and is the force that energizes high-performing systems. When we love our work, we need not be managed by hopes of reward or fears of punishment. We can create systems that facilitate our work, rather than being preoccupied with checks and controls of people who want to beat or exploit the system.

Ultimately, in great leaders and the organizations surrounding them, there is a fusion of work and play to the point where, as Robert Frost says, "Love and need are one." How do we get from here to there? I think we must start by studying change.

EXEMPLAR:
Amex Life Assurance

When Sarah Nolan was made president of Amex Life Assurance and faced the task of overhauling this American Express subsidiary in San Rafael, California, she was told that she couldn't do it. Typical of the insurance industry, responsiveness to customers was slow because there was a rigid hierarchy of workers, with little communication between levels of the organization and people doing various tasks. But Nolan had written a plan for revitalizing the business and her slogan when confronted by naysayers was, "Yes, I can!"

She concentrated on one division of the business that was doing particularly poorly and asked five managers from various parts of the business to set up an office in an unoccupied business park away from the main building. Faced with an empty office and a charge from their president, these "pioneers," as they were called, leaped into the task with vigor. What they came up with was an open office, as opposed to the rigidly divided one typically found in the insurance industry. With the use of a computer on every desk and an environment in which everybody was prepared to do every task, the levels of hierarchy in the organization were cut from ten to three. It was possible to be much more responsive to customer needs than before. In fact, the concern with customer needs has become so great that staff members leave an empty chair representing the customer at meetings. The time it took to process applications and deal with customer problems plummeted, and profits for that division of Amex Life Assurance increased 700 percent. That spirit has transferred to every part of the organization. Another division of Amex Life won the first President's Quality Award for the entire American Express Company.

The key seems to be employee empowerment and teamwork. As one senior member of the original pioneer group put it, "It's an opportunity for everyone to work together and give input, as if we were a small business. Before I came to the enterprise, I was director of customer service, under the old traditional way of running a business. I was totally isolated, I had a big office, and people came to see me by appointment. The difference now is that I'm part of the group. I get to do everything like everybody else does. I enjoy it immensely."

Another employee said, "We are treated like adults with respect and with the philosophy that any idea is not a bad idea. And that helps me with my self-esteem. I feel I have something to contribute personally."

Sarah Nolan puts it simply: "It's a staggering thing how far people will go if they own the results."

Now at Amex Life there is an enormous banner hanging from the top to the bottom of the four-story atrium in the middle of the building. It says, over and over again in large multicolor letters: **Yes, I Can!** And in the windows of the department that won the quality award are the words: **Yes, We Did!**

9

PURPOSE, MISSION, AND VISION

by James C. Collins and Jerry I. Porras

The following article presents a framework for how leaders can establish a clear sense of organizational vision. "Vision" is a term frequently tossed about by academics and practicing managers, but the concept has remained vague and unclear, with few concrete examples or case studies. Nor has there been a coherent conceptual framework to assess or evaluate the so-called "vision" of a leader or business executive.

Jim Collins is the co-author (with William Lazier) of Beyond Entrepreneurship *(Prentice-Hall) and teaches general management of the emerging venture, creativity, and innovation at the Stanford Graduate School of Business. Jerry Porras is author of* Stream Analysis: A Powerful Way to Diagnose and Manage Organizational Change *(Addison-Wesley) and Associate Dean for Academic Affairs at the Stanford Graduate School of Business.*

On May 7, 1945, at 2:41 A.M., London time, an instrument of total, unconditional surrender was signed by Germany, thus completing the destruction of the Nazi regime and bringing to end nearly six years of bitter struggle. Four months later, a similar instrument of surrender was signed by Japan, bringing the Second World War to an official close.

On July 20, 1969, at 4:17 P.M. eastern daylight time, a human being landed on the moon for the first time in history. It was the conclusion of an eight-year program to achieve a moon landing by the end of the decade.

On January 24, 1984, at 10:00 A.M. Pacific standard time, after over four years of intense effort to build a computer that would be a useful tool for people with no experience using computers, the Macintosh computer was introduced to market. Since then, it has made an enormous contribution to one of the most significant social trends of our era.

What do each of these examples of human achievement have in common?

Clearly, there is the role of a certain key individual in each situation who acted as a catalyst: Winston Churchill, John Kennedy, and Steve Jobs. These individuals played significant roles in galvanizing large numbers of people into cohesive, focused efforts.

But far more significant than the presence of these individuals is the fact that these achievements were the result of *team* efforts. No single person—no matter how talented or resourceful—could have attained these accomplishments single-handedly. Through the process of many people working together with savage persistence towards a common end, extraordinary achievements were realized.

A clear overall aim serves as a beacon—a "guiding star"—on which people at all levels of the organization can sight. It gives people a context in which to make decisions, thus increasing the likelihood that actions taken by dispersed parties will be mutually compatible.

It is impossible to have a coherent strategy or make effective tactical decisions without a clear idea of what you are trying to do in the first place. Lack of a clear overall aim was a fundamental contributor to the United States' difficulties in Vietnam, for instance.

Furthermore, without this vital component, an organization can easily fracture into divergent groups with disparate agendas. Factions may become increasingly concerned with expanding their own territory, rather than working for a common aim. Distrust, politics and destructive infighting will likely consume an ever larger share of attention.

Of even greater importance is the sense of meaning that people derive from their jobs when the organization has a compelling overall aim to pursue. Most people desperately want to do more than just bring home a paycheck; they want to *believe* in their work. They want work they can feel good about when they get up in the morning, that they look forward to and that they think is worthwhile.

The quest for work that has meaning is a powerful driving force that, for many, goes unsatisfied. Tap into this basic human desire and you need not worry about "how to motivate" people or "how to get the best" from them—they will motivate themselves. As Yvon Chouinard, founder of Patagonia, explains: "You don't need to manage self-motivated people, and nearly everyone is motivated when they are doing a job they believe in."

But, alas, the malaise that afflicts many organizations is a testament to the fact that few successfully tap into the desire for meaning and purpose. Just listen to people talk about their work. Look into their eyes. Do you see excitement? Do you see passion and enthusiasm? Do you see the type of relentless commitment that it took to defeat Hitler, put a human being on the moon or develop the Macintosh? In all too many cases, the answer is no. Large numbers of people go to work every day but leave their spirit at home.

But what makes for effective and powerful overall aim? Is it "vision"? Is it "mission"? Is it "purpose"? We believe that it consists of all three. Unfortunately, however, these terms are used interchangeably without clarity as to the meaning of each. Furthermore, these terms (especially the term vision) have taken on an almost religious or cult-like aura—as if they elude the capacity of normal mortals.

This article is based on preliminary findings from a study of historical examples, secondary sources, the examination of over one hundred talks by business leaders visiting Stanford Business School classes and our consulting work with organizations.

PURPOSE

Purpose is the fundamental set of reasons for the organization's existence—what in the broadest, most enduring sense people in the organization want it to contribute to the external world and to its internal stakeholders. In an ongoing organization, such as a corporation or an educational institution, purpose is continually worked towards, but never fully completed. That is, purpose in an ongoing organization is not a specific objective that you achieve and then say "we are done." Effective purpose is broad and inspirational, something that strikes a chord in people at a core level, and provides a clear sense of direction for the organization and its members.

In business, purpose transcends short- and intermediate-term objectives to a broader, more meaningful plane. It reflects the deep personal needs and core values of the individuals that constitute the organization, especially its leaders. Furthermore, as noted above, purpose is something that is always worked towards, but never fully realized.

For example, Steve Jobs described the fundamental purpose he felt at both Apple and NeXT as "to express some deep feeling about wanting to contribute something. I really believe that people have a desire to put something back. We want to contribute by building great tools for the mind. It's wanting to see people's eyes light up when you give them a tool that lets them do what they've never been able to do before. I don't feel that I'll ever be done. There are lots of hurdles out there, and there is always at least one hurdle that I'll never reach in my lifetime. The point is to keep working towards it."

Jim Gentes, Chairman of Giro Sport Design, described his purpose as: "Design of great products that change the face of the industry, improve safety and make people happy. Money has virtually nothing to do with it, other than that we need to make money so we can remain in business and pursue this aim."

Notice how both of these people placed financial returns as subordinate to working towards the purpose. Not that profit is inconsistent with purpose. To be sure, financial viability is necessary. But, as a central purpose, it fails to inspire people to their greatest level of performance. Purpose is something far more enduring, powerful and inspirational. In fact, it appears that organizations moving towards fulfilling their purpose usually generate significant profits along the way.

Finally, it is worth pointing out that purpose may have two components: external (what you want the organization to do, as exhibited by Jobs and Gentes) and internal (what you want the organization to be). Fred Schwettmann, General Manager of the Circuit Technology Group at Hewlett-Packard, illustrates: "Part of our purpose relates to what we want this place to be. I want to continually work towards building a work environment that helps employees attain a happy, meaningful existence—to attain self-actualization."

In sum, we believe that having a broad and enduring purpose is essential for long-term organizational health. But we also believe that having something specific to target is essential for unifying the organization into cohesive effort. This is the role of mission.

MISSION

Mission is a clear, definable and motivational point of focus—an achievable goal, a finish line to work towards.

Leaders are most effective when they translate a broad and enduring purpose into a specific, gut-grabbing mission that people can sink their teeth into. A focal point of effort will help keep people moving in the same direction and not lose sight of where they are headed. Producing the Macintosh is an example of purpose translated into mission.

But wait a minute. Isn't this a bit unrealistic in most situations? Sure, it's easy to get people all enthused about grand and noble goals, like putting a human being on the moon or freeing Europe from the yoke of Nazi tyranny. But what about the vast majority of organizations which are engaged in much less inspiring activities?

We argue that, although more difficult, it is possible. Take the case of PepsiCo in the 1970s. Selling cola is hardly on the same level as landing on the moon or defeating Hitler. Even so, the folks at Pepsi were completely obsessed with selling cola. How? By playing off the psychology of being the underdog and fixating on one overriding mission: BEAT COKE. As an ex-president of PepsiCo described it: "We believed we could do it. We never took our eyes off it. It put us on a search and destroy mission against a Goliath."

This example illustrates one of the most effective forms of mission: focusing on a common enemy or outside threat. "Us versus them" is a natural unifying force and provides a clear point of focus. This approach tends to work best in an underdog role. The key is to make the switch from a survival mode to a "we shall prevail" mode. People don't like to just survive, they like to win.

A caveat: one must be careful to not confuse mission with purpose. Because a specific mission can be so compelling, many organizations make the mistake of thinking that their mission *is* their fundamental purpose. The problem becomes: what do you do once you've fulfilled the mission? What does Pepsi do once it defeats Coke? Without a broader, more creative purpose from which to derive the next mission, there will be a crisis of direction once the mission is accomplished.

Thus, although we heartily encourage organizations to have a focused mission to pursue, we also believe that an organization should have an enduring purpose to return to for formulating the next mission. Mission and purpose are both necessary.

Now that we have discussed the two most tangible and straightforward concepts—purpose and mission—we turn to the third aspect of an overall organizational aim: vision.

VISION

The terms "vision" and "visionary" conjure up images of an almost supernatural person who can forecast the future or is given to apparitions, prophecies or revelations. There is a tendency to think of a "visionary" as someone who has the unusual ability to foresee what the world will look like in the future and has grandiose ideas or plans for meeting these expected future trends.

This is a common perception of Steve Jobs, for example. But does this view hold true? Is this what really happens? Observe what Jobs himself said about the beginnings of the personal computer industry: "We designed our first computer because we couldn't afford to buy one. We didn't have the whole idea about making a computer company until we'd built our first computer, and saw how neat it was for us and our friends. As the people it was neat for expanded, we got more excited. We didn't sit in a chair one day and think, 'My God, ten years from now everyone is going to be using personal computers!' It didn't happen that way. It was more of a gradual process."

Jobs' vision of the Macintosh was similar. He didn't sit around and dream that the future of computing was the Macintosh. No, he simply attended a demo of mouse and icon computer technology at Xerox and immediately saw the potential of what had been right in front of people for years. Alan Kay, a witness, describes: "One microsecond into the demo, Steve knew what it was about. He wanted to do it right *now*. He couldn't understand why Xerox was sitting around on its fanny."

This experience is not unusual. Gentes of Giro Sport Design, one who many in the bicycling industry call "visionary," had a similar experience: "What I saw right in front of me was the need for a lighter, faster helmet. There was no grand design, only this burning drive to create revolutionary products and a belief that *someone* had to do this helmet and had to do it *right away*. So I figured it might as well be us."

These examples illustrate that many so-called visionaries simply acted on something *right in front of them*—something they found to be immensely compelling—and thereby discovered their vision almost by tripping over it. And after the fact—after their persistence and hard work has borne fruit and resulted in success—they are heralded as "visionary." As Ted Turner puts it, "People don't *call* themselves visionaries. People get *called* visionaries. All I am is Ted Turner."

The critical component isn't a grand sweeping plan of how to respond to what the world will look like in the future. No, vision is the ability to see the *potential* in or *necessity* of opportunities right in front of you. Vision is not analytic; it is intuitive. It is knowing "in your bones" what can or must be done. In other words, vision isn't forecasting the future, it is creating the future by taking action in the present.

And, just as important, "having vision" doesn't mean walking around with your head in the clouds. It means keeping your eyes, mind and heart open and having the confidence to follow your own insights and intuition as to what can or must be done. And, just as important, it is having the burning passion and resolute conviction to immediately *do* something about it.

But what about "visualization"? Don't visionaries "picture" or "visualize" what they are trying to do? Yes, sometimes, but not always. Visualization is an effective way of seeing what can be done—of envisioning an ideal future state, the "what might be." But it is important to recognize that not all vision comes from visualization.

We do not deny, however, that the ability to communicate a vivid, imaginative conception of what you want to see happen can be powerfully motivating.

CONDITIONS FOR IMPLEMENTATION

We have found in our work a need to tailor our approach to each situation when helping leaders of organizations define their overall aim. Each situation is different and each leader has a unique style.

However, we do know that there are three necessary conditions for an overall aim to take root in an organization.

1. An Overall Aim Must Be a Reflection of the Inner Personal Needs, Values, and Motivations of Members of the Organization

Thus, the first step in setting an overall aim is to ask such questions as, "What are our values? What do we hold to be the fundamental importance and how can our purpose reflect that? What purpose would we love to pursue, would make us passionate? What kind of mark would we like to leave? What would we like to contribute? What kind of environment would give us great pleasure to create? What could we commit this portion of our lives to? What can we put our souls behind?"

2. There Must Be an Authentic Personal Commitment

Nothing will fail more quickly than insincerity. It is absolutely essential that the overall aim be an authentic and sincere reflection of your true beliefs and aspirations for the organization. You can't just put something on an overhead transparency slide that says "Vision" and expect to inspire people, unless you really *mean* it, believe in it, live it.

3. Communication and Reinforcement

Organizations tend to drift when their leaders don't keep the overall aim clear, visible and in front of people at all times. Without constant communication and reinforcement, people will lose sight of what the organization is all about and where it is going.

Take advantage of every opportunity to convey the overall aim and emphasize its central and dominant role. Put it in writing. Talk about it constantly. Have meetings where the primary point is to communicate where the organization is going and to review what progress has been made. Incessantly hammer away at communicating it, like a broken record.

Another key to reinforcement is to define and measure progress. Develop benchmarks for keeping track of how well the organization is doing. Just as a marathon runner needs mile makers to measure progress, people in an organization need to see where they are relative to where they need to go.

DOES THIS APPLY TO YOU?

Two questions often arise at this point.

First, in order to develop and promote an inspirational overall aim, does one need to be a charismatic great leader in the classic sense, like Kennedy or Churchill? Our answer is no. Charisma helps—we do not deny it—but it is not essential.

Harry S. Truman, for instance, is not remembered as being particularly charismatic. In fact many people remember him as an unsophisticated farmboy from Missouri. Yet, Truman was a driving force behind the Marshall Plan—one of the most visionary acts of the twentieth century.

Second, there is the question of whether the process of setting an overall aim is relevant at lower levels of an organization. That is, can you do this even if you are not the CEO? Our answer is yes. Not only do we think it can be done, we believe it *should* be done at all levels.

But what if there is no clear overall aim from above that you can hook in to, to ensure consistency? All the more reason to do it! In fact, one of the invaluable benefits of middle managers beginning this process is that it often encourages upper management to initiate the same process at their level.

Schwettmann of Hewlett-Packard, for example, exhibits a trait that we would like to see in managers at *all* levels: not waiting for the overall aim to come from top management but, rather, starting the process oneself. As Schwettmann points out: "Thinking about purpose and mission at my level forces my peers, those who report to me *and* those above me, to also think *clearly* about these things, which is very positive for the entire company."

It is our view that the responsibility does not rest entirely with the CEO but with every leader at every level.

10

THE PRESIDENT AS A POET: AN INTIMATE CONVERSATION WITH JIM AUTRY

by Marjorie Kelly

"We're in the midst of a turning point in the history of business," Jim Autry has written. "The last chapter on management by fear is about to be written." If the new chapter will be about management by caring, Autry is the man to write it. With his life and his presence, he is writing it.

Jim Autry is a poet. His second book, Love and Profit: The Art of Caring Leadership, *includes his poetry and his trenchant observations based on decades of business experience. He retired recently as president of the magazine group of Meredith Corporation, a Fortune 500 company where Autry ran the largest division with 800 people and over $400 million in revenue. Starting out as a copy editor of* Better Homes and Gardens, *he rose through the ranks to oversee a period of tremendous growth, taking his division from five to fourteen magazines in five years. Among the magazines he helped to launch or acquire are* Metropolitan Home, Ladies' Home Journal, *and* Midwest Living.

Autry has three sons, one of whom, Ronald, is autistic. As his friend Doug Kruschke puts it, "Jim is a man who has experienced pain in his life, and integrated it into his own growth."

Marjorie Kelly is the editor of Business Ethics *magazine.*

They leave a lot out of the personnel handbooks.
Dying, for instance.
You can find funeral leave
but you can't find dying.★

★ From "What the Personnel Manuals Never Tell You," by Jim Autry

Marjorie Kelly: *I'm thinking of the poems I've heard you read, Jim, and I'm remembering one about an employee who had cancer, and what can a manager say to such a person.*

Jim Autry: I've done a number of those, but I think you're remembering one called "What the Personnel Manuals Never Tell You"—about not knowing what to do, when a work colleague "looks you in the eye and says something about hope and chemotherapy."

I have another poem on retirement, which is a kind of death experience. I think of the retirement party as something of a funeral ritual. We have flowers, and we have a sign-up book, and visitation.

I think it's no exaggeration to say people today are closer to their work colleagues than they are to their neighbors, the people who live next door. The workplace has taken the place of the neighborhood, psychologically as well as geographically. There's an expression I like to use, and that is, *The job is the new neighborhood, and friends are the new family.* It amazes me what happens in the workplace—even in the stuffiest companies. When a woman takes maternity leave, what does she do a month later but come to the office, and they pass the baby around like a bunch of Gibbons monkeys.

Work is a community we come into, and we live in it, we love in it, we fear in it, we have anger, we cry. We hate one another sometimes. The workplace is filled with all the passions of life. So where in the world did we ever get this notion that at work you have to be this calm, impassive, detached person?

Are you?

Am I? Of course not, of course not.

Do you cry at work? Do you yell at work?

Well, I don't yell at people at work. I think one of the fundamental responsibilities of a manager is to realize that even in a community there is hierarchy, and while I may not feel the hierarchy, the people who work for me do, just as I feel it between me and the man I work for—although I like him immensely and we're friends.

Just as in a family the father or mother can create instant humiliation, so too can the manager. I refer to it as the luxury of anger. The manager is not permitted the luxury of anger *at people*. At situations, at things done wrong, yes. I have no trouble showing my outrage—yet I never focus that on a person.

But cry? You bet. I show emotion. I've had people I was reprimanding or firing who were tearful, and I was too.

You wrote a poem about that, didn't you, about having to let a man go?

Yes, it's called "Thoughts on Firing a Salesman." I've done several poems on firing, because firing takes on different aspects. Firing is like death, firing is like purging someone from the neighborhood, someone who's not fulfilled his or her responsibilities to the community.

In that sense work is a family with different rules. One of the things about blood family is you can't be kicked out, you don't have to earn your place. But business is a family where you do *have to earn your place.*

. But in the community at large, even in the neighborhood, you do have to earn your place. Because you can be kicked out.

Prison, I suppose, is a way of being kicked out of the community.

That's the extreme of it. Snubbing—an old-time Puritan technique for kicking people out of the community just by isolating them socially—that's another way. But remember I said the workplace, the job is the new neighborhood, *friends* are the new family.

I see, so you're saying the job really isn't the family.

The job isn't the family, it's the neighborhood. And within the job you may develop relationships which are family-like.

How do you create community feeling in a workplace? Do you actively work to knit the community together, or is it something that just happens?

I think everyone has to act to knit the community together, it's every worker's responsibility. I feel I have to be the leader of that, and I am.

I do some of it by talking about it, using language that isn't considered real business language. I use a vocabulary some would consider mushy, or soft. I talk about caring for each other and loving what we do. I say things like, You know, we don't have to love each other but we do have to care about each other. And I say things like, We have to take our work seriously but let's not take ourselves so seriously. It's not a traditional business attitude. It comes out of another mind-set—a realization that what really goes on in business is spiritual. It's not intellectual.

What do you mean when you say that—that what goes on in business is spiritual?

Think about business a minute, Marjorie. Where does it exist? It exists in, among, and through people. No place else. The rest of it is paperwork. The legal entity of a corporation exists on paper, but shit, it's just paper. To use a more mystical word, business is revealed through people. Just as everything important is—religion is, love is, everything important is revealed through people. It's taken me a long time to come to that.

How did you come to that? What was your learning process?

I came up through the editorial side of Meredith, and when I moved to the business side, I found the people there were much more hierarchy-oriented. As editor in chief, if I brought up an idea at a meeting, some kid three months out of college would shoot me down. On the business side, if I brought up an idea at a meeting, they'd get up from the table and do it—whether it was good or not.

So I realized I had to be less forceful in expressing opinions. Also I didn't much like that. I thought hierarchy was driving too many things and we needed to stimulate ideas farther down. I didn't know how to do that—but I kept expecting I would learn from all these systems that had been in place for years, and it slowly dawned on me that the systems simply accommodate the actions of people, they simply make possible what people do.

I saw it time and time again. You could have a sales person come into a situation judged impossible and get the business, yet a person in there ten years before couldn't. Now wait a minute, what changed? Did the numbers change, did the audience change? What changed was the person. So I realized, it's all how people relate to these factors, the factors themselves mean nothing.

It's interesting, Jim—you were explaining how you realized that everything in business is spiritual, and what you've just been talking about is people. Are those one and the same for you?

How else is spirituality realized? I believe in a universal unconscious, I believe in a spiritual realm. But let's put it another way, how is God's work done? Through people. How are things of the spirit, which have to do with ethics and morality, how are those actualized? Through people.

There are business people who never talk this way, and who would find it curious. But there are a lot more—more and more every day in business—who realize that matters of the spirit have an important place in what we do every day. People have been saying for years, Our business is people, but they haven't known how to express it.

Or felt a little embarrassed. The issue of vocabulary is key, because we don't really have words we can use without embarrassment.

One of the most liberating experiences for me was a talk, years ago, by a guy I considered my mentor, Bob Burnett. He was the chief executive officer of Meredith, though he gave that job up the first of February. Back in 1968, and this is twenty years ago, he gave a speech to our group on renewal, and he said, One of the most important aspects of self-renewal is love. The reaction in the room was palpable. Here is this big man—you know, the American story, worked his way up from sales and is head of the company—and he's looking at this group of businesspeople, most of them men, and he says, One of the most important aspects of self-renewal is love. And then he says, We have to love our products, we have to love our customers, and we have to love ourselves. It was very powerful. I've taken it as a guideline.

You know, I had heard Bob was stepping down from the CEO position, and I remembered you telling me some time ago that you deliberately took yourself out of the running for CEO.

Well, I didn't go in and say take me out of the running. What I did was decide for myself it wasn't an appropriate thing to go after. I was certainly one of the candidates, but I realize now, after Jack Rehm has been named to the job, this is really the right thing. It feels exactly right to me.

So you didn't feel competitive with Jack about this, you didn't feel regret at losing the race?

There have been times in years past when Jack and I felt competitive, but never in a nasty way. We've always been friends. There've been a few times, recently, that I've felt a little unease, a little regret— thinking, maybe I should have tried that after all, or gosh, I wouldn't mind doing some of those things Jack's doing. But I've never had any lasting feeling that it's something I should have done, just tinges here and there. I think the right person got the job.

Is Sally glad?

Oh, Sally's delighted. Her greatest fear was that I would want to go after being president of the company. She did *not* want that, and also didn't think it would be good for me. And also, you know about Ronald and his being autistic, it certainly wouldn't have been good for him.

If I could turn the situation around for a minute: you yourself have climbed a long way in Meredith—you've been there about twenty-five years—do you ever feel you did anything you regret on the way up? Did you step on anyone?

I'm not sure that other people would agree with me about that. When I look back I can remember three or four instances in which I certainly maneuvered to get a job I wanted, I put myself in the best light. I don't believe I acted maliciously, although I complained about other people a couple of times. I certainly didn't maneuver in any Machiavellian way. But yes, over the years, there have been two or three people who have felt hurt by my actions, who felt that I did them injustice.

In what way?

That I pushed myself over them. Not for jobs they would have gotten, but for attention maybe they should have gotten. I regret those things very deeply. I don't think I did anything unethical, but I have done things that were thoughtless about other people's feelings. In some cases I've actually made moves to mend those fences, and I think I've done so.

I think always we're walking the edge between the good of the group and the good of the individual. It's the most difficult challenge in business.

There's a balancing act, when you have to pass over someone for a job. A person may have worked hard and really want a job, but simply isn't qualified. It's a judgment that I have to make, and I just make it— the person must not have this job. Why? Because it will damage the group. Not because it will hurt the bottom line.

See, the bottom line follows everything else. We say in our company that profit is like breathing, it's required. So we don't pay a hell of a lot of attention to it. What we pay attention to is creating an environment, setting up the circumstances and the goals, so people can do the work that produces the bottom line. I have a little poem called "Threads," and it ends like this:

Listen.
In every office
you hear the threads
of love and joy and fear and guilt,
the cries for celebration and reassurance,
and somehow you know that connecting those threads
is what you are supposed to do
and business takes care of itself.

I wouldn't for a minute want anyone to think that's management by the wimps, or mushy, without discipline and control. It's not. It's a matter of providing the kind of environment where people exercise their own discipline and control.

One example of that environment is the flex-hours you offer at Meredith. How does that work?

There are core hours; people have to be here between 10:00 and 3:00, but they can come as late as 10:00 and work till 6:00, or they can come as early as 6:00 and work till 3:00.

And how many people do you have working outside the regular nine-to-five?

I think this makes a positive statement when I say, I haven't the slightest idea. It's up to each individual department head. Because of phoning and dealing with customers, there are work-flow requirements. But I never hear any complaints about it.

I also know Meredith recently started a fund for the homeless, tell me about that. Was that your idea?

That's through the Better Homes Foundation. And no, it wasn't my idea. It was developed through David Jordan, who is the editor of *Better Homes and Gardens*. If I had any key role in it, it was being the management advocate for the idea, taking it to the top of the company.

It's specifically on homeless families, not all the homeless. We're asking our readers to make contributions through the magazine, so it's families with homes helping families without homes.

Do you feel a corporation has a duty to do these things, or an opportunity perhaps?

An opportunity more than a duty. I'm against those who say a corporation's only social responsibility is to its stockholders. I've heard a good answer to that, which says that business is simply one part of a large and complicated ecosystem, which includes government, education, health care, really the entire social order. For corporations to say our only responsibility is to stockholders is to deny our place in the ecosystem. We have a responsibility to support schools, social programs, the arts.

Whether that responsibility extends into this homeless situation I don't know. But I do know Meredith has an opportunity to galvanize a lot of support, since it is such a major communications force. And family housing is what *Better Homes and Gardens* is all about.

If I could shift gears here, I'd like to talk for a minute about your poetry. I'm curious if people on staff know that you're a poet, or is that a hidden part of you?

People are aware of my book, published five years ago—*Nights Under a Tin Roof: Recollections of a Southern Boyhood*. Some people on staff know that I write business poetry, but not a vast number. I don't talk about it much. Hidden is the wrong word, it's not hidden, but it's not something I talk about a lot, except with people I'm particularly close to.

When do you find time to do your poetry? Do you get thoughts at work and jot things down?

It comes at almost any time. I wrote the first book pretty much on airplanes, because I travel a lot. But it comes to me at different times. My process is, I jot down lines or notes and they go into my shirt pocket, and I'll pull those out and try to organize them into envelopes of various categories. Sometimes ideas just come to me, and sometimes I actually sit down and think about a subject I want to write about. The question was how do I find time, the answer is with a great deal of difficulty.

I'm sure that's right. Yet I'm sure it's wonderful to have art in your life, here and there, balancing out the demands of business.

It is, and that's important to me. I'm not interested in spectator sports, so I never watch football or baseball on television. I'm not a golfer, and I haven't played much tennis lately. I turn instead to literature.

What have you read recently?

I read *Bonfire of the Vanities*—it's a good yarn, social commentary. *Love in the Time of Cholera*, which I thought was pretty wonderful. I read lots of collections of poetry. Interestingly enough, this past year I read the religious speeches of George Bernard Shaw, which were fascinating. And I've been reading some theology—some things by Tillich as well as some Matthew Fox. *Original Blessing*, and other things.

I never read pop novels. I'm also not a television watcher. I suspect when my little boy is older I'll be watching more TV, but the time of day I have to be with him is the time most people are watching television.

How old is Ronald now?

He's five. I take him swimming a couple of times a week, when I'm in town. But everything is a learning and teaching experience with Ronald. So it takes a lot of attention and care.

I would think that would give you a different perspective on life, and on work.

I try to let it. I operate at a high energy level, and I get fairly stressed once in a while. I try to be more meditative and reflective—and I'm much better than I used to be. I try to practice being in what Buddhists call the nowness. And part of the way I think about the nowness is to reflect on Ronald, and the fact that everything with Ronald is nowness.

He doesn't grasp abstractions. He's not looking back, he's not looking ahead, he's living each moment. I try to practice that. I remind myself that regret is a wasted emotion, that when I'm angry I'm living in the past and when I'm fearful I'm living in the future. Trying to be reflective and calm, yet still retain passion, that's the path of the warrior we read about in Buddhist literature, or the path with heart, as Don Juan calls it.

To tell you a little story, I used to have the most terrible reaction to smells, I couldn't stand changing diapers—but that turned around after a seminar I went to. The speaker asked us to recall being a child, being sick and throwing up, and to remember our mother coming with a cool rag and wiping our face. I could see heads nodding all around. Now, he said, those who remember your fathers doing that raise your hand. And there were no hands. None. He said, Just think of what your father missed.

So I went home and told Sally, I'm going after those diapers. It's changed my entire attitude. Ronald's defecation and vomiting have just become so natural a part of loving Ronald I don't even think about them anymore. That was a fifty-year weakness that was overcome in the past five years. I think what I learned with Ronald is that the unpleasant experiences—burdensome paperwork, or an unpleasant relationship with a boss, or a customer giving you a hard time—if I can look at those calmly, there's a great chance for me to learn something, and a chance to teach something by the way I respond.

And Marjorie, you're not talking to St. Jimmy here, I do not succeed as much as I would like, but I do try. And I learn some of that by dealing with Ronald.

I remember riding in your car and you had the back doors child-locked, so they couldn't be opened from the inside. Is Ronald likely to just open the doors and jump out?

Probably no more likely than any other five-year-old. But the fact is that Ronald is unpredictable, and sometimes his displeasure will expand into a tantrum without much warning. The locks are just a safeguard.

I don't know much about autism, Jim.

Not many people do. The movie "Rain Man," where Dustin Hoffman plays an autistic adult, is going to do a lot for the understanding of autism. My friends say, Could Ronald be like that? I say, yeah, he might, or he might not. We don't know.

Autism is basically drawing into oneself; preoccupation with oneself is what the term means literally. He's in his own world. Sometimes at the bottom end of the scale babies won't suckle their mothers, they don't want to be touched, they withdraw and self-mutilate, bang their heads against walls. Ronald is not at that end of the scale. He'll probably be what's called a high-functioning autistic person. He speaks, not plainly and not with any complexity of conversation.

In the movie Dustin Hoffman goes through this bit, who's on first, the Abbott and Costello routine, he says it over and over again. Ronald does some of those things too. Autism is fundamentally a profound communications problem, and it manifests as behavior problems. Eighty percent of autistic people end up institutionalized.

But you've decided not to do that?

I won't say it won't happen. The priest on M★A★S★H, William

Christopher, has an autistic son, and he took him to Europe, did all these wonderful things. And when the boy went into puberty, he started attacking his mother and others. Christopher had four grown men, therapists, move into the house and live twenty-four hours a day with him for a year, and he finally had the boy institutionalized. So you don't ever know.

Editor's note

I asked later for a poem about Ronald, and Autry sent a draft of a piece called "Leo." "It's only obscurely about Ronald," he told me. "It has to do with the pain of when we first found out." It's a poem that talks about Autry's teenage years, when the family next door had a retarded child named Leo. He was a big hulking fellow, and Leo liked to throw water on the one sparkplug in Autry's motorcycle, to force him to stay and play. "You Leo's buddy. Play with Leo now."
   In one of the concluding stanzas, Autry writes:

> *I hadn't thought about Leo in years, of course,*
> *until just the other day,*
> *just after the tests were in . . .*

That was when the pediatrician brought the news of Ronald's condition. The poem ends:

> *And I thought,*
> *sometimes God makes you write things on the blackboard*
> *a thousand times.*

EXEMPLAR:
New Hope Communications

Doug Greene, founder and CEO of New Hope Communications, provides some of the best illustrations of how business can be done in a different way. He expressed his values in his suggestion to employees as to the three principles for relating to people: "Be kind, be kind, be kind." Then the New Hope workers began to realize that often they weren't being honest in order to somehow be kind. So they changed the exhortation to "Be kind, be honest, be kind." Then Greene wanted to emphasize the joy of business, so they changed the watchwords to "Be kind, be honest, have fun."

But what if someone is not being effective and is also not having a good time? Greene tries to encourage people to be aware of this so that he and other managers don't have to find this out too late. Right at the beginning of employment, each person at New Hope is encouraged to consider quitting. As Greene puts it: "We tell people, 'We want you to quit. We want you to leave this company. We are hiring you, but we don't want you to stay forever. If someone wants you to stay forever, run as fast as you can in the other direction. You may stay for forty years or you may stay for four hours. We don't know how long you're going to stay. If our needs meet and it fits right, fine. If you quit, I want you to be as happy the day you quit as the day you joined the company.' "

In order for the company and all its participants to individually know how things are going, New Hope has experimented with a five-part paycheck, consisting of four questions in addition to the check. This allows everybody to assess how they are doing, not only in terms of money but in terms of other aspects of the meaning and value of work. Accompanying one of the two paychecks each month are these four types of questions:

Are you happy with your financial or economic package?

How do you feel about your relationships here, the people you work with and come in contact with?

How do you feel about the skills you are developing?

How do you feel about the experience of the job overall—are you at the right place at the right time in your life?

Greene and the people at New Hope struggle with the form of the questions and ways to learn more from the answers both individually and organizationally. But they find that the growth of the organization and the people in it is enhanced by this kind of questioning.

11

THE CORPORATION WITHOUT BOUNDARIES

by Robert D. Haas

How does an established Fortune 500 company maintain its position of growth and profitability while also adjusting to powerful forces of social, political, and technological change in its business throughout the world?

In the following address to the Commonwealth Club of San Francisco, the President and Chief Executive Officer of Levi Strauss & Co. demonstrates the kind of leadership that is required in today's marketplace. He responds both to the myriad complex external issues of doing business on a global level and to the personal internal development of his employees.

Here is how one important leader feels about technology, communication, employee motivation, and the disappearing distinctions between geographic countries and between managers and workers within the corporation. Only enlightened leadership can ensure a future for even the most successful businesses today.

All of us are on a wondrous and somewhat scary journey to a world vastly transformed by the forces of change. Institutions as well as individuals will thrive or decline depending on their ability to understand the implications of these forces.

The most visible differences between the corporation of the future and its present-day counterpart will be not the products they make or the equipment they use—but who will be working, how they will be working, why they will be working, and what work will mean to them.

A good first step in dealing with change is to test all your assumptions. Every day, old truisms fall by the wayside and traditional concepts are challenged. Companies intent on surviving—and thriving— must help their employees overcome old ideas and outdated notions, whether this means seeking opportunities in new markets, acting with greater urgency, treating suppliers and customers as partners, rethinking the distinction between workers and managers, or redrawing the lines between personal and professional concerns.

BREACHING BOUNDARIES

Familiar boundaries are being breached or are disappearing altogether. This is why I describe the corporation of the future as the corporation without boundaries.

In a corporation without boundaries employees are able to tap their fullest potential. They know what they're responsible for and what resources they have to get the job done. They take personal responsibility for their contribution to the business. They feel like owners, and in many cases they will be.

Technology is the most potent force we have to quickly erase old boundaries and assumptions. In the business world, technology is the most obvious means of gaining a competitive advantage.

Technology, especially in the area of computers, is a powerful equalizer. Access to information, once held captive in big mainframes and available only to wizards with the right codes, is being distributed more broadly.

If knowledge is power, that power today is being shared in many ways with extraordinary ramifications for the business world. Information can now be transmitted globally, in a matter of seconds.

People at every level are gaining the ability to work smarter and more independently. As we fully harness the computer's potential, the capabilities of all employees will broaden and improve greatly. This transformation must be overseen by supervisors who are willing to relinquish some of their responsibilities and to empower their subordinates.

GLOBALIZATION

While technology allows corporations to make startling advances, it also opens them to challenges from many new directions. Long-standing competitive advantages may disappear overnight. Boundaries that once provided an advantage can quickly fade in importance.

Also fading are geographic distinctions that have placed barriers to foreign competition. In times past, geography determined plant locations and product distribution; a country's boundaries defined individual markets. These were shaped by unique laws, customs, currencies, and language.

We already know that national boundaries are becoming less of an obstacle. The recent U.S./Canada trade agreement is one example. Western Europe's drive for economic unity in 1992 and the breaking down of borders in Eastern Europe are events of even greater significance.

Many companies are now developing businesses in Eastern European and Soviet markets. In Hungary, Levi Strauss & Co. has made a profit and found new customers. In turn the Hungarians have gained new technologies and better wages than ever before.

We're witnessing the globalization of the manufacturing process. This represents a triumph over old geographic limitations. Our company buys denim in North Carolina, ships it to France where it is sewn into jeans, launders these jeans in Belgium, and markets them in Germany using TV commercials developed in England.

Remaining a truly global corporation requires tapping new resources. Key among these is the diversity of cultures and perspectives held among employees around the world.

From a business perspective, one of the most important new resources available because of globalization and supported by technology is access to new capital. The ability to move funds electronically has literally transformed capital markets into a 24-hour, world marketplace. Shouldn't a truly global company be open for business 24 hours a day?

The ability to compress time can yield a competitive advantage. Conversely, failure to deliver products and services to impatient customers can spell doom for any enterprise.

Speed, is essential, not only in delivering your product to a breathless market, but in other dealings as well. Telephones, fax machines, and electronic mail link the world. Business partners know that, theoretically, you can have near-instant access to information. They expect you to respond quickly with decisions—if you don't, someone else in the marketplace will.

Technology alone cannot make your company sufficiently responsive. To interact with business partners in a timely manner, global corporations must rely upon well-informed employees who can be trusted to make decisions and accept the responsibility for results. Here again, empowerment is essential for success.

The value of empowerment is nothing new. History is filled with examples of opportunities lost because someone's on-the-spot representative would not or could not make a decision.

WORKFORCE 2000

The workforce is the most critical area of change. Let's take a look at the United States between now and the year 2000. First, there will be a significant decline in the percentage of white males, traditionally America's workers and managers. At the turn of the century, these men will account for only 15 percent of people entering the workforce. Women, on the other hand, will represent two-thirds of the new entrants.

We can also expect an increasing proportion of minorities among the new employees. Some will be skilled entrepreneurs or technicians with a track record of success; others will be new to the world of business. Some will be immigrants, and some will not be comfortable with English.

The U.S. Department of the Labor has identified what's called a "skills gap." This points to the disparity between the skills new jobs will require, and the education and background new entrants bring to the workforce.

Many young people are not staying in school, and those who do may not be acquiring the skills they need—reading, writing, critical thinking, problem solving, science, and mathematics. At a time when the global marketplace makes it increasingly important to understand geography and to learn a second or even a third language, we are graduating students who can't find Boston—not to mention Brussels—on a map.

Many new entrants to the workforce are not well-equipped to learn and succeed at the jobs that need to get done. We need to discard the old thinking that says, "You're not a student, you're a worker." The concept of life-long learning—the willingness and ability to master new material—must replace the notion that education takes place only in schools.

For the first time in our history a majority of new jobs will require a post-secondary education. The skills gap is widening. Who is going to close that gap? The Department of Labor reports that private business is already spending $30 billion to $40 billion a year for formal on-the-job training. You can expect that number to go up. Way up.

NEW ATTITUDE

In coming years we will see even more two-wage-earner families and single-parent heads of households. This change is influencing how people feel about work—about their need for more flexible hours, willingness to relocate, and desire to do some work at home. Employers will have to re-think the boundaries between their employees' personal and professional lives.

In the future, employees will challenge old distinctions and seek greater flexibility on how and when they work. This seems only fair since companies have begun discarding the traditional ground rules of employment.

In the "good old days" employees offered their loyalty in exchange for job security, decent wages, and fair working conditions. Upheavals in the business world, however, have raised uncertainties in the relationship between employer and employee. Corporations in the future will have to earn the loyalty and support of their workers in many new ways. This will require new ways of managing.

Companies have always understood that customers are volunteers. We need to see that employees, too, are volunteers. They have options. If we're going to persuade the best people to choose us and stay with us, we must develop a new kind of work environment.

We still have to provide competitive pay and benefits, but we need to do much more. Employees want to be consulted and to understand the thinking behind decisions. They want communication, not direction. They want recognition. And they want to be empowered to make decisions.

Companies will have to restructure. They must streamline to speed decisions. They must also provide more information, authority, and responsibility to those who are closest to products and customers. Many companies, including our own, have already begun this process.

EMPOWERED ORGANIZATION

Corporations will also have to commit themselves to reworking one of the most rigid boundaries of all—the line that distinguished workers and managers.

This means some basic assumptions must be challenged: Why can't some employees set production goals? Why can't they monitor plant efficiency? Why can't they hire and fire new workers on whom they are increasingly dependent? And why can't they benefit directly from their initiatives which result in higher profits?

The corporation without boundaries must also have a truly international outlook. It will be committed to a cross-fertilization of ideas and values among its domestic and international workforces. It will constantly seek ways to inform and educate people so that they can challenge their own ingrained ways of thinking.

Also, its managers will do as much listening as talking. A commitment to two-way communication will result in a workforce that shares a common vision, sense of direction, and understanding of values, ethics, and standards. Without this individual decision-making is crippled.

To promote initiative, creativity, and commitment in the corporation without boundaries, managers must shed traditional authoritarian practices. They must be coaches, facilitators, and role models. The corporation without boundaries will also reduce the distinction between workers and owners. Its employees will gain an increasing stake in the success of the company and a proportionate say in discussions of company policies.

I am describing the empowered organization, the most advanced form of the corporation without boundaries that I can envision. Sometimes empowerment takes hold, sometimes it doesn't. It isn't just a tough change for managers. It's tough for employees as well. Often both are reluctant to let go of their traditional roles and power.

MANAGING CHANGE

Pessimists envision an America that shortly will find itself a second-rate competitor in the global marketplace. I disagree. Change is creating new markets and radically remaking existing ones. The key is flexibility, innovation, and a workforce that can seize the moment.

We cannot underestimate the magnitude of this challenge. Managing change is not a simple matter. In fact, nothing is more difficult. Implementing change within ourselves is tough enough. Implementing change among groups of people throughout institutions is exponentially more difficult.

Still, as the world continues its radical transformation, corporations intent on success will have to draw on every resource available. Mastering technology, having global presence, and compressing response time will all prove invaluable.

But the most important resource of all lies within people—their talent, energy, and commitment. A corporation without boundaries will best utilize all of these resources. It's my hope that businesses and other institutions will also strive to overcome their own boundaries and unleash the potential of their own people. The result will be a more exciting, prosperous, and humane future for ourselves and for our children.

12

BUILDING COMMUNITY AS A LEADERSHIP DISCIPLINE

by Kazimierz Gozdz

If the new paradigm and the practices associated with it are, by definition, appropriate for these times and their challenges, why are we having such difficulty implementing them? What should we be moving toward and how can we get there? And what kind of leadership is necessary? In the following article Kazimierz Gozdz provides some answers to these questions.

Community and the new paradigm can be developed and maintained when leadership makes a commitment to it, engenders a community discipline, and understands the inevitable cycles in and out of community that happen in any organization. Gozdz's experiences have led him to be realistic rather than falsely hopeful. But the recommendations here, supported by a number of actual examples, are the kind of serious steps that are needed in this time of transition.

Kazimierz Gozdz is an internationally known facilitator of community building in organizations through his firm, Gozdz & Associates, and as a consultant to the Foundation for Community Encouragement. He devoted himself to this practice in 1987 after a successful career as an entrepreneur and degrees in business administration, chemistry, and training and development. He has had major responsibility for such projects as an attempt to bring community to an entire county of over fifty thousand people in Washington State, a $750,000 effort to introduce community into the Louisiana State Prison System, and conflict-resolution work in organizations in Russia. He is completing his doctorate at the Institute of Transpersonal Psychology.

As organizations struggle to find appropriate structures for a new paradigm in business, they need to incorporate the principles of community. If they wish to become learning organizations, they need to realize that the learning organization is by definition a community.

While the word "community" often refers to a geographical location or a group of individuals, for the new paradigm organization it is much more. An organization acting as a community is a collective lifelong learner, responsive to change, receptive to challenge, and conscious of an increasingly complex array of alternatives. As leaders work to maintain community within organization, a new kind of leadership, involving virtually everyone in the organization, emerges.

Dr. M. Scott Peck has provided an excellent guide to community in his book *The Different Drum*. His form of community has been implemented in business and other organizations through the Foundation for Community Encouragement (FCE). Virtually all of the examples in this article come from FCE's work. My experiences in working with FCE and on my own have led to my belief that community is a process rather than a state; strong leadership and commitment must be mustered in order to maintain it; only through purpose and discipline will the community process be maintained; and attention to the developmental cycles of community will help ensure that it is sustained.

The struggle to develop and maintain community is identical to the struggle to develop and maintain a new paradigm way of business. In fact, when we look at what Peck means by community, we find that it is quite close in concept to what most people mean by new paradigm business. Peck's idea of community reveals what work life with other people could be. In the first place, community to him is inclusive (it does not exclude anyone who really wants to be part of it), while also celebrating diversity. It is not like a stew in which all the ingredients are cooked so long that they are a gooey mass. Instead, community is like a crisp salad in which all the ingredients (in this case people) retain their individuality, yet make something greater than the sum of the parts.

With true community, there has to be commitment, a willingness to coexist. It is not a leaderless group but rather a group of leaders. All capabilities in the group are utilized in a flow in which different people lead or contribute when it is appropriate.

This type of community is a safe place where people can be vulnerable and where love can flourish. But the conflict that is often necessary for creativity and innovation occurs too. People can fight gracefully in an empowering, understanding, and compassionate environment. A community contemplates itself and examines itself. It is realistic, because it takes everything and everybody into account. Not surprisingly, decisions in this environment are made by consensus, rather than by a majority vote or fiat that might leave out the contributions and inclinations of some individuals.

In many ways the new paradigm organization seeks to build and experience community, yet many organizational leaders are without the necessary tools for creating such a framework. After all, the development of community-building technology is extremely recent and has not yet become a core requirement in management training.

Often community occurs briefly because of crisis or at least a strong necessity. In the case of one national trade organization, for instance, board members learned about community as a result of conflicts caused by a merger. Two regional trade organizations representing East and West decided to merge to give their constituency national political power, and to expand the level of service they could provide. One year after the merger, having undergone a whitewater rafting trip and other team-building processes, board members still had not been able to put behind them the controversial fight over the original merger. Recognizing their anger, resentments, and unfinished grief from the transition, the chairman took decisive action to rebuild the board's ability to direct the association. A strategic-planning process to set the organization's five-year vision plan was combined with a process of establishing the board as a community.

In a community-building workshop, individual board members were able to express the loss they experienced from the merger. Some spoke of fear of losing their board seats if the organization grew too quickly. Others discovered that they were afraid that they would lose contacts they had made on the board. Some felt anger about how individual personalities and leadership styles seemed to dominate the board's decision making. Having developed a safe place to appropriately grieve its past, the board became an effective learning group that was able to envision its future as a national organization.

This idea that community occurs naturally at times of great need is a major factor that makes building community within organizations confusing. At times, in response to an external threat or a challenging task, community is palpably present. But, once the group resolves the crisis or moves to another level of organizational maturity, the sense of community disappears, leaving leaders with a desire for renewal of a lost sense of spirit.

However, there is a way to make the process less mysterious and to understand the natural ebb and flow of the feelings of community. This article presents this more effective approach by focusing on four aspects of community: the experience of community; community-building as a process; the organizational framework for the mastery of community as a discipline; and the developmental cycles of sustainable community.

THE EXPERIENCE OF COMMUNITY

An experience of community in the workplace is a special encounter with work as a creative and enriching part of life. Often unforgettable, it is a time when a person feels most alive and connected to the world.

Most often community is associated with the meaningful occasions of life. This was certainly the case for Jill, a middle manager in a manufacturing organization that was constantly beset by technological change and a chronic sense of impending doom. Troubled by layoffs and downsizing, management looked toward an experience of community to break the cycle of decline. In a three-day community-building experience attended by managers from three levels of organizational hierarchy, they were able to be openly disappointed and angry with one another.

Understanding the dynamics of grief, the facilitator reframed the group's despair. When the tears and sadness were expressed, an opportunity for creative problem-solving led to task-force initiatives to sustain the change. Having achieved a sense of community with this group, Jill likened the experience to the birth of her child. Once she endured the natural pain of childbearing, she had experienced an overwhelming sense of well-being that seemed to extend to everyone in the hospital and beyond. Similarly, the initial pain of authentic communication with people she worked with every day (and yet strangely never knew) opened her to seeing them with new eyes. Authentic shock and grief transformed her work with them into creative opportunity.

Mihaly Csikszentmihalyi, in his book *Flow*, wrote of the psychology of optimal experience. Community, like flow, is characterized by a certain quality of attention. It is a focus so clear that little else matters outside that awareness.

For example, Burt, an MBA candidate, saw that community-building work within a class, which led to the group's resolving differences and working together, was like the experience of his college rowing team. Over the course of many years of training, the team had begun to communicate nonverbally. With the slightest cue, he had known exactly how to compensate for an oar dipped too low in position two or for a slow return in position six. On occasion the team would transcend individual limitations and perform beyond the sum total of each person's individual capacity. It was as if the team, quite separate from the individuals that comprised it, had begun to row. With the class community work, Burt touched moments of the same type of collaboration. For him, community-building was a recollection of one of the best periods of his life.

So it is with many who experience community in a workshop setting. It is as if our beliefs and expectations within our organizations formed a thin film that seems to block a group of individuals from peak performance. With the right guidelines, commitment, and facilitation, groups routinely find this membrane to be permeable. Crossing over into an area of extraordinary skill and competency, they experience community.

Community, in its basic form, involves a group of people who have committed themselves to a process of ever-deepening levels of communication. Such a group becomes capable of learning, self-reflective behavior, and the capacity to balance individual and group needs. Building community is a process, not a place, a feeling, or a particular type of organizational structure.

The communication involved in an experience of community is honest and clear. It is uncharacteristically loving. For an ex-POW who experienced community with a group of sixty people in a workshop, it was reminiscent of communicating in a prison cell where tapping on walls and floors was a communication that said another human being existed. Brief, spaced with silence, yet carrying an essential message to stay alive, communication became love.

The question, then, is not whether community *can* be experienced, but do we have to wait for a devastating crisis to initiate it? How can organizations experience such states with deliberate intention? If community is sometimes achieved as a result of attention to a pressing crisis or important task, why is it so difficult for organizations to achieve a sustainable, continuous sense of community deliberately?

The first part of the answer to these questions involves an exploration of the process of building community as developed by Peck. Elaborating on his work and my own applications of his technology to the new paradigm organization, the next section discusses building community as a short-term process. This leads to a discussion of the discipline needed to extend that process over the productive life of an organization.

THE FOUR-STAGE PROCESS OF COMMUNITY-BUILDING

The process of building community requires a new view of the organization's stakeholders. Although comprised of individuals, large systems and subsystems, it is important they be seen as one entity. This is the community, composed of the interactive process of many, yet by itself capable of growth, development, consciousness, and learning. Having made the fundamental mind shift from fragmented parts to one interconnected entity, it is possible to conceive of nurturing this community. Such nurturance requires a disciplined act of love, in which everyone in the organization can participate.

In his book *The Road Less Traveled*, Peck defines love as "The will to extend one's self for the purpose of nurturing one's own or another's spiritual growth." Later, in *The Different Drum* and *A World Waiting to Be Born,* he extended the realm of spiritual growth to groups and went on to lay the groundwork for an actual technology of building and sustaining community in organizations.

An organization desiring to become a community is trained to use a four-stage process model. Experientially, the group breaks down its barriers to communication. Eventually individuals and the group as a whole begin to learn and transform. Peck's four stages of community-building are presented here from the view of a learning organization.

• *Pseudocommunity*. During this stage the group pretends that it already is a community and that differences do not exist. The decision-making process and the nature of relationships go unchallenged.

• *Chaos*. The sense of apparent control and order is disrupted when deep differences emerge. The group tries to obliterate these individual differences by changing each other. Replication and duplication of what has worked in the past is mandated, with decisions by competition and control.

• *Emptiness*. Having failed to control or organize its way into community, the group steps into true chaos; uncertainty and ambiguity replace control. The group begins the work of self-examination, giving up personal obstacles, barriers, and agendas. It is the beginning of true listening, where the group's decision-making process becomes collaborative.

• *Community*. Having emptied itself of its mental models, the group is available for authentic communication. Characterized by flow or Spirit, differences are embraced. A context for the underlying interconnectedness in the diversity becomes apparent. In this safe place, creativity emerges. The group as a whole makes decisions co-creatively, learns as an entity, and innovates as a whole.

As a result of this process, which the community-building technology facilitates and hastens, the group begins to see that the differences with which it is most frequently preoccupied are distractions. As a learning organization, the community turns its attention away from organizational roles, meaningless activities, religious, gender and ethnic differences when they are irrelevant and attends to true differences that are causing conflict.

Leadership in community is more a context than a person. It takes strong leadership to move people to get into the process of community. But once that state is achieved, the group becomes a community of leaders. Everyone knows that he or she has a contribution to make to the group. When the time, situation, or need is right, anyone can take up the staff of leadership. Even though there may be a hierarchy in place, when individuals hold to the process of community, that hierarchy becomes an efficiency rather than a power system. It allows everyone to know his or her responsibilities. The responsibility of the leader at the top of such an organization is to be a facilitator rather than a dictator. As one such leader said in an organization that had developed a community, "I just stand back and let everybody do their jobs."

Given these benefits of community and the learning organization, why are there so few organizations capable of sustaining a sense of community? Once this powerful sense of spirit has been achieved, why does it invariably decay with time? Establishing a framework where community can be held as a disciplined process of mastery is the next skill in building sustainable community.

COMMUNITY AS MASTERY AND DISCIPLINE

There are two reasons why organizations that may briefly experience a sense of community during special moments fail to become organizational communities. First, we examine the failure to understand community as a discipline. Second, we look at the frequent inability to make this discipline part of the organizational framework and philosophy.

In the short run, the community-building process can be used to achieve the flow state, the stage called "community" in Peck's model. It can resolve existing problems or conflicts and facilitate collaboration. These are a strong set of benefits. Content with these immediate results, organizations often stop short of taking the next essential step to community development and organizational transformation: the commitment to community as a discipline.

Such commitment is required for its long-term success. Most often the experience of community is so successful in and of itself that organizations and individuals routinely fail to plan for its inevitable cycles. Most frequently they never make this critical connection to community.

In one case, a large group-medical practice in the South had difficulty retaining professional staff and, as a result of this decline, low morale pervaded the office. Having had thirty physicians, the group declined to seventeen before exploring community-building as a solution. But the success of community-building led to a weakening of commitment. When the morale in the office increased and the organization entered a rapid growth phase, group members seemed to forget where the success came from. Interest in sustaining the work of an ongoing community decreased. Ultimately the leadership tired of fighting an uphill battle for involvement and commitment, and another cycle of decline toward an impending crisis began.

This scenario is a familiar pattern in organizations striving to use community-building technology in the workplace. Another example is a Fortune 100 company that arranged community-building workshops for its labor management contract negotiating teams. Having moved toward a sense of community, the teams were able to translate competitive positions into creativity, avoiding a strike. However, they felt that both teams had to conceal that they had experienced community. Revealing to labor or management this alternative conflict-resolution technique would not have fit the old paradigm model of antagonistic, secretive negotiating. Regardless of the outcome, the team felt they would be held as suspect within the operating cultures they represented. And thus the potential for them to expand the community process was diminished substantially.

This typical pattern of crisis, intervention, resolution, and re-emergence of crisis in a new form can be stopped if an organization commits to the disciplined practice of sustaining community. Leaders have to hold the commitment and keep the process going, even though some in the group may become complacent. There is an illusion that once a sense of community occurs within an organization it will remain constant. This is not the case. The sense of community or flow state is repeatedly lost. It can be deliberately regained at ever greater levels of organizational maturity, but only when sustaining community is seen and accepted as a path to developing mastery. This path is community as a discipline. It does not mean endless drudgery or meaningless forced work. It means commitment that aligns and directs courses of action chosen from a basic philosophy that enriches each individual's life. Such discipline, practiced personally in relationship to community, over time leads to ever-deeper levels of mastery.

A leader must practice the discipline of community and nurture and maintain it in the group so that everyone begins to act as a leader and takes up the discipline as a natural way of working. At that point everyone learns that this sort of discipline is ultimately freeing and powerful. As Peter Senge says in *The Fifth Discipline:* "By 'discipline,' I do not mean an 'enforced order' or 'means of punishment,' but a body of theory and technique that must be studied and mastered to be put into practice. A discipline is a developmental path for acquiring certain skills or competencies. As with any discipline, anyone can develop proficiency through practice."

Such a sustained course of action is required, because to create a sustainable community, an organization must invariably pass through stages of frustration, grief, and instability. In his book *Surviving Corporate Transition*, William Bridges refers to a phase in the transition of organizations as the "neutral zone," very similar to Peck's "stage of emptiness." Helping people to navigate this cycle in organizational life requires a good working structure, to which we now turn.

AN ORGANIZATIONAL FRAMEWORK TO SUPPORT COMMUNITY-BUILDING

A commitment to community by an organization's leadership has to be reflected in the framework that defines the very reason for an organization's existence. Some call this framework a "purpose"; others an "organizational mission"; still others, a "vision." Key to its use in building sustainable community is the understanding that it is never completely achievable. The leaders of the organization are called to make a statement of the importance of the principles and process of community.

Most often managers are perplexed as to how to introduce community-building into their organizations. Those who are willing to move in this direction are confused as to how to enroll others in the process. They can start by declaring the commitment to community as one of the organization's reasons for existence.

This commitment to community adds an overall continuity and context to the process that is vital in helping teams and subgroups understand that others hold the same values as they do. Groups that have never interacted before can begin to understand that the ground rules they use for meeting are supported by the organization's culture.

The task will not have to be the only reason why individuals can treat each other with a sense of respect and openness characteristic of community.

Consider how often this scenario has occurred in organizations. An organization has simultaneously assigned work groups to tasks. Within time, a sense of cohesion and "team" is achieved in each group. Within a large organization, they may know only of one another's existence on paper. When the task is over for each group, they return to the normal operations of the organization and its culture. The sense of team is lost, and most often people even need time to transition to a less-productive working environment. With the end of the tasks comes the end of the reason to relate in a special way.

An organization that constructs its framework to incorporate community as its overall culture would give each of these team members permission and a context within which to carry out the norms they had developed in the smaller group. Within the larger culture individuals would begin to expect and relate with others, knowing they had probably achieved a sense of cohesion elsewhere within the organization. They would have permission to practice the discipline of community outside of the task group. It would be an expected part of the ongoing culture.

An organizational guiding philosophy is a set of values from which an organization operates. These can become guideposts, a lighthouse that attracts individuals with similar values as well as lending permission to these dormant qualities in the existing organization.

Discipline may be a good idea, but how can it ever take hold in an organization that currently is not disciplined toward community? The basic building blocks are within its organizational guiding philosophy. These are fundamental assumptions or values that form the basis of the way the organization behaves.

Implicit within the process of community, these are some of the many ground rules which can be adopted as a portion of such a philosophy:

- Systems thinking and long-term thinking
- Equal responsibility for the development of community
- Flexible and continuous learning
- Inclusivity
- Encouragement for everyone to assert his or her leadership abilities
- Commitment to authenticity and truth telling

SUSTAINABLE COMMUNITY
DEVELOPMENTAL CYCLES

If the organization envisions community-building as an ongoing discipline and is purposefully dedicated to it, it will realize that it must go through the transformational stages over and over again. The four stages of the community-building process become four development cycles, each having stages built within them.

Again, the job of the leaders in this situation is to keep the life of the community process alive by constantly keeping everyone's attention on the process. Just knowing that this process has these developmental stages allows organization members not to lose heart, but rather to gain motivation for the task.

Everyone will know that the old community inevitably becomes the new pseudocommunity. As a spiritually growing entity, the organization's previously achieved level of maturity shortly becomes one of immaturity when new exigencies are faced, and the growth cycle must be repeated.

The leader in one situation was a state governor. He appointed a task force to form a work group focused on the issue of substance-abuse prevention. The group could make little headway in developing guidelines that were workable across the twenty agencies involved. They described themselves as natural competitors. The first time the two-day community-building approach was used, the group did pass through the four stages, but honest and vulnerable communication was far too threatening to be sustained.

What did happen, however, was that the pseudocommunity that the organization reverted to soon broke down. During a second event, new people came into the process. This group also went through the four stages of community, but their cycle went deeper. Prevalent control issues were exposed. Then the group was more capable of honest communication and of including new people into the process. If the group continues to air its differences, eventually it may lead to emptying itself of its roles and pass into a still more authentic sense of community.

By following the path of mastery of the discipline of community, the individual, the group, and the organization all go through a similar transformation process. The benefit is that, having committed to this process, both the group and the individual have an internal instruction manual on how to facilitate transformation. Born from their own experiential learning, such inner preparation facilitates the outer organizational changes. An old paradigm organization's transformation into a sustainable community is characterized by these developmental cycles.

• *Pseudocommunity developmental cycle.* Here a group attempts to decide whether it wants to transition to a new paradigm or keep operating in the old. There is much ambivalence, yet new ideas are imported as quick-fix solutions. The organization calls itself a community and has occasional teams and groups that touch that goal, but the experiences are fleeting. Everyone knows that the organization is not a safe place; management likes to pretend that it is. Often the group feels powerless to make change and manipulated by those in power.

• *Chaos developmental cycle.* Here hidden secrets and conflicts begin to emerge. Long-stored resentments and past hurts become part of the working day. Individuals begin to challenge themselves and the norms of the group. Long-term silent agreements start to be broken as individuals begin to believe there is another way. Control in all forms, from leadership to organizational structure, starts to be challenged. Differences in power, commitment to the process, and life-styles all become part of a cultural re-examination. There is a belief that if enough of the right people were excluded things would get better. Control is used to bring the system back to where it was before, by organizing or problem solving out of this phase. If this cycle is not faced directly, another level of pseudocommunity is created in the organization.

• *Emptiness developmental cycle.* This cycle is characterized by a loss of hope. The question, "Why did I do this?" is always present. Many things have gone wrong; the old systems no longer work, nor does the new. No one seems to have the solution. It seems apparent that the effort toward community is not the dream it started out to be. Many ideals have been shattered, yet the undeniable growth of individuals is apparent everywhere. There is clashing of paradigms and inevitable communication breakdowns because the same words and ideas now mean two different things, one interpreted from the new paradigm perspective and one from the old.

• *Community developmental cycle.* Starting with glimmers of hope and almost with a mysterious sweep, another order of complexity is integrated almost overnight. Things begin to make sense, and the quality of communication alters significantly. A new appropriate structure becomes apparent, and with it a clear sense of energy and activity. Creativity is free flowing, and a sense of spirit seems to pervade the work. Appropriate leadership emerges, with each individual finding a way to contribute as a co-creator or leader in their own way toward an overarching purpose. With this integration a new status quo is established until another cycle of pseudocommunity begins.

The more conscious of itself the leadership and the learning organization becomes, the more quickly it will be able to diagnose its new stagnation and efficiently move through the developmental cycles again.

REFERENCES

Bridges, W. (1988) *Surviving Transitions*. New York: Doubleday.

Csikzentmihalyi, M. (1990) *Flow: The Psychology of Optimal Experience*. New York: HarperCollins.

Peck, M. S., M.D. (1978) *The Road Less Traveled*. New York: Simon & Schuster.

———(1987) *The Different Drum*. New York: Simon & Schuster.

———(1993) *A World Waiting to Be Born: Civility Revisited*. New York: Bantam Books.

EXEMPLAR:
North American Tool and Die

Tom Melohn, Former Head Sweeper (his self-appointed title was meant to show his commitment to serving his workers) at North American Tool and Die, turned a sleepy metal-stamping plant into a thriving and advanced corporation that he sold to his employees. How did they do it? By adhering to a set of very basic values without compromise: honesty, trust, mutual respect, openness, and creativity.

And how well did this approach work? Sales were up 28 percent compounded annually since 1978, and pretax earnings increased twenty-five times. NATD achieved a return on investment that was the equivalent of that achieved by the top 10 percent of the Fortune 500. The company's stock prices grew 47 percent a year compounded each year. Productivity was up by 480 percent, while absenteeism dropped to less than one percent, turnover to less than 4 percent. And the reject rate at NATD is one tenth of one percent on parts produced by the company since 1980.

Melohn says about creativity: "You generally think about writers or artists. But I think that creativity can be anything. Our toolmakers take a great big piece of steel and make it into an absolute jewel with tolerances to one thousandth of an inch. That's creativity. Our engineers take a dumb blueprint and read it and design a die that will make a part that has a tolerance of less than one-fourth the thickness of a human hair. What we try to do is to create a climate where people can be creative on the job, where they can express themselves. That's how you get no rejects. They care about their work. And they watch out for what is happening."

Melohn feels that people work for pride and recognition, as well as for money. He gave cash bonuses each month for innovations and extra efforts by employees. One such honoree at NATD was Jim Norsworthy, a shop maintenance worker. The company uses large quantities of oil. If it isn't dealt with properly, it can become toxic waste and is costly. Norsworthy bought an oil-recycling device that has a double-sided filter system. That way the oil could be reused, instead of being disposed of and replaced with new oil. The machine paid for itself in the first week of operation.

Melohn represents the love and caring that is exhibited by a new type of manager and leader. Whenever he is reminded of his "gang," as he calls his former employees, his eyes get teary and he expresses how much he misses them.

Part III

ORGANIZATIONAL TRANSFORMATION

This is a world of permanent white water in which we're all roaring down a wild river, none of us feeling like we either understand or control what we're in the middle of.

PETER VAILL

The problem is not to introduce change. The issue is to recognize it—it's already there—and help people through it. It's not that there aren't some very powerful high human technologies—but the bottom line is you can't play by the old rules.

HARRISON OWEN

There are those opposed to the principles of New Management and who use every downturn in profits, stock price, or the economy as an opportunity to lobby for a return to the "tougher-minded" practices of the Old Guard.

JAMES O'TOOLE
Vanguard Management

Actually, any organization that plans to wait for the methods for transformation to be proven effective is probably writing its own epitaph.

RALPH KILMANN ET AL.
Corporate Transformation

INTRODUCTION

How do we get there from here? That is the question of the times. How do we transform our organizations and keep transforming them as the world changes? How do we maintain our purpose in the face of this change, keep relationships strong, deal with stress, balance our personal and professional lives, and nurture our spirit when the pull of external rewards and the chance of losing them is ever present?

We are told that the only constant in the world is change and that the change now is greater than it has ever been. For instance, Layton Fisher of Imperial Oil told a conference of the International Center for Organizational Design about the exponential increase of information in the world. He pointed out that if all the world's knowledge could be represented by a book in 1980, we would need two books by 1987, four books by 1994 and so on. In fact, some experts estimate that the world's knowledge is now doubling every three and a half years. Fisher concluded, "Trying to manage your life or your organization in a world changing that rapidly is like dancing with a gorilla. You don't stop when you get tired. You stop when the gorilla gets tired."

The articles in this section show that these assertions about the rapid pace of change and our helplessness in the face of it are partially wrong. They leave out one essential constant: the human spirit. While we must respect the explosive river of change, we can learn to flow in harmony with it in our attitudes and actions. The challenge is to live and prosper through the tests of constant change by applying our inner resources of consciousness and creativity.

All the successes of business transformation reported in this section are based on a trust in the human spirit in the face of great demands. There is consistent evidence that the more an organization moves in this spiritual direction, the greater will be its success in terms of the standard business measures, as well as in those measures of human values and environmental effects that are increasingly being applied.

But because of fear, short-term thinking can sometimes prevail. More often than not, when there is success with a new approach in a division of a company, there is a cycle of top management questioning the approach, instituting cost-cutting or other repressive measures, and killing the initiative. Or the necessary changes are made from the top but in such massive steps that the stress on the organization leads to a failure of what could be effective approaches in the long run if they were carried out in a measured, organic way.

When you look at the full potential of the new paradigm way, it is hard to imagine that this type of business doesn't spread at least as fast as the changes in the world are demanding it. Most people would like to work in a setting without the "we-they" mentality, in which people are treated like adults, and with open sharing of information throughout the business. They would thrive in a workplace that offers widespread authority for task and strategy and allows an experience of community without hierarchical or division barriers. They would appreciate doing business when it gives flexibility to workers and offers trust and freedom for dissent. They would benefit from a policy that honors individuals for their diverse qualities and their connections to each other, that gives personal development equal priority with making profits, that has an orientation to the surrounding society and environment, that places an intrinsic value in the product or service, and that offers ownership for all.

But such organizations have trouble maintaining themselves, partially because changes in structure are often made before there are changes in mind. Often people do not have the interpersonal skills for dealing with organizational changes; things simply move too fast. Often there is not enough success in the beginning, in terms of standard bottom-line measures, to support staying with the new approaches. Or, as with a shift to a new paradigm in science, the changes are met with resistance by those who were prospering under the old ways. They fear the unknown or suspect that these new ways will not work.

Whatever the reasons, Tom Melohn of North American Tool and Die says that the only way to overcome these difficulties is by scrupulously holding to certain values. He says that all kinds of fads come and go—including management by objectives, zero-based budgeting, visioning, self-directed teams, empowerment, communitybuilding—and they all have their contribution to make. But none of them is going to work over the long term without a solid foundation of values in the organization. He put it this way: "I'd like to sell you your most important corporate asset—your fellow employees. But you see, they're not for sale—at least not for *just* money alone. It takes a different kind of currency. It's called honesty, trust, equality, mutual respect, self-worth, dignity, recognition, teamwork, and caring. Most of all—caring."

Values are at the heart of all the innovations and breakthroughs in organizational transformation that are in this section. The good news is that even though there is always resistance toward a new way of doing business, the heart and skill of those involved will inevitably lead them into a process that befits the change. There are, indeed, ways to "get there from here." You can be assured that when we get there, we'll just keep moving down the river of change in fine style.

13

THE ART & PRACTICE OF THE LEARNING ORGANIZATION

by Peter Senge

What is a learning organization? Senge's use of the word goes beyond taking in information. It's more about creating and building something, enhancing capacity. An organization that can operate in an active, generative manner that continually enhances its capacity is in a state of learning. Such an organization also must overcome entrenched, old paradigm "learning disabilities," such as "I am my position" and "the enemy is out there."

The new organization, according to Senge, will instead make a commitment to five basic disciplines, by which he means a theory translated into a set of practices. Much like an artist or spiritual practitioner, the new paradigm organization may never master each discipline; however, it will create the skills and tools that enhance its capacities.

Peter Senge is Director of the Systems Thinking and Organizational Learning Program at the MIT Sloan School of Management and a founding partner of Innovations Associates Inc., in Framingham, Massachusetts. He is the author of The Fifth Discipline: The Art and Practice of the Learning Organization. *The selection that follows was initially edited by Colleen Lannon Kim.*

One morning a few years ago during a little quiet time it hit me that how organizations learn or fail to learn was going to become a hot topic. Having lived through the buildup of ideas such as vision, alignment, and empowerment and not having written anything for wide distribution on those subjects, I thought maybe this was a subject where we ought to stake out some turf. Since then, I've seen the term "organizational learning" used in a lot of ways which make me glad I wrote the book, because, although they are interesting, they are not very profound.

By and large, the term has been used to describe organizations that are "fast on their feet." We all know that the world is very turbulent today, that organizations with many layers of hierarchy can't adapt quickly, and many won't be around very long. But the idea that learning is about adaptation seems to me woefully inadequate. The very word "learning" has lost most of its meaning in contemporary speech. It has become almost synonymous with "taking in information." We might say, "Well, I learned all about financial accounting for executives yesterday. I went to the class." But what are we really saying? It's that I pulled up a chair and took in some information, and now I can replay some of it.

The schoolroom is a pretty powerful metaphor for the idea of learning as taking in information. Most of our formal education reinforces this perspective—we are taught to believe that there is some information that the "expert" has that we don't have, and once we can repeat it back to her or him with some fidelity and reliability, then we have "learned" it. But of course none of us learned to ride a bicycle that way, or to walk, or talk, or any of the other things that are genuinely called "learning." So learning has very little to do with taking in information. Most fundamentally, learning is about enhancing capacity. Learning is about creating and building the capacity to create that which you previously couldn't create. It is intimately related to action, which taking in information is not. One of the reasons traditional learning is so boring is that taking in information is very boring; it's very passive. But real learning is always "in the body"; it's intimately connected to action.

So learning organizations are organizations that are continually enhancing their capacity to create. This concept of the learning organization echoes the idea Innovation Associates has been committed to from the very beginning: that groups of people can potentially operate in ways that are fundamentally more generative, empowering, and inspiring than the ways in which we normally operate.

The central idea of [my] book is that a set of—let me call them "ideas" for now—is gradually crystallizing that will make learning organizations a realizable, reliable phenomenon. We will no longer struggle to surmount the predominant tendencies of traditional, authoritarian organizations to destroy people's spirit and change only when they must. Organizations will become predominantly learning-oriented rather than controlling. Why? *Because the way people think and interact in those organizations will be different.*

But, first, we need to look a bit deeper at why new ways of thinking and interacting are needed. We need to better understand the learning disabilities that afflict most contemporary organizations.

LEARNING DISABILITIES

The second chapter of [my] book is called "Does your organization have a learning disability?" In it, I talk about what I think are the fundamental reasons why real learning doesn't occur in organizations. Almost all of these learning disabilities are illustrated in the infamous "beer game." Over the years, I have come to see it as a wonderful metaphor for life in general. You remember when you played the game that, after a relatively short period of time, you really were hunkered down managing your position—you were a retailer, or a wholesaler, or a brewery. And that's the first learning disability, "I am my position." The way organizational life operates is that, after a little while, people form an intense identification with their position—who they are is what they do.

I first started to realize how serious this identification is ten years ago. A friend of mine had a booming business that involved retraining workers in steel plants that were closing down. He said that, in reality, these people were fundamentally untrainable. The reason is that if you've been a lathe operator for twenty years, in your mind who you are is a lathe operator. Until you can get people to see that who they are is different from what they've been doing all this time, you can't train them for anything else. The consequence of operating in organizations as if I am my position are incalculable—the loss of dignity, the destruction of intellectual curiosity, and from a systems view, doing my job "right" but screwing up the system as a whole. As the beer game illustrates, when people concentrate on handling their position well but don't understand what's going on around them, they never see how their own actions contribute to their problems.

That leads to the second learning disability, "the enemy is out there." When we think of who we are as the position we play, or the job we do, then if things don't go well we conclude that somebody out there "screwed up." When I draw this boundary very tight around myself, and my sense of identification is rooted in my position, it's very natural to look at the people outside that circle as enemies once problems arise. One of the great ironies in companies is that people often have more animosity towards other people in their organization than they do towards the competitor. Isn't that interesting when you think about it? But it is the natural consequence of this self-identification.

The third learning disability is the "myth of proactiveness." Proactiveness is a phrase that is often used these days, but it usually means

"I'm going to get more active fighting those enemies out there." For example, early in a project at an insurance firm where we've done a lot of systems work over the years, the claims vice president came up with a proactive strategy for fighting litigation.

The litigation crisis has been growing for many years in the U.S. property and liability industry, which you all know. What you might not know is that about 80 to 90 percent of the cases that get litigated are never taken to trial by jury, but are settled out of court. The reason is that within a month or two the claimant's lawyers usually know much more about what happened in the situation than the insurance company, so the insurance company has to settle. The vice president decided that to fight this they would boost their litigation staff and not get "taken to the cleaners" anymore. "We're going to get proactive" was their motto. The vice president had written a speech, which he was about to deliver, proclaiming the new policy.

The project team sat down one afternoon and built a very simple computer model—the types of calculations you could really almost make on the back of an envelope. We looked at the likely fraction of cases that would be won or lost and the cost. We estimated the cost regardless of the outcome of the trial because there are certain costs involved in taking cases to court, depending on how long the litigation process takes, the overhead costs, the indirect costs, etc. We found that there was no set of assumptions the team could provide where the firm would be ahead financially by taking more cases to court. The reason was that the quality of investigation of the claims in the first place was so shoddy that the insurance company rarely had a good case to defend, no matter how many lawyers they hired. Being "proactive" was an illusion.

The vice president was being proactive in a very reactive mindset. The root of reactiveness is in the way we think. If our state of mind is that the enemy is "out there" and we are "in here" (a fundamentally nonsystemic way of looking at the world), then proactiveness is really reactiveness with the gauge turned up 500%.

There are several other learning disabilities I talk about in chapter two. One of them, "the parable of the boiled frog," has to do with the fact that we are very good at reacting to sudden threats to our survival, but we're very poor at recognizing slow, gradual threats. That is similar to a frog that will sit in the water and let itself be slowly boiled to death because it doesn't perceive the danger.

I think the most ponderable learning disability is what I call the "illusion of learning from experience." Here's the dilemma: it's pretty evident that most of the real learning most of us have done in our lives has been through experience. How did you learn to walk, ride a bicycle, or talk? You learned from doing something and observing the outcome—you fell off the bike and got up again, rode some, fell off and got up again, rode some more, fell off and got up again, and all of a sudden you sort of got it, right? So human beings learn wonderfully from experience—most of the time, but not always.

In fact, we learn reliably *only* when the consequences of our actions are apparent quickly and unambiguously. The reason why bicycle riding is such a good metaphor for learning from experience is that it's a near perfect example of seeing the consequences of our actions *immediately*. But, what if the rider was blind-folded and drugged, so that when she or he fell they only learned about it when they awoke, several hours later? It would then be virtually impossible to master riding through simply trying again and again.

As marvelous as children are at learning, think about what happens when a child first starts to interact with other children. Very different dynamics come into play. You do something that hurts another child's feelings, but he or she doesn't say anything, so you don't notice. Two weeks later you notice that the person who used to be your good friend just isn't very friendly to you anymore. But you don't make the connection—cause and effect are not obvious because the consequence occurs "out there," at some distant point in time. By the time you feel the friendship waning, you probably can't even remember what you did. You conclude that "people are hard to understand." Thus starts a lifetime of slow and unsteady learning about relationships.

The dynamics that preclude learning from experience in organizations are vastly more complex. Think about the important decisions we make. What makes them important, what makes them "strategic," is that the consequences occur in the future, and often in distant parts of the system. They're not local. They're not clear and unambiguous. And they are very, very hard to learn about.

I don't think organizations learn much from experience at all. As Rick Ross says, "Most managers' twenty years of experience are really one year relived twenty times." There is nothing we have that we could really call twenty years of meaningful experience. I think this is quite an interesting dilemma, the fact that we learn best from experience and yet we don't "experience" the consequences of our most important actions.

Then there is the "myth of the management team," the idea that complex inter-dependencies and dynamics can all be figured out by a talented group of people who bring together diverse backgrounds and points of view. The reality is that most of the time management teams don't work. They are held together by a superficial facade of "all for one" camaraderie that comes apart when there is any real pressure. The collective IQ of the team is half that of the least swift team member.

For difficult problems, vastly more creative solutions would be generated if one or two people just went off and dealt with problems unilaterally instead of agreeing to the watered down consensus that emerges from "the team." One reason is that teams have pre-programmed responses to protect each other and themselves from pain, threat, and surprise—what Chris Argyris calls "defensive routines." The result is "skilled incompetence," where groups are highly skilled at protecting themselves from threat, and consequently keeping themselves from learning.

So those are the learning disabilities. Obviously, they are written with the idea of getting people's attention, because they tend to pose some troubles, some difficulties. But they are really just setting the stage, because the book is not about learning disabilities.

What I think potentially could be the enduring contribution of the book is the idea that it's truly possible to build a different sort of organization. But it will take a radically new strategy: a commitment to certain basic disciplines, which will shape how we think and interact.

The word "discipline" has a couple of different meanings. One is that a child should sit still and be "well disciplined." But another is the way it's used in the phrase "artistic discipline" or "spiritual discipline." In this context it means a particular theory, translated into a set of practices, which one spends one's life mastering. You never "have mastered" a discipline. No matter how much you learn you realize how much more there is to learn.

The first discipline is that of *building shared vision*. Now, everyone in this group knows about this discipline because it is has been a focus of Innovation Associates' work for a long time. The question I addressed in the book was first "what does it mean to have a vision?" and second, "what does it mean for it to be shared?" The idea of *building* shared vision stresses that you never quite finish it—it's an ongoing process. Even if one group starts to see very clearly a picture of the future about which they care deeply, others will see it less clearly or remain unconvinced, or simply can't see how this picture relates to them and their job. This is why the "let's write a vision statement" fad that has run rampant in recent years is so off-base. Many executives want to get "this vision thing" over and done with, so they can then get back to work. They don't grasp that the "vision thing" *is* their work. Those leaders who understand the distinction between vision as a set of inert words and vision as a living force in the hearts and minds of people know that what matters is continually reflecting on and talking about what people really want to create.

A lot has happened in the last 10 years since Innovation Associates began to work in this area—everyone now talks about visions. But the idea is still a long way from practice. I think one of the reasons that shared visions are not common is that very few corporations have any real idea the sort of commitment you have to make to the *individual* for genuinely shared visions to operate.

The second discipline, the discipline of *personal mastery*, elaborates this commitment. The bottom line with shared visions is that individuals must have their own visions before a shared vision can exist. If people have no real sense of what truly matters to them, the best they can ever do is follow someone else's vision. This is the fundamental distinction between commitment and compliance. What needs to be recognized is that this is exactly the state of affairs that traditional authoritarian organizations have always sought: compliance to the boss' goals. *Work*, in the sense of "doing one's work," then becomes *labor*, "a factor of production," along with plant and equipment and materials. To change this state of affairs represents what might well be the most radical position advocated in the book: that learning organizations must be fully committed to the development of each individual's personal mastery—each individual's capacity to create their life the way they truly want. Despite much rhetoric to the contrary, I think this commitment is still pretty far ahead of us, although there have been a lot of changes in the business world in recent years in this direction.

Personal mastery involves not only vision but also holding an accurate picture of current reality, thereby generating "creative tension." People with high levels of personal mastery have a great tolerance for living with creative tension. They actually relish it. Martin Luther King spoke of "creating a tension in the mind, so that individuals could rise from the bondage of myth and half truths," and indeed felt that fostering such tension was his core task. This is why he sought to "dramatize" the actual conditions of racism and prejudice, while simultaneously holding forth his personal dream of "racial brotherhood . . . where my four children will one day live in a world where they will be judged not by the color of their skin but by the content of their character."

People with high levels of personal mastery can distinguish creative tension from the "emotional tension" (sadness, disappointment, hopelessness, anger) that may arise when we are truthful with ourselves about the gaps between where we are and where we want to be. Emotional tension for them becomes simply another facet of current reality, and as such is subject to the senior force of creative tension.

I think there is a great deal more to be learned about how organizations can actualize this "commitment to the truth" required for true personal mastery. I mean, what *is* current reality? The answer is not actually as straightforward as we might think. Take this flipchart. Some people might not know what a flipchart is. They'd think of it as a mass of papers. Some other people might not know what paper is, and think of this as some strange substance. So our vision of current reality has everything to do with the third discipline—*mental models*—because what we really have in our lives is constructions, internal pictures that we continually use to interpret and make sense out of the world.

The idea that people create internal representations is the cornerstone of cognitive psychology. But from a managerial and organizational perspective, what makes this idea pertinent is that our individual representations are all different, and we do a hell of a good job obscuring these differences from ourselves and one another. Recognition and communication of our mental models requires reflection and inquiry skills possessed by few managers. This part of the book is where I first start to draw very heavily on the work of Chris Argyris, Don Schon, and others who have worked to better understand the nature of reflection in the managerial setting.

One of the key concepts of the discipline of working with mental models is the need to balance inquiry and advocacy. In the organizations I've known well, most managers are trained as advocates. They were taught to be forceful, articulate spokespersons for their point of view. Very few organizations reward inquiry. When was the last time anyone was promoted for asking tough questions that challenged established policies and practices?

The irony is that as you rise in an organization, more and more you are dealing with issues that *don't* have simple answers. The really important issues that confront senior management are what E. F. Schumacher (the man who wrote *Small Is Beautiful*) called "diverging problems," which require seeing issues from multiple points of view, identifying trade-offs, and making choices while continually remaining open to discovering errors in one's reasoning. Yet the very people we're relying on to sort out these issues have been conditioned for all their professional lives to be forceful advocates, not incisive collaborative inquirers.

There are many other important aspects of working with mental models. One critical idea is what is called "levels of abstraction." Our minds work so fast that we literally confuse what we directly observe and the images our minds form based on what we observe. We leap from "data" (he is speaking loudly) to abstraction (he is insensitive) in the flicker of an eye, and then treat the abstraction as if it was data. This is why our mental models are so hard to see—to us they are what *is*, not our interpretation of what is. The idea that we relate through our mental models has all sorts of fascinating implications for managers. The basic puzzle is how do you surface, expose, and bring into a conversation people's assumptions about the world so that shared mental models can continually improve. Behind every strategy is a mental model. We can argue like cats and dogs about the strategy, but without any way of getting at the assumptions behind the strategy the argument is virtually pointless, because we have no way of achieving a deeper, shared understanding.

Now I am already starting to imply the fourth discipline, which in the book I call *team learning*. The mental models that really matter in an organization are the shared mental models, the implicit assumptions that "this is the way the world is." Individual learning, no matter how wonderful it is or how great it makes us feel, is fundamentally irrelevant to organizations, because virtually all important decisions occur in groups. The learning unit of organizations are "teams," groups of people who need one another to act.

To appreciate the discipline of team learning, let's start with the difference between discussion and dialogue. The word dialogue comes from the Greek dia • logos, *dia* meaning "through," and *logos* meaning "meaning" or "word." In its original sense, it described a conversation where the meaning moves *through* the group. So, to truly have a dialogue is really a different state. It no longer consists of individual thoughts, but a group "sharing in a pool of collective meaning," in the words of David Bohm, an eminent physicist who has spent the last eight years trying to understand the nature of thought. Bohm points out that *discussion* comes from the same roots as *percussion* and *concussion*, and literally means "to heave one's views at one another." A discussion is always a game of win or lose—the prevailing opinion is the one left on the field once the battle is done. I'm not saying that discussion is always bad and dialogue is always good. Discussion is often very important for making decisions, particularly when there's time pressure. But without the enrichment of dialogue, collective learning will rarely occur.

The Laws of the Fifth Discipline

- Today's problems come from yesterday's "solutions."
- The harder you push, the harder the system pushes back.
- Behavior grows better before it grows worse.
- The easy way out usually leads back in.
- The cure can be worse than the disease.
- Faster is slower.
- Cause and effect are not closely related in time.
- Small changes can produce big results—but the areas of highest leverage are often the least obvious.
- You can have your cake and eat it too—but not at once.
- Dividing an elephant in half does not produce two small elephants.
- There is no blame.

Team learning was the discipline I felt the most uncertain about when writing the book. Much of what I learned for the chapter on team learning I discovered after I'd written the first draft. After I encountered David Bohm's work, I had a richer theoretical framework for talking about a lot of things I had been struggling with before. David's basic premise is that thought is primarily collective, but that humankind has, over the past several thousand years, lost the capability it once had to truly think together—that is, we have lost our ability to be conscious of our thinking and therefore to originate new thoughts that can lead to new, more collectively productive actions.

THE FIFTH DISCIPLINE

The last discipline, the one that ties them all together, is *systems thinking*.

Systems thinking is vital to the book and to learning organizations on two quite different levels. First, it offers a critical set of tools for understanding complex policy and strategy issues. Everyone pays lip service to the fact that the world is daily becoming more complex, that change is accelerating. "Change has changed"—or so the saying goes. Yet, there is little serious attention to how our predominant ways of thinking must change in order to be prepared to understand and manage in a world of increasing inter-dependency.

In the book, systems thinking is introduced in a novel way that we have been developing at Innovation Associates in the past year or two—through understanding and using certain basic "systems archetypes." I have become convinced that this offers the lay person an intuitive and usable avenue for beginning to think systemically, without having to first spend 532 days studying at MIT or some other equally distant venue. The systems archetypes are "story lines" that keep recurring in diverse personal, organizational, and social settings. For example, many systems grow and then stop growing, often prematurely. Yet most people push on all the wrong places when they want to keep growth going. Rather than seeking out and removing the sources of limitations to growth, they "push" on the growth engines. This usually results in a brief resurgence, and then things just get worse again.

The "limits to growth" archetype is one of eight identified in the book. It may take some time to come to understand these archetypes, but I think those who do will find them to be invaluable for their own thinking and for talking about complex issues with others.

Second, systems thinking is vital as a philosophy and set of principles that integrates all the learning disciplines, and keeps them from being just a list of favorite ideas and clever techniques. The more you understand the systems perspective, the more you can begin to practice the other disciplines.

For example, I really question whether you can build shared visions without systems thinking. Most people believe their "current reality" was created by somebody else. I have long held that the best definition of systems thinking is "understanding how our actions shape our reality." If I believe that my current state was created by somebody else, or by forces outside my control, why should I hold a vision? The central premise behind holding a vision is that somehow I can shape my future. Systems thinking helps us see how our own actions have shaped our current reality, thereby giving us the confidence that we really can create a different reality in the future. Without a systemic viewpoint, I believe the visions are wishful thinking at best and the seeds of cynicism at worst.

Likewise, systems thinking provides critical linkages that support the other disciplines. It illuminates the subtleties of personal mastery, such as the nature of compassion and our connection to the larger world. It is vital to the practice of working with mental models: it provides tools that can help us surface hidden assumptions and construct mental models focused on inter-relationships and processes of change rather than static images.

Lastly, the very cornerstone of team learning, dialogos, arises from a profoundly systemic worldview that illuminates the subtle connectedness in our patterns of thought. So it is no wonder that the tools of systems thinking prove uniquely well suited to fostering collaborative inquiry and building shared mental models that encompass different individuals' unique points of view.

So you see, systems thinking is the discipline that integrates the disciplines—that's why [my book is] called *The Fifth Discipline*.

EXEMPLAR:
Ben & Jerry's
Homemade Ice Cream, Inc.

Ben Cohen and Jerry Greenfield of Ben & Jerry's Homemade Ice Cream, Inc., have been doing business in new ways since they founded what has become one of the top superpremium ice cream companies. As Ben puts it, "We didn't have any intention of becoming businessmen. Neither one of us was really into that image." And Jerry, who admits that "I've got no idea what a balance sheet is," emphasizes their underlying vision when he says, "The purpose of our business is to spread joy and not to make money."

This kind of thinking has led to some of the best implementation of new paradigm ideas and also some of their worst problems. Jerry and Ben have been criticized as being overly paternalistic and concerned more with the welfare of people in other countries than with workers at their own plant. But they have always responded to these criticisms with positive actions, and they can be credited with holding to values that are central to them.

To answer the question of how a company honors individuals within the company and also contributes to the surrounding community, they offer a salary program that limits highest salaries to a ratio of five times the lowest salary. When top executives complain that this limits their salaries, Ben points out that all they have to do to raise their own salaries is to raise the salary of the lowest-paid individuals—so that everyone moves up with the success of the company.

At the same time, all employees share in 5 percent of pretax profits, and every employee has been made a shareholder. Even the corporate health insurance is planned for equality: they set the deductible at one percent of each employee's salary.

These policies are transferred to partnership in ways that are becoming quite common in business now but which were unusual when Ben and Jerry started. As Ben says, "In our company the constituencies are the employees, the shareholders, and the community." They give 7½ percent of their pretax profits (15 percent after taxes) to the Ben & Jerry Foundation, which supports community projects. They produce products such as Peace Pops and Rain Forest Crunch that benefit particular social causes.

Ben reports that stockholders are quite supportive of such community activities: "The shareholders have been really happy because the price of the stock has been going up quite a bit. So they've never had any problem. We've never taken a formal vote of all the shareholders, but at our annual meetings I usually ask them—just a show of hands, it's nonbinding—if they support the company's supporting the community and giving away what are really their profits. And they're all in favor of it."

14

BUILDING A COMMITTED WORKPLACE: AN EMPOWERED ORGANIZATION AS A COMPETITIVE ADVANTAGE

by Dennis T. Jaffe and Cynthia D. Scott

Organizational transformation always requires a shift in power. Executives and managers must learn how every level of the organization can be mobilized to strengthen its resources, productivity, and organizational vision.

But how can such a radical shift in power be achieved? How can a workplace entrenched in the old paradigm transform itself into an organization with a fresh concept of communication, joint decision-making, and shared responsibility? How can you actually change individual mind-sets, personal and intergroup relationships, organizational policies and structures?

In answering this question, the authors discuss a new organizational form that is more interdependent, customer focused, flexible, and responsive. They demonstrate the kinds of new leadership, collaborative processes, and community-building required to initiate an organizational transformation.

They also are frank about the resistance to such change and the ways in which managers can undermine large-scale organizational transformation through impatience, emotional illiteracy, elitism, insecurity, poor modeling, anger, and alienation.

Dennis T. Jaffe, Ph.D., is a professor of Human Science at Saybrook Institute. Cynthia D. Scott, Ph.D., M.P.H., is a principal with HeartWork Inc., a San Francisco organizational consulting firm. They are the authors of Empowerment, Take This Job and Love It *and* Managing Organizational Change.

Enhancing the capacity of employees, teams and whole organizations to produce higher-quality, customer-focused results is the goal of an empowered workplace. In this workplace people at all levels feel directly responsible for results, are continually learning and developing their skills, feel the trust to share their best ideas, and work together in teams that contain not one, but many, leaders. "Empowerment" has become a buzzword which represents a range of initiatives—training programs, motivational speeches, and structural shifts—that help organizations develop this new style of operation. However, as we suggest in this article, it is not so simple.

Empowerment means that the organization shifts from limiting the power to determine its future and how it will get there to a few top executives, to include every level of the organization in the process. This organizational workstyle, which mobilizes the inner capacity of all employees to contribute to the benefit of the organization, has become the core of organizational development in the 90's. As organizations have depleted their capacity to tap non-renewable resources for competitive advantage, their human capital (creativity, innovation, and intrinsic motivation) has become the key to success. After generations of using coercive, manipulative or controlling methods to motivate performance, organizations have lately become compelled to develop environments which foster the fair and voluntary exchange of human resources in a continuously renewing interchange. This challenge of creating an empowered organization has propelled our work for the last ten years.

BALANCING FREEDOM AND CONSTRAINT

From our consulting experience, we see empowerment as an initiative that strives to balance individual freedom and organizational constraint. Every organization has structures that demand close organizational control and constraint and others that are premised on allowing individual freedom and autonomy to make decisions and to get things done. Empowerment is often mistaken for an environment where only personal freedom is maximized. We see it differently. It is not an either/or dichotomy. The empowered workplace is one where everyone is constrained by commitment to organizational "visions," and accepts the organization's need for control of resources and exchange of information. In other ways it allows each employee, not just those at the top, to experience freedom and autonomy to grow and do the best possible work. It is not, as some managers fear, unbridled freedom. It is facilitated, or coordinated, freedom, where many people work in harmony to produce results that they all want.

How can a workplace accustomed to tight control over employees become empowered? We initially approached this challenge with the tools of the human potential movement: self-awareness, self-regulation, stress management, and health promotion. After individual techniques did not produce organizational change of the desired magnitude, we began to look at resistance to change from a psychological and structural/organizational viewpoint.

Why is it so hard for people to change, to try things in a different way? Our clients struggled with empowerment in the face of increased competition and global pressures to produce higher quality. They were trying to increase trust and freedom, at a time when everyone felt threatened. Under these conditions, people can initially become closed, upset and defensive. Our clients pushed us in dialogue and in action to answer questions like:

- How do you reduce resistance to change?
- How do you create shared ownership of corporate results?
- What are the most empowering organizational structures?
- What are the limits of empowerment?

We found ourselves returning to our systemic roots as behavioral scientists looking at the interconnection between individual competency and organizational structure. In between these two exists the "immune system" of the organization—that interactive subtlety which provides the inner fuel—empowerment. How do you enhance this "immune system"? What are the points of intervention that encourage the organizational structure to re-balance and re-new itself in the midst of unprecedented challenge and pressure? This essay outlines our learning from organizations as they move along the path toward becoming healthy, empowered organizations.

THE NATURE OF EMPOWERMENT

Empowerment is not an individual process. A bunch of empowered people do not necessarily create an empowered organization. You cannot lead a workshop for managers in empowerment skills unless the organization/context in which the person works is ready to make structural changes that will support the new behaviors. Many organizations invested heavily in training interventions which gave individuals new skills and ideas, only to send those same employees back to work environments and relationships which had not changed. This "workshop high" tended to produce momentary resolve to change and then bitter disappointment and cynicism. People attend teamwork retreats, but return to a reward system based only on individual results, or to a supervisory system where advancement was based on "who you know."

Our model for moving toward empowerment notes that change must occur on three levels. Empowerment is not just built into individuals but has to be built into the organizational structure. When focusing our consulting efforts we assess the following:

Level One: Individual Mind-sets:

- Do the individuals in the organization believe they are capable of making changes and of being the source of creativity and innovation?
- Do they listen to themselves?
- Do they seek new ways?
- Do they believe in what is or what can be?

Level Two: Personal and Intergroup Relationships:

- Are people willing to behave in self-responsible, self-managing and accountable agreements with each other?
- Have people learned the skills of collaboration, trust, communication, shared problem-solving, conflict resolution, and mutual respect?
- Do they know how to create a learning team?
- Do people create informal links between groups, and communicate and cooperate across groups within the organization?

Level Three: Organizational Policies and Structures:

- Do policies and procedures support and encourage individual and team empowerment?
- Is the culture, mission, value, and vision clear and accepted by everyone?
- How can people make input into these policies?
- Is security and fair treatment guaranteed?

UNDERSTANDING ORGANIZATIONAL LEGACY

To understand some of the historical background for this challenge, many of our largest traditional organizations have had their day, and are threatened and challenged by the new business environment. Over one third of the Fortune 500 of a decade ago no longer exist. Giants that previously were synonymous with good management and stability—IBM, GM, Sears, Chrysler, Macy's—now find that their inability to change endangers their existence. These large companies want to renew themselves, and craft strategies to accomplish that. Yet they fail more frequently than they succeed in reaching their goals. Our thesis is that along with strategic redefinition, new technology, new products aligned to customer needs, and intercompany alliances, the challenge of the future is for a company to fundamentally redefine the nature of the way people work together.

The last century has been the story of the success of the bureaucratic organization. Procedures, control, and level in the hierarchy were the essence of an organization where change was slow and incremental, and competition was minimal. In this traditional organization, people were considered machines, and thinking was confined to the top. Factories and capital was more valuable than human creativity or commitment. Stability was the expectation, and people were rewarded for passivity, which was labeled "commitment." Today, organizations are realizing that these assumptions won't work in the emerging world-business environment.

A new organizational form is in the making. It has been called the "network" by Charles Savage, the "circle" by Scott and Jaffe, the "shamrock" by Charles Handy, and the "learning organization" by Peter Senge. Each of these new organizational models points to a more interdependent, customer focused, flexible and responsive structure. These new forms are in the generative stages and are currently being experimented with in organizations. It is still too early to say definitively which elements of the emerging styles are the most successful. The future organization will most likely be a synthesis that fits the needs of the organization, its employees, and its customers. But defining the qualities of a new model does not tell an organization that has operated within the traditional style how to shift to the new form.

MISCONCEPTIONS ABOUT CHANGE

Many organizations see change as something that can be declared, and implemented without much difficulty. They are still operating on a 19th century view of human nature, where people are motivated by appropriate reward and punishment. With money, or the threat of termination, people will go along. Managers assume that if they order people to change, they will. They do not recognize the tremendous internal struggle, the emotional dynamics, the upheaval, and the nature of the learning process that organizational renewal poses for individual employees. Viewing change from the executive perspective, a study of top executives found that 80% felt their companies had to change. However, only 20% felt that *they* had to change. People see the need for change, but not the immensity of the personal and professional disruption it entails.

Ironically, many of the actions of top managers actually increase alienation, anger, frustration and add to the confusion. They say they want empowerment, but intentionally or most often unintentionally, they produce the opposite. Some of the common underminers of large organizational transformation include:

1) Incongruence between the stated goals and what they do (e.g., act directive and controlling, while asking for empowerment).

2) Emotional Illiteracy, not understanding the complex emotional dynamics of people faced with drastic and total shifts in the nature of their work.

3) I Don't Have to Change, "They" Do. Feeling that the leader is an exception, and not available and open to learning.

4) Not Giving Up Control. Empowerment is accompanied by trust, rooted in understanding that the leader alone can't solve the problems. Employees need to be allowed to come up with innovations, and trust in their goodwill. This is difficult for men who have held on to power for most of their lives, yet some learn to do it, with spectacular results.

5) Isolation. The leader doesn't come out of his office, and doesn't really seek out and listen to distressing information from employees. One of the easiest ways leaders maintain illusions is by staying on the phone with the central office, traveling a lot, and relying on subordinates to tell them what's going on. The essence of this behavior is fear of listening, and inability to manage people in distress.

6) No Models of New Behavior. People can't be ordered to change, give up control, or take more responsibility, if they have never learned how to do it. That is the dilemma in the Eastern Bloc countries today: they want freedom but they don't know how free workers act. People need to see and practice new models of behavior, and they need time to learn, and space to experiment and even make mistakes.

7) Impatience. Many promising programs are discontinued just as they are on the verge of payoff because the management feels it isn't working, or worse, they find a new fad or program and move on to that. The key factor in successful change seems to be persistence in a direction, with prudent feedback and course correction along the way.

8) Middle Management Entrenchment. Middle managers are an endangered species, and in many change efforts they are the most threatened. They are expected from above to produce results, and they feel the pressure of newly empowered, newly competent people from below. Under threat, they dig in. They need support, security, and help in learning new ways.

9) Failure to Understand People's Needs for Psychological Security. Change is terrifying and the company needs to provide some form of psychological security. That does not mean job security, which doesn't exist, but at least offer clear information on what is happening, options and possibilities, and then allowing people the time to move through the phases of transition.

Most of these pitfalls are almost unconscious, yet their effect undermines the goals of renewal. It is imperative for leaders to develop the self-awareness to understand that unless they see these pitfalls, they themselves become the problem, the reason why change isn't going well. Those who fall into these traps have elaborate theories of who's to blame: unmotivated employees, lack of resources, corporate policies, bad competitors, or the economic pressures. But the truth, which they deny and avoid, is that the major obstacle to change in many large companies is the lack of self-awareness in top management, their lack of capacity to see that they themselves need to change in ways they at first do not fully comprehend, that they need to let go of control and allow the power of the people below them to grow.

Empowerment requires a deep transformation of management style. Managers need to shift their attention from other people to themselves. It takes time, conscious and careful planning, and a series of steps that teach people new ways and move toward new structures.

RENEWAL TAKES A GENERATION

Organizational renewal takes a long time, and must be pursued with persistence, clarity, and care. Richard Pascale, in *Managing on the Edge,* talks about Ford's transformation. Common wisdom suggests that change begins at the top, but Ford, like many successfully changing large companies, discovered its formula for change in one of its divisions. Team Taurus was charged with designing the next generation of Ford cars, responding to the challenge and success of Nissan, Toyota, and Honda. Their success a decade ago was based on a collaborative approach where self-managing, multi-disciplinary teams, empowered to make decisions and working together by consensus without the need for top management approval, produced extraordinary results at unprecedented speed. They were able, while pursuing their new product design in record time, to shift their structure from the pyramid to the circle. Their success in morale as well as the bottom line was subsequently adopted by Ford's top management as its future model. This was no easy task, and took quite a while, because, as we have seen in the ill-fated Soviet coup of 1991, top leaders are reluctant to give up behaviors that have brought them rewards and success in the past. With empowerment, it may seem to top management that they are losing prerogative, privilege, and freedom. And in some ways, they are. In other ways, though, their work will become more rewarding and the organization will work better.

It will be a few years before it is clear whether Ford has really changed fundamentally, and whether the shift can be transferred to the entire company. The transformation of a large organization, as Kuhn suggests in his study of scientific paradigm shifts, takes almost a whole generation. Hopefully, we won't have to wait 20 years to see the fruits of at least some intermediate changes in these large companies, because none of them can last that long.

15

A WORK IN PROGRESS AT DU PONT: THE CREATION OF A DEVELOPMENTAL ORGANIZATION

by Carol Sanford and Pamela Mang

Here is a systematic analysis of how one Du Pont chemical plant near Memphis, Tennessee, undertook a complex organizational transformation in 1989 that continues today. The plant was a successful and profitable organization, but top management realized that to remain competitive in a changing world, they had to undertake a radical internal transformation. Their ultimate goal was to become a Developmental Organization—an organization in which every employee is a source of creativity and in which all employees are self-organizing.

The authors describe each step in the process: the formation of Core Teams that take on some of the roles traditionally played by management but also serve as a vehicle for building important individual capabilities such as self-reflection, evolutionary systems thinking, personal development, and performance improvement. The emphasis here is on individual as well as organizational development, on personal growth and change as fundamental to the corporate effort on every level, leading to a new consciousness that gives all workers a creative, responsible vision of themselves within the organizational system.

Carol Sanford is a partner in Sanford and Ely Associates, based in Washington State. Her published works include The Culture of Continuous Improvement, Science into Technique: A Structure for Research and Development in Organizational Science, *and* The Scientific Basis of Developmental Organizations. *Pamela Mang has over twenty years of business experience in managerial and consulting capacities in the private and public sector. She is a member of the Board of Governors of the World Business Academy.*

The Du Pont chemical plant outside of Memphis, Tennessee, sprawls across the flat green prairie like the tentacles of a giant squid. Started up 40 years ago, the plant today employs 850 people, produces 7 product lines of industrial chemicals for a world-wide market, and is a provider of highly valued basic chemicals to the global marketplace. For most of its existence, the plant has been a classic example of a well-run, traditional American manufacturing plant. Reasonably profitable with no major problems, it was not a self-evident candidate for a major organizational transformation, yet that is exactly what it is engaged in now.

WHY CHANGE?

In September 1989, when the change effort was launched, employees of the Memphis plant were well paid, physical working conditions were as good or better than most, and, from the perspective of business profits, it was providing a sound return to Du Pont. So why invest in a long-term, fundamental transformation of the organization?

To plant manager Bob Porter, the need was clear—"I knew how we had worked in the plant wasn't going to be sufficient for the future. We needed some profound changes." While Porter was the initiating force, every level of participant is now able to articulate their own understanding of the need for change. When one clerk was asked why he thought change was initiated, he offered that "Du Pont had the reputation as number one in being competitive, producing good quality product, paying people good salaries . . . they also recognized the fact that the world was changing and to compete globally, they have to change. In order to do that you have to have input from all people, you know everybody that's gonna make this thing work. They didn't get to be number one not recognizing those things."

"I think the world is almost shrinking so it's becoming a neighborhood," noted a supervisor, "and I feel that in order for this company or whatever company to succeed in the future, it's going to require people to work as a team. You're going to be pitted against people who are working as a team, and I think you have to use all your resources available." A manager, asked the same question, added that he thought "that to a large extent the people that are involved have gotten to a point where their basic needs are met as far as a sound financial basis for living, and are looking to satisfy other internal needs now, to having some control over their destiny."

OVERVIEW AND THEORY BASE
OF THE CHANGE EFFORT

The Memphis change effort was born in the fall of 1989 when Bob Porter and Dick Jensen met with two consultants from Sanford and

Associates. Out of these initial meetings grew a series of development sessions in which, starting in early 1990, teams of plant employees began working with the consultants for 2 days every 6 weeks. Made up at first of managers only, each team is now a "holographic reflection" of the total plant makeup—i.e. the makeup of each team is reflective of all the key perspectives in the plant such as function, age, experience, and gender.

One of the more fascinating aspects of a hologram—the three-dimensional image produced by a laser beam—is that if you break up the beam, rather than reflecting fragments of the original image, a whole image is reflected by each part of the beam. This concept, of having each part contain a reflection of the whole, is fundamental to the design of the Memphis change effort and will be referred to often in the following pages.

The number of teams, which are called Core Teams, has grown from 3 to 11, including one team from a customer plant. The Core Team serves as a steward for the continuously increasing harmony between the business unit and its environment. To do so, they take on some of the roles traditionally played by management, as well as others that were not played by anyone. The Core Teams, in turn, set up other teams on-site—some focused around long-term improvements, others around specific projects—to whom they transfer their learnings while working together on joint improvement efforts.

The ultimate aim of this effort is to transform the plant's culture in order to create a Developmental Organization—an organization in which every employee is a source of creativity and in which all employees are self-organizing and working together to create a self-organizing business. As a foundation for achieving this aim, the critical initial stages of the effort focus on building a systemic set of four interwoven capabilities, each of which nourishes the development of the others:

(1) **Self-Reflection**—Being able to see, in any situation and at any point in time, the patterns that dominate my thinking and interactions, and to understand their source. This is the essential first step toward the development of self-accountability.

(2) **Evolutionary Systems Thinking**—Being able to hold in my mind, while engaged in my day-to-day activities, a picture of myself as one of a series of dynamic, evolving systems. Each of these systems constitutes a different level of system that is nested within the next. Furthermore, each is continuously engaged, directly or indirectly, in a multitude of complex interactions and associations with the other levels. Thus, I see myself as part of a team whose performance and well-being I impact and am impacted by. My team impacts and is

impacted by the business unit within which it is nested and which, in turn, is within the plant which is within the corporation and so on out in ever-widening spheres of influence. Within this context, I can understand and appreciate the implications and significance of my patterns of thinking and interacting and, through that, take a second step toward self-accountability.

(3) Integration of Personal Development and Performance Improvement—Being able to utilize every effort to improve business performance as an opportunity to develop myself, and vice versa.

(4) Holographic Approach to Work—Being able to bring to every decision-making process a total perspective that holds within it a reflection of all the critical elements which make up the whole of the business and the nested systems of which it's a part.

Each one of these capabilities can be developed only to the extent that the other three are also developing. While they build on each other, they are best developed in an iterative and systemic way, rather than by working on them one at a time in sequence.

In May and June of 1991, we had an opportunity to do some reflecting with employees in the Memphis plant on their experiences during the 18 months spent working to develop these capabilities and improve their business. Over 90 people were interviewed. They were asked to talk about what has changed in them and in the plant; what has been most difficult and what kept them going in tough times; what has been most rewarding; and what they have new hope for as a result. In the following pages, we draw from these interviews to look in more detail at how the Memphis plant's change effort is unfolding.

(1) SELF-REFLECTION: USING REALITY AS A MIRROR

With the rapid popularization of "Self-Managing Teams," there has been a tendency to mistake form for substance and equate a self-managed team to a team without a manager. One of the unfortunate results, seen in many companies, has been a focus on organizational shuffles as a way of achieving self-managing teams, even leading, in some cases, to competitions over who can eliminate the most managers in the shortest period. At the Memphis plant, change in organizational structure will be a long-term output of, rather than an input to, the change effort.

As one of the line managers puts it, "Let's stop trying to change the organization all the time and get down to business . . . that's what's happening here. We're doing something that doesn't revolve around reorganization, but yet it's going to lead to significant change."

At the heart of the Memphis effort is the increasing capability of every employee to be truly "Self" managing—managing of the self by the Self. The premise underlying this aspect of the effort holds that the success of self-directed teams in the workplace is directly related to people's capability for self-reflection in their own thinking and in their interactions, a capability which is foundational to their ability to be self-accountable.

As a line manager noted, "The whole key really is personal development. The plant is going to grow as each one of us grows. I think that's where the rubber meets the road in this system." "It has to start with us at the beginning," notes plant manager Bob Porter, "if you want change to occur, *you* are going to have to change."

The plant is working on developing this capability by attempting to integrate into every aspect of work processes that enable people to learn how to reflect on the mental patterns that dominate their thinking and doing, to see the sources of these patterns, and to choose and put in place the patterns that will best achieve the destiny they desire.

What changes are people seeing in the plant as a result? The growing value for understanding the thinking behind one's own ideas, opinions and actions has led to greater interest in and openness to the thinking of others, as well as to cooperation across traditional boundaries to a degree not seen before. "So far as myself," one operator notes, "I've seen some changes where I'm not just thinking about myself but I'm reflecting and starting to learn how to reflect on what other people feel as well as what I feel. I'm able to listen to people and try to understand where they are coming from and what happened."

People are learning to ask why someone is thinking a particular way before rushing to judge the output of their thoughts. As an operator in one of Du Pont's customer plants that is going through the process with them says of himself: "It's made me value everyone's opinion. You listen and you think 'Why are they thinking this way?', rather than 'That's a dumb thing.' " These changes gain added significance in light of a recent survey of American workers by Northwestern National Life Insurance in which 33% of those interviewed pointed to co-workers as the major cause of their job stress—stress which they said lowered their productivity and adversely affected their health.

Another evident change is the extent to which people at all levels in the plant are discovering and applying their own leadership capabilities. People who had never participated in any kind of work session with upper management are finding themselves speaking up with ease, making presentations and initiating improvement efforts when they see a problem. The trust that people build in their own inner knowing as a result of the self-reflective processes they are engaging in is foundational to developing leadership at every level.

An operator describes a pattern he discovered in himself and how it has affected his ability to be a leader. "Looking back on myself, my life, childhood on up, you're programmed to react to what someone else says, to do what you've been told and not to take the initiative so it's kind of hard to change that pattern all of a sudden . . . First you've got to focus on what kind of changes you want to make, and constantly reflect and see where you are to make those changes. To be a leader you've got to make decisions, not just sit there and be told what to do. Never having had a chance to do that, it's hard to make that change but you constantly work toward it—it's just a constant battle."

(2) EVOLUTIONARY SYSTEMS THINKING: SEEING THE INTRICACIES OF THE WEB THAT WEAVES LIFE TOGETHER

The increasing ability to access intrinsic sources of creativity and wisdom that results from reflective processes is recognized as necessary, but not sufficient for the Memphis effort to achieve its goals. Being able to bring one's thinking patterns into alignment with purpose does not necessarily contribute to the whole if one's purpose remains narrowly focused. The next step required helping people learn how to extend their thinking to encompass relationships between and associations with ever-widening sets of nested systems or wholes. That is, to be able to mentally connect with other units in the plant, the plant's suppliers, its customers, its customer's customers, and the chemical industry and its environment, and to see how each level is evolving and the implications of that evolution for their own activities. To accomplish that, the Memphis effort introduced evolutionary systems thinking as the second core capability.

As with self-reflection, processes which engaged evolutionary systems thinking are integrated into work tasks wherever feasible. Improvement tasks undertaken by the teams require that people extend their thinking beyond the entity or entities immediately impacted. Symbols are used when people are working together to depict graphically the relationships and associations that will be impacted by a decision or an action.

Evolutionary systems thinking is essential to making sense of the complexities and dynamics of life and to organizing oneself to be the creator of one's own destiny. In the Memphis plant, as managers and wage role employees operate increasingly from the same mental picture of the business and its evolving environment, teamwork is improving and individual motivation is increasing as people see greater significance in their work.

An operator describes how "Beforehand, the thinking . . . was more of a blame-type situation as to these guys will screw up and we are going to end up having to shut the plant down. Well, now it's more . . . 'What can I do for the business to make it better to keep us from shutting down.' The blame factor seems to be disappearing."

The mental scope of responsibility each person holds is also expanding. In planning and problem-solving sessions, workers talk about their impact on future generations, and about their impact on and stewardship for the chemical industry—its overall health and its impact on the environment. Projects with increasingly long-term implications, such as seeking raw material replacements that are more environmentally sound, are being generated from the bottom of the organization.

Another operator describes his own evolution, "As for being involved in the core team, it has helped me to see that there's a larger whole outside my little work area . . . As time's gone on I've begun to see the ramifications of some of my actions or inactions, and it's just helped me look at the bigger picture."

With every step that the individual employees take toward seeing beyond themselves, the Memphis plant is finding it increasingly possible for the organization as a whole to see more of its place in the world. The result, they are finding, is a system which is increasingly capable of evolving itself, not just responding to feedback or direction from its environment.

(3) INTEGRATION OF PERSONAL DEVELOPMENT AND PERFORMANCE IMPROVEMENT: BRIDGING THE GAP BETWEEN VALUING PEOPLE AND PRODUCING PROFITS

This third layer of core capabilities is based on the premise that to build continuous creation into a business, people must work on self-creation in every act of work—that personal development and performance improvement are a necessary dyad that supplies the essential energy required for continuous improvement. As countless managers have found, few things kill the spirit of a change effort faster than learning new skills and having no place and no freedom to apply them. At the other end of the spectrum, and equally deadly to continued change, is ungrounded involvement—people using their new skills to start projects or make decisions which don't match business needs.

A line manager in the Du Pont plant describes how he sees their effort as different: "I think one of the keys to this approach is that we continually try to keep the effort business focused, and some of our previous attempts at developing people and changing our management styles were not always connected to the business. And I think that is what has allowed this approach to go as far as it has."

The Memphis effort was designed to provide structured opportunities for involvement that grow in concert with people's capabilities to manage themselves and their capability to use evolutionary systems thinking to identify business needs. At first the needs that were identified focused on small issues which hindered the day-to-day work. Over time, as capabilities have grown, the teams are increasingly focusing on business needs which reach far into the future. For example, out of gaining understanding of how their customers and their customers' needs are evolving came a recognition of how current product formulations will not meet those future needs. As a result, there are now operator and R&D teams working on the chemical redesign of these products.

In addition to structured involvement opportunities, managers are encouraged to introduce in day-to-day work interactions whichever element of the development/improvement dyad is missing—asking how people engaged in problem solving are working on themselves, or requesting specific ideas for application of new learnings from people who attend training sessions. A supervisor describes his role: "Not only do you evaluate how well you accomplish a specific task, but how well have we developed the people now working on that task to be better able to handle other tasks in the future . . . it forces you to sacrifice some of the perhaps short-term gains in a specific solution while developing the capabilities of people going more and more on their own in the future."

As people are able to manifest the personal change they are experiencing, those changes take on greater significance and meaning, and their motivation to continue the difficult task of changing themselves is reinforced.

A mechanic reports that "The change I've seen in myself and this group is that we feel more positive about what we're doing because we see changes, we've made some decisions, we've done things that are affecting the plant. In the past, you had to go through so much red tape and get so many blessings, that the original idea had changed so much that you didn't even feel a part of it. So now I think it makes you more motivated because you can actually see a change being made."

Integrating a change effort with day-to-day work also alleviates the feeling of being overwhelmed by new responsibilities. From a supervisor: ". . . this is not in addition to your job; this *is* your job. And that helped me because I'd been struggling with, I've got all these other things to do, and it seemed to be taking away from doing these other things."

While the benefits of integrating personal development into the daily work are clear to the Memphis participants, they're equally clear about how difficult it is to sustain this integration. Development, while profound in its eventual impact, is, by its nature, rarely a rapid process. Our culture, however, is focused on instant gratification and driven by crisis motivation. For most of us, our attention span is so short, we want change to happen overnight even though we know the conditions we're trying to shift took years to form. No matter how much we come to value our and others' development, keeping sight of that value when under pressure from external sources on the job or at home requires constant vigilance in light of these cultural constraints. As an operator notes, "It [working on personal development] helps . . . yet it can be very hard. Especially when you're into the day-to-day types of problems and you're not thinking at the time about development."

(4) HOLOGRAPHIC APPROACH TO WORK: CREATING WHOLENESS FROM VALUING DIVERSITY

The fourth core capability, developing a holographic approach to work, returns to the concept mentioned earlier of having each part contain a reflection of the whole. It is based on the premise that hierarchies of power, where those at the top are seen as "smarter," prevent distribution of creation and leadership throughout the organization. The only way of shifting that hierarchy is to move to holographic decision-making processes—processes which honor the unique capabilities, perspectives and contributions of every individual, as well as the synergy that comes from these individuals working together.

As with self-managed teams, the temptation around hierarchy has also been to focus on form rather than substance in change efforts.

Holographic decision-making processes are mental phenomena, not physical. They do not require polling or otherwise involving everyone every time a decision is made. Rather, they depend on the degree to which people are capable of self-reflection, of evolutionary systems thinking and of sustaining the mental polarity of personal development and performance improvement.

The Memphis plant utilizes teams which are holographic reflections of the business and which operate parallel to the management structure, providing leadership to the change effort. These teams, which serve as developmental instruments for both the business and the individuals, provide an arena for people to apply and build on their self-reflective skills, serving to further reinforce self-confidence, while working on business improvement.

Two operators describe their experience: "In the meetings we have learned to be equals . . . And that equal sense is really giving people incentive to participate. You know, I see myself when we go to staff meetings . . . I can with no shame at all speak up my mind. . . . And I think you have a lot more sincere respect for what you can do for the business." And, "By being a part of this group I have gained a lot more self-confidence. First is being not quite so reluctant to speak out; the other thing is beginning to see myself in a leadership role. I've always thought of myself as a doer and a follower. And I think somebody has seen something in me that I didn't see, so I believe I can become a leader."

The impact on management is described by a supervisor who says, "It has helped me to see the total picture, the total plant operation from management point of view all the way down to the assistant operators' point of view because of the mixture of people in the room and the problems I hear them talk about. You know it has helped me to open my mind up and accept the problems they have more readily."

In addition to enabling simply better thinking and decision-making, the holographic make-up of the teams is also an important source of motivation, especially during the early stages of a change effort. When asked what keeps her going in the face of difficulties, a clerk says, "It's the commitment that I see from upper and middle level management here on the team now. How hard they struggle with it and how they keep coming and they're trying their hardest, and as long as they're trying, I'm going to hang in there and try with them."

LOOKING AHEAD

In addition to organizational and personal improvements made over the last 18 months, all teams cited accomplishments resulting in substantial fiscal savings or gains for the Memphis plant. Employees involved in the effort are excited about the changes they've seen in themselves and in the business, but there is also a strong recognition of how hard they have worked and of how difficult it has been to break old patterns. As a manager seeking change, it can feel very comfortable to let employees make decisions, until those decisions differ from one's own.

A line manager advises those who would undertake a similar effort, "Have people really reflect on, are they really ready to let go and trust people. I don't mean just to say it, but to the point of letting go so much that it hurts, that you are really exposed and you have to trust people to keep you from getting in serious trouble." These old and inhibiting patterns are not the sole domain of management, however. It takes equal effort on the part of operators to overcome patterns, one of the most common being the fear and/or cynicism that this is just another "program of the month."

The difficulty of sustaining change is being reconciled by recognition of the many changes that have occurred at all levels of the plant. Decisions which in the past were routinely made by top management are now being made by teams; when direction is set for the business unit, it is done by the Core Team, which is reflective of the perspectives of the whole unit. VIP visits, formerly the domain of staff, are now planned and conducted by teams of operators and supervisors.

An operator, excited about what was happening in the change effort, sent Du Pont C.E.O. Ed Woolard a letter inviting him to come see for himself, an invitation Woolard accepted. In the past, when people had a problem with someone in another unit, they would pass it up through the chain, across and down. Now people talk directly to the person with whom they are having a problem. Responsibility for plant improvement is also no longer exclusive to management—as many improvement projects are initiated from the floor as from management. Even more important, the people who create the idea now carry it through to evaluation. There is no longer an artificial separation between the idea generator, implementor and evaluator.

While change can be seen throughout the plant, there is also recognition of how much still remains to be done. Dick Jensen, the manager who has been responsible for guiding the change process plant-wide, is quick to point out that "The biggest challenge in front of us now is extending the changes in capabilities and vision to the rest of the folks who have not yet been touched; and that takes a lot of patience, and remembering how hard it was for us at first."

Bob Porter also adds that "some people are still wondering 'why change?' That is partly because we haven't connected everyone to all the relevant business information and partly because we are not yet totally consistent in how we are working with people. This is what we are working on now, and have quite a way to go."

SUSTAINING A CHANGE EFFORT

Most managers in American business have long believed that people will change only if they see something in it for themselves, specifically some material reward or personal advancement. Perhaps one of the most significant aspects of the experience of the Memphis Du Pont plant is that it is bringing into question this long-standing truism. Managers there are discovering that the most powerful source of change may, in fact, be people who have the opportunity to give of themselves.

In the eloquent words of a clerk speaking on behalf of herself and her fellow workers, "We're really beginning to recognize that there is untapped capability here and an untapped desire to experience being an individual who contributes something to the business and is recognized for that contribution, and so I think part of what drives a group like this is that sense of being able to touch and manage and shape in some way their destiny."

EXEMPLAR:
General Motors

The Fremont, California, General Motors plant had one of the worst records for employee relations. Called the "Battleship," it had four shutdowns in twenty years and was finally closed by GM in 1982. But in a new partnership with Toyota as New United Motors, at least 60 percent of the old work force was hired back. In the past there was no mutual trust. Today trust, equity, employee involvement, and teamwork have turned the plant around.

Employees began to have a sense of ownership. Authority was pushed down to the lowest level. Employee satisfaction, productivity, and cost savings increased. Management became trainers and facilitators rather than trying to impose rigid rules. One manager talked about how a $20,000 suggestion program in a stamping plant led to $2.3 million in savings in one year. He viewed that as an example of the power of allowing everybody to contribute. He claimed that the more decisions made at the lowest level, the higher the productivity and the quality and the lower the cost.

GM also has innovated in a new paradigm way with the production and distribution of the Saturn automobile. Its Spring Hill, Tennessee, plant is a model of technology and manufacturing design. The plant has won four environmental awards. The distribution system is revolutionary.

But Saturn's president says that the real revolution is in the people side of the equation. Management and unions tossed out their old ways of doing things in order to achieve a total integration of people, technology, and business systems. Hierarchy and perks for management were eliminated, while responsibility was pushed down to the lowest level. An electronic mail system called R.S.V.P. allows any worker to send anonymous messages to upper management and receive timely responses.

Clearly, dramatic changes are happening at even the largest corporations.

16

THE LEVERAGED BUYOUT
AS A POSITIVE FORCE

by Eric J. Weiffering

Since certain leveraged buyouts have become notorious for junk bond entrepreneurs, overpriced acquisitions, and enormous fees for key operators, it may be surprising and difficult to consider them as a positive force for social and economic change. But George E. McCown has a totally different approach to leveraged buyouts, viewing them as a constructive process for the revitalization of underperforming divisions of large companies.

McCown, CEO of McCown De Leeuw & Co., has pursued only friendly LBOs, avoiding junk bonds and short-term, exploitive turnovers. Instead, his company has used leveraged acquisitions as a vehicle for the transformation of both the capital structure and hierarchical management of a company, increasing benefits and worker participation. In each case this new paradigm management approach has brought down-to-earth results. Since its formation in 1984, his company has acquired 17 companies and has helped them to complete over forty growth acquisitions. The companies remaining in its portfolio generate over $1.3 billion in annual sales and employ more than 15,500 people.

Eric J. Weiffering is a freelance business writer whose work appears in Corporate Report, Minnesota, *and* Barron's.

George E. McCown, the recently elected chairman of the World Business Academy, is passionate about two things: mountain climbing and leveraged buyouts. One is his avocation, the other his vocation. Given current popular opinion regarding LBOs, McCown might seem an odd choice to chair an organization that describes itself as a network of executives "involved with personal and business transformation," a network working to create "a positive future for the planet."

McCown sees no irony, but then, McCown De Leeuw & Co. isn't your stereotypical LBO firm. The company, with offices in Menlo

Park, California, Ann Arbor, Michigan, and New York, shuns the kinds of deals that have dominated Wall Street and been reviled on Main Street: expensive acquisitions motivated by assets that can be sold and the enormous fees that can be generated. McCown De Leeuw pursues friendly LBOs, usually with management as a partner, and it works to transform the management philosophy of the company, flattening hierarchies and giving employees control of their destiny.

"If you challenge people, if you give them the incentives and the time to go and create, they'll be happy, and they'll be successful," McCown says. "That's how business works best."

It's a philosophy that's worked well for McCown De Leeuw and the individuals and institutions who have put $120 million into its various partnerships. Since its formation in 1984, the LBO firm has provided investors with an average annual return of 160 percent on the companies it has bought and sold.

It's a philosophy that is also right at home at the Burlingame, California–based World Business Academy, which serves as a forum for what McCown calls cutting-edge organizational and business strategic thinking. "We are an academy in the traditional sense of the word, a place where executives can exchange thoughts and get new ideas," McCown says. The central theme is new-paradigm management, which, as the September 1989 WBA newsletter explained, represents a shift from hierarchy to employee empowerment, from rigidity to adventure, and from secretiveness to openness.

Like most LBO funds, McCown De Leeuw uses high leverage, but it has turned to junk bonds only once. And instead of going for the quick kill, McCown De Leeuw works to genuinely revitalize its companies, putting in place a capital structure that supports growth. While the firm does sell some assets, it often does the opposite, acquiring competing companies that help expand market penetration or geographic reach.

"There is a very genuine attempt on the part of McCown De Leeuw to add value to the corporation," says Dan Wertenberg, president of Building Technologies Corporation in Cincinnati, which was acquired by McCown De Leeuw last year. And adding value can mean something other than increasing revenues. Shortly after paying $71 million in 1989 for Van Doren Rubber Co., the Orange, California maker of Vans tennis shoes, McCown De Leeuw began offering English classes to its Mexican-American workers. To reduce the anxiety LBOs can cause, McCown makes it a point to include existing management in most deals, and he shares information openly with employees.

McCown came to the LBO business after twenty-five years at Boise Cascade Corporation. His experience there confirmed a belief he'd had for a long time, that a workplace that was psychologically and financially dynamic, or entrepreneurial, made for a more successful business.

Preferring to acquire small or under-performing divisions in large companies, McCown likes to buy divisions that contribute less than 10 percent in sales to the parent company's revenue. Often, those divisions are ancillary to the corporation's strategic plan, and thus possess huge unrealized potential. "Once a division falls below 10 percent, it usually doesn't get much capital or much management attention," he explains.

Beyond leaving market potential untapped, such neglect often leaves corporate morale depressed, McCown says. Resigned to their fate, or resentful of it, employees and even managers come to believe they have little control over their destiny. They become convinced the people in charge have little interest in their opinions. "Our biggest job," Mc-Cown says, "is reversing that thinking."

After an acquisition, McCown's staff meets regularly with employees and managers, to impress upon them that it's no longer business as usual. They hold three-day training programs, and encourage managers to organize and take part in Outward Bound seminars. "We tell everyone, 'You guys are in charge. We want all of you to be engaged, because if you don't make it work, there's nobody here to save you,' " McCown says. "We make them feel accountable. We try to strip away the corporate rigidity."

The Building Technologies Corporation acquisition in July 1989 typifies McCown De Leeuw's kind of deal. BTC was a division of the publicly traded company Building Technologies Inc., and with sales of $188 million, the BTC division had strong industry name recognition and geographic penetration. But it had been hurt by the financial difficulties of its parent, as well as a slowdown in new construction. In acquiring the company, McCown De Leeuw joined with BTC's senior management, plus Hambro International Venture Fund. "When McCown De Leeuw put the deal together they spent a lot of time explaining it and presenting things to managers and employees," says BTC President Dan Wertenberg, who was a partner in the acquisition. "There was a tremendous amount of information sharing."

But even McCown acknowledges that whittling away those old attitudes and carving new ones is not easy. "Often it takes two years before attitudes change from being oriented toward pleasing the boss to being in charge," McCown says.

McCown began thinking about how organizations work, and how people best function within them, in the late 1950s and early 1960s, while he was serving in the military and later working in business. Even then, he says, he was struck by how assiduously organizations seemed to work to stifle creativity, to impose a rigid hierarchy upon employees.

At Harvard Business School he came under the tutelage of the late Georges F. Doriot, a legendary professor who spent his professional life addressing the same issues—and putting his theories to the test with American Research & Development, one of the first venture capital firms.

"Professor Doriot had a philosophy that emphasized the quality of people and the quality of the work environment," McCown recalls. "He had a great reverence for the creative process and for the entrepreneur."

McCown shares that philosophy, and he's been in the business world long enough to see the pernicious results of management structures that emphasize authority and control. "It was always my observation that for most people, work was not a place where they got a lot of satisfaction," McCown says. "And when you think that work is the place where we spend most of our adult lives, the human cost of that dissatisfaction is mind-boggling."

When work can be made enjoyable again, the potential benefits are enormous. "If the worker is happy, chances are his family is happy and he will be a more productive member of the community," McCown says. It goes without saying, he adds, that business will also be more profitable. For proof, McCown need only point to his own track record.

17

GIVING VALUES A VOICE: MARKETING IN THE NEW PARADIGM

by Terry Mandel

Many would say that of all aspects in the world of business, marketing would be the least likely to reform itself in the wake of new paradigm transformation. How can you sell something without hype and manipulation?

In fact, marketing can be even more effective when it truly communicates our values, when it balances attitudes and actions with honesty and vision. Many companies today are able to discover what inspires and moves their work and to convey that, to commercial advantage, in their marketing.

Terry Mandel is the founder of a San Francisco–based marketing and management consulting firm. She speaks and publishes nationally on "Marketing with Integrity," "Selling Successfully Without Selling Out," "Ethics in the Marketplace," and "Authentic Communications at Work."

Depending on one's perspective, we're either on the brink or in the midst of a global paradigm shift. The systems orientation fundamental to this new worldview will enable us to reintegrate all that's been fragmented since the 17th century, when power eclipsed spirit as the currency of human exchange.

Far from discarding power, however, the new paradigm promises a balancing of power with spirit, of human invention with natural systems, of image with substance. The iron grip of "either/or" is being softened by the healing salve of "both/and."

The transitions from international to global markets, from multinational to multicultural companies, from hierarchical to horizontal organizations, and from transactional to relational interactions are more than semantic. Making and understanding these distinctions linguistically is the first, crucial step towards applying them in our work and lives.

Baby Boomers, now culture *shapers* as well as culture *shakers*, are bringing the values of the '60s into the '90s. The increasingly widespread acceptance of participative management, ESOPs, intuition in the workplace, flextime, and socially responsible business practices parallel the Boomers' rise on the corporate ladder.

In spite of this generation's growing influence on how business is done, however, one major arena remains virtually unchanged: marketing. We've been bombarded with lies for so long that truth is a real novelty. Is it any wonder that a national attitude survey reported in the *Boston Globe* revealed that "43 percent of Americans—and more than half of those under age 24—believe selfishness and fakery are at the core of human nature"?

THE HEART OF MARKETING

Even people committed to running businesses that reflect their inner convictions often use traditional marketing strategies that play on people's fantasies and fears.

I believe the antidote to this cynicism and stagnation is a new model of marketing that mirrors the new paradigm. Instead of discounting marketing as merely a vehicle of information, we can learn to use it as a tool for transformation.

Admittedly, this requires something of a leap. Most of the advertising we see is insulting, much of the junk we get in the mail is aptly named, and many of the salespeople we encounter are intrusive. But what has been sullied in the name of greed can be reborn in the service of truth. Freed from the stigma of how others use or abuse it, marketing offers us the power to give voice to that which most inspires and moves us in our work. When we share our visions with others, we build bridges between our world and theirs.

Most people think marketing with integrity is an oxymoron, like jumbo shrimp, or honest politician. But this new paradigm of marketing speaks to the possibility that we can successfully promote ourselves and our ideas and profitably sell our products and services in ways that are consistent with our individual and corporate styles, values, and intentions.

And what *is* marketing, anyway, if not a process we use, consciously or unconsciously, to communicate our values? We market with integrity when we balance our attitudes and actions with our values and vision. Surprisingly, the result is a competitive advantage that can raise the standard of operation within an industry while rewarding everyone involved with a greater sense of purpose.

This redefinition shifts the usual focus of marketing from the organization outward to include the inner organization, as well. By building a bridge between inner and outer worlds—within ourselves as much as in our companies—we make possible the integration of our values and actions, our inspiration and expression, our work and spirit.

Marketing with integrity creates a context in which an authentic and abiding relationship is not only possible, but very nearly irresistible. The dark side of that ideal is the false chumminess and relentless pushiness that characterize traditional marketing and advertising. The safeguard for that is integrity, which is not about moral superiority or perfection, but about balance and wholeness.

I explore with clients marketing's untapped potential for making a deep and lasting connection with their audiences. When we fan the sparks within us, they become irresistible beacons for the sparks in others.

MEETING YOUR MARKETPLACE FACE TO FACE

It's easy to imagine the true excitement Henry Ford's first automobile generated among the horse and buggy set; the breathlessness of early advertising accurately reflected the enthusiasm with which the public greeted products unlike anything they'd ever imagined, much less seen before.

Since then, the unchecked proliferation of consumer goods to meet every whim—and create new ones—has understandably dampened our enthusiasm for the constant stream of new product introductions. The breathless tone that once excited now just grates and irritates.

The inflated expectations most marketing efforts create are often punctured by the customer's eventual experience with the product, service, or company. Like so much else in our post-industrial age, marketing has been relegated to a mostly one-way function designed to inflate a product or company image at the expense of its substance, reduced to hucksterism and the quest for the holy buck.

Everyone longs to be seen and heard. By creating products that promise to fulfill us and using advertising to play on our yearning to belong, traditional marketers meet the deep collective longing to connect with superficial and artificial substitutes, both in products and promotion. When we sell our souls by forgetting the sacred contract we have to honor life, we sacrifice nothing less than our humanity. This diminishes us all.

The most innovative customer service work being done today treats the customer, as neither the *subject* of study nor the *object* of new products or behavior, but as an active *partner* in developing win-win solutions. There's no more "them" when it's all "us" in this together.

THE EVOLUTION OF SYSTEMIC CHANGE

Working over the years with a wide variety of clients—traditional as well as progressive organizations, nonprofits as well as multinationals—I've discovered that, while most want to grow and transform, many are afraid to try anything too new or different in marketing—even if their success was built on being new and different!

Not long ago a client more or less said what many have felt: "I want things to be different as long as I don't have to change."

I have found there's a wide gap between accepting new paradigm principles in *concept* and applying them in *practice*. Resistance to change and fear, its constant companion, may not be rational, but they're real enough to short-circuit many well-intended efforts. Even small movements towards integrity, however, are powerful magnets. When values are put into action, they become a beacon to which both internal and external customers are drawn.

New paradigm proponents, however, can be trapped by the old "all or nothing" approach by insisting that systemic change must, by definition, happen all at once. Paradoxically, making systemic change in large organizations may only be possible step by step. Though evolution is our teacher in this regard, my experience suggests that marketing with integrity can help us leverage that process. Communicating our values consciously and comprehensively through our work and workplaces can only bring us closer to our colleagues, corporations, customers, and communities.

One businessman's commitment to marketing with integrity helped him address a specific, thorny problem without requiring him to remake his entire organization. As Jeff Salzman, co-founder of CareerTrack, the largest producer of professional development seminars in North America, explains it, "We had a very successful, lunatic seminar leader who also offended many customers. I was about to fire him when I said to myself, 'Let's try to just tell the truth about him.' It worked! In a side-by-side test of brochures promoting his seminar (which, incidentally, teaches people to maintain calm and productivity under pressure), the version in which we capitalized on his unorthodox style beat the traditional approach by 42%, a *lot* in our business (or any, I would think). Since the format of the traditional brochure normally beats the one we tested, these numbers are even more significant. The copy otherwise was 95% identical."

Most companies valuing customer satisfaction would just have let the presenter go. But Salzman's creative and financially-rewarding solution acknowledged his unhappy customers without forsaking those who appreciated both the seminar and its iconoclastic leader.

By using the "problem" as a doorway to the solution, CareerTrack was able to preserve its relationship with both one of their best seminar leaders *and* their customers. Highlighting the very qualities that turned some of their customers off allowed people likely to be offended by the presenter's style to avoid his seminars. Telling the "whole" truth at the customers' decision-making stage ensured that they wouldn't feel betrayed by a promotion that omitted crucial information. Customer expectations and experience were thus brought significantly closer together.

GIVING BIRTH TO THE NEW PARADIGM IN MARKETING

The promise of the new paradigm is the coexistence of industry and intimacy. This unlikely marriage is the essence of integrity.

But there's no wedding possible without coequal partners. The denial of the feminine principle has left our workplaces and marketplaces spiritually—and increasingly, financially—bankrupt. The drive for short-term profits at the expense of long-term considerations, the focus on results regardless of process, the drive to do more, better, faster (witness the tyranny of many TQM implementations) has had devastating human and environmental costs.

Even in organizations, the thigh bone's connected to the hip bone; the consequence of ignoring that interconnectedness is that many large organizations have become lifeless structures, skeletons stripped of all vibrancy and aliveness. The structure's been preserved, but nobody lives there anymore.

I bring this up because it's easy to dismiss values and integrity as "soft" issues, with no honorable place—or damn business!—in business. It's curious that something supposedly so trivial evokes such strong reactions from both men and women. The feminine has been revered and reviled for centuries because it embodies the unknown, the mysteries of creation.

Marketing with integrity, however, does not supplant the dynamic and direct energy of the masculine with the receptive and contextual energy of the feminine, but seeks to integrate the two.

Let me illustrate with a direct mail success story that considered *how* the message was conveyed as much as *what* was being said. *Yoga Journal*, not your usual hard-sell publication, nevertheless had been using a typical "breathless" package to attract new subscribers. The pitch: yoga can relieve your back pain. The package: 4-page, hyped, letter with lots of little pictures of celebrities they'd had on their covers. The promise: if you send money with your order, we'll send you a FREE book on the yogic way to pain relief. The problem: it wasn't working.

When we sat down to design a test package, it became clear the magazine's driving force was less about pain relief than about the profound harmony that yoga promotes. The new pitch: "Just say the magic words and we'll leave you in peace." The new package: A short, sweet, letter with "sell" and a brochure that unfolds—subtly mirroring the unfolding of the body and consciousness *YJ* readers are drawn to—to reveal images and quotes from past issues with only a bit of copy to tie it all together. The new promise: if you pay for your subscription with your order, take a dollar off the price. The result: the new package pulled 150% better than the old, and cash with orders increased 250%, significantly increasing cash flow as well as cutting the expense of repeated billing. We served the objective of selling more subscriptions by exposing the heart and spirit of the magazine to its natural audience.

While answers—a symbol of the masculine—are credited with changing the world, both for better and for worse, it is the questions—a symbol of the feminine—that precede them that point the way. As we are increasingly challenged to change our ways or perish, we must begin to entertain questions that, even in the asking, will open us to new possibilities.

If our organizations are to become members of the larger world community, our sense of responsibility must encompass stakeholders as well as stockholders. By taking the time to listen—to ourselves, individually and collectively, inside the organization and without— we foster relationships that can stand the test of time. Instead of glorifying transactions at the expense of relationships, business can re-energize itself as a high-voltage conduit of human connectedness.

There's an Ethiopian proverb that says, "When the heart overflows, it comes out through the mouth." By applying new paradigm principles in the realm of marketing, we have the opportunity to make the language of the heart the lingua franca of the marketplace.

18

THE QUESTION OF
EMPLOYEE OWNERSHIP

by Rolf V. Osterberg, Tamas Makray,
and Terry Mollner

Employee ownership has long been hailed as an idealistic panacea for improving the productivity, profitability, and psychological life of a company. And yet, it hasn't always worked. Problems of conversion, labor versus capital, and cooperative control have been acknowledged as ongoing issues that need careful consideration in each situation.

What follows are three different views on the question of employee ownership. They appear in the following sequence: Rolf V. Osterberg, author of Corporate Renaissance, *held the positions of President of the largest Scandinavian film company, Svensk Filmindustri, Chairman of the Newspapers Association, and Executive Vice-President of the Dagens Nyheter Group, the largest newspaper company in Scandinavia. Tamas Makray was born in Budapest, and is presently Chairman of Promon Tecnologia S.A., an employee-owned company, operating in engineering and electronics in Brazil and other countries. Terry Mollner is founder and Co-President of Trusteeship Institute, an economic and social policy think tank best known for its consulting to corporations converting to an owner-worker cooperative based on the Mondragon model.*

I. ROLF V. OSTERBERG

Let me first settle that what we are talking about is *direct* ownership by employees and not indirect ownership as in socialistic systems, where it is sometimes claimed that the fact that the production means are owned by the state is a form of citizen/employee ownership.

Let me also settle that by "employee ownership" I mean that the enterprise in question is owned *only* by its employees, each one with a more-or-less equal share. Thus there is no group with a voting majority and there are no absentee owners.

The first thing to underline is that, as I see it, the reason behind employee ownership has nothing to do with the idea of creating wealth for the employees. The present, rather common programs of letting employees buy shares or convertibles might be considered as progressive but *is* another extension of the old way of looking at employees as tools; the idea behind it is that the possibility to get rich would make the employee work harder, be more loyal, etc.

No, the difference between the predominant ownership pattern of today (and I see no borderline between the capitalistic and socialistic systems) and employee ownership has to do with *distance* on the one hand and *interconnectedness* on the other. It is the difference between *mechanical* and *living* companies.

Let us take a look upon nature. It is so clear to me that everything is interconnected. Every part of nature is linked to every other part. Furthermore, nature is a self-generating system; it creates its own energy and sees to it that the energy is circulated in the system in an exactly appropriate way. Nature is indeed a living system.

Why should business diverge from the pattern of nature? Why should business follow special laws? I see no reason.

Nevertheless, we have created an economic system and a way of looking upon business which is far from, and in many cases, directly against nature. That in its turn is a natural consequence of the mechanical way of thinking we have been continuously developing for several centuries now—and developed in absurdum. One of the key elements in that thinking is distance.

We have distanced ourselves from nature to the extent that we have completely lost perspective. We no longer perceive nature as our life source. Instead we look upon it as a tool, a tool that we, "the masters of nature," use for our own selfish purposes.

We have created distances, not only to nature but to ourselves. The consequence is the ever increasing distance between humans (between parents and children, between soldier and general, between citizen and government, between union member and union leaders, between employee and company, etc.).

It is then no wonder that we, when building up our business systems, have chosen ownership forms which per se mean distance. By doing that we have built up mechanical companies—*machines* instead of living entities.

What do I mean?

Let us see a company as an energy system. Profit is generated primarily by the employees' energy in form of cash flow. In a non-employee-owned company, however, the energy generator—the employees—are not part of the system; they are outsiders, they do not belong, and they are alienated.

Looked upon from the owner's side, the *employee* is a tool to fulfill the owner's goals, be it wealth, profit, power, etc. Looked upon from the employee's side, the *company* is a tool to fulfill the need to get money for survival, to get a position in the society, to get power, etc. It is not a place where s/he *lives*. There is no feeling of belonging. The mutual relations between the company and the employees are mechanical and without real life.

Is that what we want?

I don't think so. On the contrary, I think that in any company every employee (be it the president or the ordinary worker), when allowed to think about it, will find a deep yearning for another relationship to his or her working place. Despite the distances we have created there is deep within us this sense that everything is connected, that everything belongs. Deep within us we feel a strong yearning to leave the I-thought and replace it with we-thought. We are longing for harmony with ourselves—harmony with the creation. And that means interconnectedness.

As far as I have seen there is no other form of ownership than employee ownership which provides a natural environment for interconnectedness to occur. In an employee owned company the employees can *be* the company and only then the company is *living*.

So, to conclude: The reason I argue for employee ownership is simply that I see it as the basic provision for creating living companies. It is when we have living companies that our working places become something more than somewhere to go to earn money. With living companies our working places become somewhere we primarily go to thrive and develop as human beings. A living company is a place where that enormous creativity we all bear within us has a chance to blossom.

Machines have no creativity. Living entities do.

II. TAMAS MAKRAY

Our company was started very conventionally in late 1960 as a 50/50 joint venture between a Brazilian and an American contractor [see Exemplar: Promon Tecnologia S.A.]. We offered integrated engineering services for the process industries in Brazil. The company was small, investment irrelevant, with the owners staying at a distance, letting the business be run by its managers.

When the political and economic situation deteriorated in Brazil, the American partner considered getting out of the country. It was expected that the company would be closed down. A group of key employees prepared for the worst and registered a partnership to continue the business in the case of liquidation. That was in 1964.

The economy improved, the company was not liquidated, but the American stockholder had no interest in staying. After two years of negotiations, the employees' partnership acquired the shares of the American contractor.

Growth and diversification brought conflict of interest with the Brazilian contractor, owner of 50% of the company. Another two years of negotiations resulted in the purchase of their shares also by the employees' partnership.

The year is 1970. The company has a staff of 500. The ten years of struggle have taught some lessons:

• It is terrible to be an employee and depend totally on the owners of the business. You may be sold, merged or closed down without your slightest participation in the decision.

• The staff spends most of the day at the workplace, may spend their entire professional lives in the company with colleagues and friends, so what happens there is very important to them—often more important to them than to the owners.

• Privileges are so ugly. We should try to be equal. Ideally all employees should be more or less equal shareholders and participate in at least those decisions that affect them directly.

• Conflict between capital and labor (owners and staff) is mortal. It goes against the very nature of any venture that is based on cooperation, or even better, co-creation, by all stakeholders.

The basic structure of the organization today is as follows:

The partnership formed by the key employees in 1964 controls the organization with the prime objective of ensuring that basic principles and policies are complied with. Seventy active senior members of the professional staff own the company. Participation is by invitation, consensus is necessary, and maximum ownership is limited to 6% per person.

The original engineering company's scope was amplified and today it coordinates operations in various areas of technology. It is jointly owned by the partnership (55%) and some 2,000 shareholders, all employees of the organization. The total staff is around 3,000, and 41% are university graduates.

Nineteen years of experience as an independent, totally employee-owned organization has resulted in the following rules and operational procedures:

Acquisition: Shares must be purchased by staff members; they are not given.

Value: The price of shares is the audited book value, adjusted for contingencies.

Access: All employees are encouraged and even expected to become shareholders. A gradual build-up of ownership is normal during the career of the professional. Shares are not inheritable in case of death, they cannot be donated and cannot be sold to outside parties.

Purchase back provision: Contracts include a provision whereby the company repurchases shares in the event of death, retirement or termination of employment.

Ceilings: A maximum of 6% in the holding partnership. A maximum of 2% in the operating company. That means that combining indirect and direct ownership nobody can have more than about 5% of the capital.

Transactions: Staff members are free to buy and sell shares from and to the company but it has to be understood that equity ownership is a means of financial engagement in the company and not a form of financial investment.

Phase-out: In the partnership there is an "equity phase-out" provision, whereby staff members who approach company age limits reduce their participation on a steady basis, over up to 10 years.

Profit destination: In principle, 70% of the results are distributed and 30% retained in the company. The distribution is in equal parts as dividends and as profit-sharing, the last according to merit and performance.

Return on investment: Over the years, the shares have afforded their owners levels of profitability reasonably above those of alternative non-speculative investments.

Financing: The private pension fund of the employees extends loans to those who may need financing for the purchase of shares.

Election of directors and officers:
Elections are held every three years for Board Members and Officers. Conditions to be eligible are to be a member of the partnership, have a management position and be under company age limit and, of course, to be a willing candidate.

The first selection is made in the holding partnership, a second in the operating company. The vote is secret, collected by independent auditors. A minimum of a 50% vote is required as it is felt that a massive support is essential for a strong management.

Equilibrium of this model of ownership:

This ownership model postulates a minimum rate of return so that the system generates funds that increase employees' revenues by dividends and profit-sharing that in turn enables them to finance capital requirements.

Whenever profitability falls below certain values the model may experience some operational imbalance. This situation may be further compounded when a significant number of shareholders leave the company.

Naturally this model seems to be more compatible with service industries than with capital intensive investments. We pay particular attention to maintain the level of fixed assets as low as possible. Certain activities which would unduly increase the book value of the shares are practically excluded from the options. For example, land and buildings were the object of a spin-off years ago to make equity participation more accessible to new staff members.

And, of course, this model is immune to hostile takeovers and guarantees stability in rendering professional services for long term major programs and projects.

To conclude these incomplete observations, I should like to stress that the essence of this "professional community" model is participation in the life of the organization, not only in its capital. To buy shares is relatively easy, but it does not mean by itself that you are engaged in a creative, living, dynamic community. And as you read in our Charter, we believe the purpose of Promon is to create conditions for professional and personal fulfillment and realization.

III. TERRY MOLLNER

If we assume, as many do, that *successful* employee ownership and control would be an improvement of the psychological life, productivity, and profitability in the workplace, then the reason there have not been a flood of conversations of corporations to employee-owned cooperatives is because those of us who are interested in doing it have not as yet figured out how to do it well. This is self-evident. The obvious question becomes, "What have we been doing wrong?"

Both capitalism and communism are based on a world view which we now know to be false. I call this world view the Material Age (or "Two-or-moreness") world view. It is the assumption that the universe is an immense number of separate parts which primarily compete with each other for their own self-interest. The other possible fundamental world view I call the Relationship Age (or "Oneness") world view. It is the assumption that the universe is an immense number of connected parts, each of which cooperates with all other parts in the interest of the universe first, and only secondly cooperates or competes in the interest of themselves or any sub-group of parts.

Obviously, therefore, people who are operating on the Material Age world view would not find it natural to cooperate except as enlightened self-interest: self-interest is primary and cooperation is secondary. People who are consciously or unconsciously operating on the Material Age world view would not be able to create a successful owner-worker cooperative. For the emotional life of the worker, productivity, and profitability, under these conditions one boss is better than 500 or 500,000 bosses who are primarily competing. Only those who have made the shift to the Relationship Age world view would be well advised to give the owner-worker cooperative model a try.

Therefore, the first responsibility is to invite the workforce to shift the psychological pattern of their thoughts into the Relationship Age context. If this is so, then the main mistake we have been making has been that we have not been dealing with the conversion process at this level.

What we have been doing is shifting the ownership of the stock and the control of the corporation into the hands of employees in ignorance of this pre-requisite. A shift in world view from the Material Age to the Relationship Age is essential. Only people who believe that it is natural to give priority to cooperation with all things at all times because they are parts of one's self will be able to freely and consistently give priority to the good of all over their self-interests.

If this is so, then the next question becomes, "How do we go about shifting the psychology to the Relationship Age world view?"

The first thought which crosses the minds of most people is to run workshops to educate the workforce to the new world view. Although this will certainly be part of the process, to give it priority would be naive.

A corporation is not the products, computers, buildings, etc. Those are its possessions. A corporation is a set of agreements. Those agreements are an extension of either the Material Age or Relationship Age world view. Those agreements are the context within which all else occurs. They are the behavioral modification box. Without changing the behavioral modification box, no amount of talking and persuading will change people's behavior unless they are naive people.

Therefore, the first three new policies of the current owners must be to:

1) change the agreements to reflect the Relationship Age world view,
2) maintain a veto power over all decisions until the psychological change in the workforce is complete, and
3) try to never exercise the veto power.

In this context the education will be received and the new world view will be given a genuine try. If it is indeed the correct world view, personal experience will prove it to be so to each employee and there will be no stopping the psychological change to the Relationship Age world view.

"What are the corporate agreements which reflect the Relationship Age world view?" The Mondragon Cooperatives in Spain have provided the leadership here. What I am about to suggest is that the corporation be reorganized into one based on the agreements and structures of the Mondragon Cooperatives *underneath* the existing Board of Trustees (BT). The latter will delegate all the operational decisions to the Worker Board of Trustees (WBT) elected by and comprised of only workers. Thus, the change is only a management change, not a legal change in ownership and control. However, the BT tries to never exercise its veto power. Instead it does its best to work out all differences by achieving a consensus with the WBT. Of course, if necessary it exercises its veto.

The purpose of doing the conversion in this manner is to be able to switch to the Relationship Age agreements and processes on the first day of the conversion process while leaving the ultimate power in the hands of those who have been managing the business successfully during the learning phase. It is not possible to learn the Relationship Age system while continuing to do the Material Age system. At the same time the business must be kept alive during the learning phase or the learning phase will not be able to continue. Finally, leadership is necessary to make the committment to convert to a Relationship Age corporation and to stick with the process until it has been accomplished. The current owners are the only ones who have the authority to either provide this leadership or to do so to the extent that they hire a consultant to lead the company through this change.

The first operational agreement change is that the top priority of the company is the good of all, not just the owners or workers. This is the good of all in all directions at all times, not just by providing one service or product to the community.

Secondly, the workers themselves decide what that is in each situation through a consensual rather than combative process. The invisible hand of competition is replaced with the visible hands of consensus.

The workers elect a WBT. Only workers can be on this body. At least one person is elected from every division of the company. The BT delegates all of its powers to this body as soon as it is capable of receiving them. The BT only retains the power to guide the company through this transition to the Relationship Age model backed up with a commitment to sell the company to the employees once the task has been accomplished. The WBT chooses the Chief Executive Officer (CEO) and must approve the CEO's selection of his or her top management people.

The CEO establishes a hierarchical management system without hesitancy. Because the CEO is hired and fired by the workers through a democratic process, the hierarchical system of operation ceases to be a power system and becomes an efficiency system. People who have never escaped the arms of the Material Age have never had the experience of a hierarchical system which was not a power system as well as an efficiency system. However, once the power aspect is removed from the hierarchical system, people love hierarchy because of its efficiency and they do not find it to be a barrier to healthy relationships with each other. Also the number of levels of hierarchy can be greatly reduced because of the commitment and self-regulating integrity of a Relationship Age management system.

Each group of 10 to 50 workers in an area elects a representative to a Social Council. It is a committee of the WBT which is responsible for determining salary scales, working with the personnel department to do individual worker evaluations, determines fringe benefits, etc. It attends to the functions which are normally the focus of unions, but it is a committee under the democratically elected WBT; it is not in conflict with it.

There is also an internal social and financial Audit Committee of three people elected by the workers. It is also available to assist any worker with any issue. Finally, there is also a Direction Committee made up of the senior members of the BT, WBT, and top management which meets at least once a week to make sure everyone's actions are co-ordinated with each other and all are supportive of each other's actions.

If possible the owners voluntarily begin to take a reasonable fixed return on their equity and the rest of any profit is distributed as follows: 50% to the workers as bonuses, the size of the bonus based on each person's wage level; 40% is held in a Trust Account never to be distributed to individuals; and 10% is donated to social, charitable, and educational activities in the community. The bonuses are not distributed to the workers in cash. Rather, an internal account is established for each worker. The worker's bonus is placed in this account and treated as a loan from the worker to the company. An interest rate above the inflation rate but below the prime rate is paid on this loan in cash each year. This internal account can also be used as collateral by the worker to secure a loan. The result is that the worker also has use of the money if necessary at a net interest cost of only a few percentage points. At the same time the money remains in the business to be used to create additional owner-worker jobs for the community. The 40% in the Trust Fund is also used for this purpose. Only the 10% to charity leaves the company. As you can see, this profit distribution system clearly gives priority to the good of all by using 90% of the profits to create additional jobs in Relationship Age companies. At the same time it does not do so by making the workers into martyrs.

When the company has successfully converted to the Relationship Age model psychologically, not just in talk, the BT then sells the company to the employees. In other words, only when the conversion to employee ownership and cooperative control is a formality because psychologically and operationally it is already operating as such should the legal changes be made. Ownership is a skill which must be learned and Relationship Age trusteeship and control is even a more difficult skill to learn. The current owners need to love their workforces enough to provide for the leadership necessary to successfully achieve this conversion. It may take years. If they are not willing to make the commitment which is necessary, then they should sell the company to someone who is willing to do so or to turn it over to others so they can do it. The others may be consultants or current employees of the company. It is not likely that it would be all the employees of the company. One thing, therefore, is certain: someone or a group which is capable of doing so will have to be allowed to lead.

As you can see, the changing of the operational agreements and structures to have them be clear extensions of the Relationship Age world view is more important then educating the workers to these ideas. However, educating the workers to the ideas is also essential. It empowers the workers to become masters of their own lives while moving in concert with everyone else. Like artists, they also become highly motivated and productive without the need of enemies or conflict. And that is what the Relationship Age is all about.

Therefore, I would recommend that company owners give priority to the psychological change in the conversion process over the legal change to employee ownership and control. I would also emphasize that they be committed to the legal conversion to ownership and control as soon as it would be a formality to do so and not allow this process to be used to motivate workers without giving them the opportunity to step fully into the Relationship Age at their place of work by actually becoming the owners and trustees.

EXEMPLAR:
Promon Tecnologia S.A.

CHARTER

1. Promon is a professional organization engaged in technical and consultancy services in the fields of engineering and architecture. It performs studies and research, and conducts scientific and technological development activities.

2. Promon's permanent objective is to provide its clients with services of a high technical standard, with strict observance of the principles of professional ethics.

3. Promon is the expression of the merit of its professionals; it is the result of the cooperative efforts of individuals with related vocations with the purpose of creating conditions for their professional and personal fulfillment.

4. Professional and personal fulfillment will be assured through:

—stimulating creativity and respecting the dignity of the individual;
—providing opportunities for the development and advancement of all, according to the qualifications and merit of each;
—membership in a cohesive, stable working community;
—fair compensation

5. Participation in the community implies the willingness to waive individual interests for the sake of the group.

6. Individual participation in the management of the company is to be encouraged. The search for consensus shall always be present in the decision-making process and in the exercise of authority.

7. All Promon's professionals, and they alone, shall have access to ownership of the company's equity capital. As an independent organization, Promon shall enter into no commitments that might detract from its impartiality in the examination of technical and economic matters with which it is entrusted.

8. While constituting an indispensable prerequisite for the stability and development of the company, profit is nevertheless not one of its basic objectives. It is, rather, a means for the achievement of its ends.

Guiding Concept: A Quest for Excellence

When we think of excellence, we think of quality. Excellence goes beyond quality and sets limits to it—an excess of quality is not excellent because it lacks value. Excellence is a more comprehensive concept, which includes the technical quality of our work, but also the quality of our people and of their life in the organization. It implies high technical standards.

It requires that we maintain high level relations with our clients, associates and suppliers and among ourselves.

It means professionalism in the way we manage our employees and our resources.

It demands that we make our company a better company and that we contribute to the societies where we live.

Excellence is a moving target. If we ever think we have attained it that will be the moment when it will have been lost. Actually, rather than speaking of excellence we should talk about search, quest, or pursuit. What this means is that we have to work for it, or better yet, to be alert and responsive at all times. This pursuit is an attitude, a state of mind. Fortunately it is contagious and self-reinforcing, so it is a matter of getting started.

Part IV

SOCIAL AND ENVIRONMENTAL RESPONSIBILITY

We cannot devise, within the traditional modern attitude to reality, a system that will eliminate all the disastrous consequences of previous systems. . . . In a world of global civilization, only those who are looking for a technical trick to save that civilization need feel despair. But those who believe, in all modesty, in the mysterious power of their own human Being, which mediates between them and the mysterious power of the world's Being, have no reason to despair at all.

VACLAV HAVEL

Business is the only mechanism on the planet today powerful enough to produce the changes necessary to reverse global environmental and social degradation.

PAUL HAWKEN

The question is not what do we do about the environmental crisis but rather what is the earth doing about us?

THEODORE ROSZAK

Business has become, in the last century, the most powerful institution on the planet. The dominant institution in any society needs to take responsibility for the whole. Every decision that is made, every action taken has to be viewed in the light of, in the context of, that kind of responsibility.

WILLIS HARMAN

INTRODUCTION

How can business take this responsibility? How can the most powerful institution turn around the negative effects by which it has gained its power?

The new theories and findings of science provide some answer to these questions. They tell us that we are in a world that has wholeness and connection between parts—to the point that, technically speaking, it doesn't really have any parts, only an extended ecosystem. But on the surface this system is highly complex and chaotic. It is not linear or step by step. It operates creatively in ways that are understood only on reflection, and even then only vaguely and with uncertainty.

It is not surprising then that the components of new paradigm business are linked in seemingly strange ways also. In the context of this turbulent world, new forms of business and leadership develop. Then, individual businesses make progress toward implementing these new forms until they reach a threshold, and perhaps that form of business will become the accepted one for a period of time. This should lead to personal development for those working in the organizations to the point that the goal and result of the business will include service to the surrounding community and concern for the environment. This means that the social and environmental responsibility of business will blossom into the contribution of business to the well-being of the world, which is beset with the problems of constant change. Thus we come full circle from the old context, to the new forms, to their implementation, to their contribution in the new context.

Of course, this cycle is going on at many levels and in every part of the process. The idea from the new physics of the holographic universe indicates that every part has the whole embedded in it. We begin to see that the beliefs and experiences of the various spiritual traditions match the findings of the new science. Even in the discipline of economics (sometimes called the dismal science), the combination of ancient spiritual traditions and modern science has been remarkable and contributed to the change in business.

So when we begin to explore the social and environmental responsibility of business, we must realize that this aspect is not separate from the other parts of the paradigm change that is occurring in individuals, business organizations, and the world. Like Russian dolls contained inside each other or, more appropriately, like the parts of a hologram, they are not just related to one another; they actually are within each other and the whole entirely.

The slogan "Think Globally, Act Locally" is an apt one for our times. It reminds us that as we make changes in our individual lives, in our working groups, and in our organizations, we can, if we keep the global imperatives in mind, make a change in the larger world and the way it operates also.

One of the best conceptualizations of this process at the organizational level has been developed by Terry Mollner. He describes the current shift as one from the "Material Age" with its assumption of two or moreness, to the "Relationship Age" with its assumption of oneness and interconnection of an infinite number of parts that interact in a cooperative way with each other. According to Mollner, the Material Age starts at the lowest level of human maturity, such as war, and exists through the next-higher levels of competition and enlightened self-interest. Even the latter, however, is still part of the Material Age, because it assumes separate entities that compete rather than cooperate.

We are operating more in line with the Relationship Age, says Mollner, when we practice self-conscious cooperation. Beyond that is what he calls the highest level of human maturity, self-conscious consensus or harmony. In this relationship mode of behavior we self-consciously make every decision and choice in line with what is simultaneously good for us, good for the organization and good for the social and physical environment. We will want to behave in this way if we are to carry out business's true responsibility for the whole.

Movement toward this type of life is made on the basis of strong values. Reflecting in *Forbes* on Americans' false sense that capitalism won the war over communism, Ralph H. Nelson writes: "So capitalism needs new moral arguments and spiritual dimensions if it is to endure; efficiency is no longer defense enough. If no such spiritual endorsement is forthcoming, capitalism could end up winning the war with communism, but losing the peace."

Brenton R. Schendler, in *Fortune*, attacks the business value of individualism without a corresponding value of community and concern for the whole. He asks: "Is this, then, where our vaunted individualism has brought us? To seek shelter in isolated lives, surrounded only by those who share our immediate personal, cultural, and economic interests, while the larger society atrophies? What about our other ideals, such as concern for the community, religious and ethnic tolerance, equality before the law, thrift, and respect for hard work? Have they become irrelevant? Might we not strike a new balance in the Nineties, one that could redirect toward bettering our society more of the selfish energy that spurs people to work, entrepreneurs to create, yuppies to acquire, and corporations to streamline?"

The purpose of this section is to begin to attempt to answer such difficult questions. Our search is to determine not how business can solve each of the problems that beset our planet, but rather to determine which systematic view can allow us to take responsibility for the whole, so that every one of our thoughts, decisions, and acts is done in harmony with that larger context.

19

CAPITALISM AT ITS BEST

by Marjorie Kelly

Is capitalism inherently evil? Is it doomed to corrupt and exploit the earth's population and environment until there's nothing left?

With new paradigm business practices increasing in our corporations, some attitudes and practices are changing. Some American companies have exhibited a 180-degree shift in environmental policies, worker participation, and other aspects of social responsibility.

As a result, old-fashioned stereotypes of capitalism are falling away. In the following essay, Marjorie Kelly, the editor of Business Ethics *magazine, argues that it's time to realize that despite conventional prejudice, capitalism is in fact becoming a primary tool for social and political change.*

To my mind, the item was front-page news of the fundamental sort, worthy of a weighty editorial, but *The New York Times* had tucked it away in the business section, and if my read-through hadn't been more leisurely than usual that morning I would have missed it entirely. (Only the very idle or the very bored read pieces titled, "Electricity Price Plan Is Backed.") Yet here was news of a New York state court ruling that utilities could set electricity prices based on *power saved,* rather than on power used. Instead of coupling profits to rising sales, the new rate system couples profits to reduced demand. In a strategy known as "demand side management," utilities subsidize efficiency improvements for customers, and recover the expense through electric charges. As a brief filed on behalf of the National Audubon Society stated, "We cannot expect power companies to take conservation seriously unless there is something in it for them."

I read the piece several times through, fascinated, for here was tangible evidence of a truth I have long believed: that the profit motive is not inherently wicked, but is rather a powerful engine that can be harnessed for virtually any purpose—including a socially responsible one.

In recent months, there has been a good deal of evidence of this truth—the most prominent being the speed with which business is gaining environmental awareness. I'm thinking, for example, of the recent special section on the environment in *Business Week*—a publication that serves as an unfailing barometer of mainstream business sentiment. In the magazine trade, special sections are known as pure advertising vehicles, covering safe and non-controversial subjects. And for *Business Week,* the mantle of non-controversy apparently extended to topics like "The Global Commons," zero toxic emissions, sustainable development, deforestation, CFC elimination, energy conservation, and alternative fuels. Everybody and their v.p. wanted into this section—which ran a surprising 107 pages—and featured CEOs of Monsanto and PG&E alongside the chairman of the Earth Island Institute. On the issue of business and the environment, the magazine concluded, "an abrupt about-face has begun."

I'll say.

And it's not the only about-face on social issues I've seen lately. South African divestment began as an issue of little concern to anyone beyond college age, but it ended up as front-page news in the *Wall Street Journal,* when the smattering of companies leaving South Africa became a stampede. Green products that once showed up only in health food stores are today the hottest concept—predicted to be in the '90s what "lite" products were in the '80s.

Even more dramatic is the change in the prospects for defense work. I have a friend who at one time was CEO of a defense company and was considered a peacenik in the industry, leading delegations to the Soviet Union and exploring ways to convert to peacetime production. My friend was considered on the fringe then, but it turns out to have been the leading edge. Able to see the handwriting on the wall before his more traditional colleagues, he sold his company in the nick of time—fetching twice what he could have gotten had he waited even six months.

It seems to be occurring with greater frequency and speed today, that ideas which begin on the periphery move into the mainstream. Companies that once looked like mavericks, with their socially responsible practices, turn out to have been the harbingers of things to come.

Herman Miller was virtually alone when it instituted worker participation and teams in the 1950s, but today *Fortune* calls self-managed teams "*the* productivity breakthrough of the 1990s." Even the conservative National Association of Manufacturers has endorsed employee involvement in decision-making, calling it "a revolution that will transform the way work is organized."

When I read the business press for signs of change, it's unmistakable to me that something new is stirring. The evidence is overwhelming: A more socially responsible way of doing business is taking shape.

But not everyone sees it that way. In his new book, *Making Peace With the Planet,* Barry Commoner flatly declares that capitalism can create nothing but environmental degradation. Profits, he writes, are inherently in conflict with the environment. In downtown Minneapolis last week, I picked up a free copy of *New Unionist,* which tells me that "corporations can succeed in the competitive capitalist market only by exploiting the Earth." Even *Management Review* recently headlined an article, "Is Business Ethics Really an Oxymoron?" If I had a dime for every time I had been asked that question, I could retire today a wealthy woman.

Sometimes I want to stand on my chair and shout, Can't you *see* it? Can't you see that business is changing? The signs to me are as obvious as the stars in the sky—yet I could cite evidence all day long, and someone like Barry Commoner would never see what I see. Our difference lies deeper than rational discourse. It's a difference at the level of paradigm—a level that has less to do with assembling facts than with having a worldview in which those facts make sense.

Someone who believes capitalism is inherently evil can no more "see" socially responsible business, than the American settlers could "see" the wisdom of Native Americans, when they assumed them to be savages. But times change. Truths that we thought were solid and unchanging parts of reality turn out to be images we carried in our heads, and those images from time to time need updating.

The notion of capitalism as evil is firmly rooted in our collective mind-set, yet it is an image increasingly at odds with reality. We haven't updated our image of business since the days of the Robber Barons, and it's time we did so.

We may cling to the notion that nice guys finish last and the ruthless get ahead, but today the reverse seems to be true. When Frank Lorenzo played hardball with the unions, he ended up driving Greyhound into Chapter 11. In the 1990s, you don't have to be a saint or a genius to figure out that it doesn't pay to alienate workers and turn them into enemies.

And you don't have to be a prophet to see that social responsibility is more and more a requirement of good business. If the about-face on the environment weren't evidence enough, if the rise of worker participation weren't evidence enough, there is the wave of legislation washing over us in this post–Reagan era. In the last few months alone, we've seen bills passed or close to passing that update the Civil Rights Act, mandate new clean air requirements, expand the employment rights of the disabled, and contemplate everything from better food labeling to bans on cigarette machines.

The paragons of business today are companies like IBM with its no-layoff policy, Johnson & Johnson with its effective handling of the Tylenol incident, Herman Miller with its employee involvement. They're the ones who show up on *Fortune*'s list of the Ten Most Admired Companies—where environmental and social responsibility is one of the key criteria.

A new paradigm clearly is emerging, and it is time we recognize it. The old view of business as a jungle, where only the vicious survive, is giving way to a new view of business as a community affair, where only the responsible get ahead.

That's not to say business is wholly transformed and now 100 percent pure. But it does mean that our picture of what constitutes good business has matured. There's a new way of looking at capitalism: not as preying upon society, but as serving society. It's an image, you might say, of capitalism at its best.

EXEMPLAR:
National Payments Network

Lou Krouse was a middle manager at a telephone company who had an idea about how he could help the poor and make money too. On the day his boss was congratulating him on his twenty-fifth anniversary at the company and saying that he was looking forward to another twenty-five years with Lou, Krouse said, "No. I won't be back tomorrow." He had an idea.

He knew that approximately 20 percent of American households have no bank account, so they can't write checks. In order to pay their utility bills, for instance, they have to take time to go to the company office and pay in person. Or they have to purchase money orders at a dollar and a half apiece.

Krouse planned to place a system of electronic machines in stores. His company would pay the stores a fee to install the machines, and the stores would have the prospect of fifteen hundred extra customers coming in to pay bills each month and also purchasing other goods there. Utilities would pay Krouse a fee because they would get a payment record in twenty-four hours and the actual payment itself within two days. Most importantly, people without bank accounts would be able to pay their bills near their homes with cash and without any extra expense.

That was Krouse's idea. But he had to travel the country for months to secure capital to get the company started. Finally, a bank gave him the support and hooked his terminals to their electronic fund network—all for a half stake in the business. At that point Krouse was about one month from personal bankruptcy. In under three years, however, National Payments Network had revenues of about twenty-six million dollars a year and three and a half million customers in nineteen states.

Krouse says that there are as many opportunities for businesses like this as there are social problems, and that it truly is possible to do well by doing good.

20

MICHAEL NOVAK:
THE THEOLOGIAN
OF CAPITALISM

by Marjorie Kelly

Michael Novak has set out to articulate a theology of capitalism, a spiritual framework that can help society understand and judge modern corporate activity.

"No system has so revolutionized ordinary expectations of human life— lengthened the life span, made the elimination of poverty and famine thinkable, enlarged the range of human choice—as democratic capitalism," he says. Central to Novak's thinking is the concept that capitalism cannot be considered in isolation, but only as a part of the cultural and governmental system in which it is based. He says of capitalism what Churchill said of democracy—a terrible form of government except for the alternative.

A former socialist and a Catholic who once studied for the priesthood, Novak has authored many books, including The Spirit of Democratic Capitalism *and* A Theology for Radical Politics. *He holds a chair in religion and public policy at the American Enterprise Institute.*

Marjorie Kelly: *How is it that you began working on a theology of the corporation? It's a fairly radical idea.*

Michael Novak: Not for a Catholic, because the Catholic vision is that religion permeates everything, as a yeast does dough. Everywhere we act, grace is also present. All worldly occupations are a form of worship. Coming from this background, it struck me as odd that one of the greatest inventions of modern times, the corporation, has received so little attention from theologians.

The corporation is an image of something in the nature of human beings. As Aristotle said, we're social animals. There's very little we can provide only for ourselves. Even the alphabet, even our words, are a social achievement. So in a way, our thoughts are social as much as they're personal.

Most objections to capitalism are aimed at the corporation, primarily the large corporation. It's intriguing to look at the large corporation and find criteria for judging it in a theological way. What would a good corporation, fulfilling all its possibilities, look like from a theological point of view?

And what is your vision of the ideal corporation?

That can't be said in a sentence. But you might begin by saying a good corporation pays special attention to its human capital, and nourishes the skills of its whole personnel—because a lot of joy comes from doing well what we do. It should also attend to the quality of intercommunication. There's nothing worse than working in a group riven by animosities and feuds and mistrust. Human beings are only imperfect, so you never get a full family sense in a corporation, but it should approach that ideal. It should be a place where people like to meet, where they get some comfort in their sorrows and help in their necessities.

At many places in your writing, you make the point that the capitalist system is in fact based on a deep morality, a very commonplace morality.

It's very realistic. Our framers knew there's no use building a new republic for saints. There are too few saints to fill a republic, and the ones there are, are impossible to live with.

They intended to build a new republic that would last—*Novus Ordo Seclorum*, they put on the seal of the United States, meaning, the new order of the ages. Most republics in history had dissolved within a single generation, so they took up building a republic as a challenge.

We're building, Madison wrote, a republic for which we found no model, no precedent on the face of the earth. For it to last through the ages, it had to be built for human beings as we are. Women and men are not angels. If we were angels, government would not be necessary. But we're not. You've got to build a government that will work with sinful people.

You seem to have a conception of America as having a unique mission, almost a city on the hill for the rest of the world.

Well, I'm a little uneasy with city on the hill because that was the sanctimonious strain in American politics. I liked the other side, the ones who said if we're going to make a republic for the ages, we'd better make a city in the valley where people are. It's the city in a valley I like best. Which by the way from an airplane at night is just as beautiful. Most cities actually do sit in valleys.

So by city in a valley you mean . . .

Down where human beings are, with all our flaws.

So if we live in a republic designed for sinners, I'm curious what you think are the sins of corporations today. You've written that the corporation makes the riches of creation available to the mass market, and this is the standard by which its deeds and misdeeds should be judged. By that standard, what are the corporation's misdeeds?

I doubt there is a human sin that a corporation has not committed somewhere, because corporations are only associations of human beings. And human beings do bad things. Take the idea about handing on the riches of creation to human beings everywhere—to an extent, corporations have done this. Corporations are the main instrument by which a commercial republic brings goods and services to the entire people. And surely never in history have so many goods and services been so widely distributed. But where corporations carelessly pollute, or make shoddy products, or in other ways disfigure creation, they are not fulfilling their mission. People feel it and say so. I would guess every corporation has its sins.

So you feel corporations need government regulations?

Yes, the concept of democratic capitalism means you must have a firm political system. In fact, businesses will be the first to ask for fair rules and a level playing field, lest their competitors cheat and destroy the reputation of the industry. They're all against regulation, except they want all their competitors regulated.

And what is the proper role of the corporation in reducing poverty?

Well, as a society we can never attain equality of income. But we should try to make sure that people on the bottom have opportunities to move out, to live at certain levels of decency, and to find improvement from decade to decade. Everybody should feel they're moving up.

What I would urge on corporations is that the more they attend to such things and become creative agencies in helping things move along, the less the state will have to do. It's in the interest of the corporation to help provide for the poor in its area, because the more we do that privately, one human being to another, the less we are forced to turn to a large bureaucracy to do it, the more likely it will be a success.

Why is it, Michael, that executives are so reluctant to discuss things like ethics and values in the boardroom? Why are they seen as inappropriate topics?

I think of it this way. In the Victorian period, people in polite company—in the equivalent of a cocktail party—wouldn't dare dream of discussing sex, but they would talk freely about prayer and meditation and sermons they had heard. Today the inhibitions are reversed. You can say almost anything about sex, and people will just laugh. But if you begin to talk about prayer or meditation, there's a distinct discomfort. Talking about ethics makes a lot of people squirm, not because they're unethical, but because they think that's rather a private matter.

Don't you think it has something to do, also, with this notion that corporations are entirely about profit, and questions of human values are outside that?

Some businessmen have been taught that. They feel they should always sound hard-nosed, stick to profit and loss. I remember a journalist telling me about his interview with a man who was closing a plant in Gary, Indiana. And throughout the interview, the businessman kept a tight upper lip and focused on financial reasoning, here's why we have to do it.

When the two of them later went down and had a beer, the guy cried. He said, you know, I've lived in this community thirty years, I know the manager, I've had him to my house. I know the men. Where will they go for work? But when he was playing businessman, he didn't feel emotion was correct for him. Like a soldier doesn't discuss his fears.

I think that's beginning to change. I certainly hope that it is.

Oh, it is, but I'm just saying, it's the running start with which we come onto these problems. One reason is that in a country as religiously divided as this, we made an implicit contract years ago not to argue about religion and values publicly. But we're discovering you cannot make a good business system move without thinking about its human implications, its implications for the environment, for families. To be a good businessman these days means thinking about the ethical and the political dimensions, as well as the economic.

That's central to your view, isn't it, trying to promote more thoughtful values in business?

Yes, because only good and creative things survive. What is vice? Vice is a form of behavior that kills. I think of it like a moth eating at good wool. Vice is a breakdown, a gap, where something good and strong and living should be. All vices corrode those involved with them. A greedy corporation is a corporation on the way to its death. It will infuriate and make suspicious everyone it deals with, and it will attract to itself great hatred.

Your passion about corporate matters, I'm wondering if that springs from experience. Have you ever worked for a corporation?

No, I haven't. In fact I studied for the priesthood for many years, but I found it wasn't my calling. I also didn't think I'd live well a life of celibacy. So I left.

In your work now, do you feel a sense of calling?

Only in the remote sense that I think every human being has a calling. I don't feel it like a mission in the sense that there's something I must do before I die. The sower is not the reaper. I can only do what I think needs doing and use the talents that I have.

And what you think needs doing is to ground capitalism in its proper theological framework.

That's part of it. I'm interested in the religious quest, the moral quest in everything. I think it's one of the most neglected topics of our time. We're more illiterate about religion than any other matter in our lives. Our training in religion is primitive compared to our training in statistics, literature, or history.

But I've explored a lot of things. I've written a book on sports, which is one of my very favorite books. I've written another book called *The Experience of Nothingness*, about the other side of liberty— meaning that when you have full liberty over your life, what you will do, who you will become, you occasionally become terrified. You may not like the way you have been living, but looking at other possible scenarios, you don't like those either. A great wave of nothingness floods over you, which is a kind of formlessness. You don't know what kind of form to put into your life, and when you lack form, it's hard to act.

The first sign of this is that people begin to sleep a great deal. It affects college sophomores distinctly; they stay in bed a lot because they don't know what they want to major in and why they're doing what they're doing. Sleep is the best retreat, a kind of image of death.

Have you had that experience of nothingness and formlessness in your own life?

Oh often, often. I think it's a daily companion of people aware of their liberty. So often I'll face a number of options, and I'll be so unsure of what to do that I can for a few moments get overwhelmed. And actually, that's good. It's good to taste the depths of your own liberty and quietly draw it in—to realize that what you are about to do is take responsibility for creating something. It feels like creating out of nothing. I suppose you must have felt that in creating a new magazine. I think it's a common experience for the world of business, as it is in the world of the arts.

It's curious to me that you talk about an experience of nothingness in your own life, yet your writing is suffused with a great optimism and what seems to me a great faith that all is in good order, that we have in fact constructed a good society and we're living well in it and there's room to advance. I wouldn't have thought of you as a person who often experienced nothingness.

But you see my optimism is based on a very profound pessimism. It's because of being Slavic and from Eastern Europe, where nothing good has happened in a thousand years. I'm accustomed to how bleak life can be. In fact, I'm even uncomfortable when things are looking good. I feel more in tune with reality when things are going badly, otherwise I think I'm being deceived.

Some people are shocked that there is vice in the world. I am constantly amazed by how good people are, when they don't have to be. I saw a mother the other day, talking ever so gently to her son, who was two or three, and patiently teaching him the letters in a book. And I just thought, what patience, what joy in that patience. What a wonderful thing. Of course, it's just ordinary mother love, but she could be batting the kid around, telling him to be quiet, telling him to be still.

I wrote a book on crime and character. Again the problem is not why is there crime; the amazing thing is there is so relatively little of it. It's amazing that everybody isn't just criminal, getting what they want, being like babies and grabbing, being violent. Most people aren't. I think that's quite astonishing.

I've been wanting to tell you, Michael, when I was coming up with the idea for Business Ethics, *I stumbled across one of your pamphlets in the library, "Toward a Theology of the Corporation." I was stunned. Really, I must have read it four or five times. I had never heard anyone say the things that you say. I still don't.*

It's a relatively new field, the interaction of theology and economics. When I was beginning to write *The Spirit of Democratic Capitalism,* I was amazed to find that there are whole rooms of books on the questions of theology and politics, or theology in marriage, but on economics, you could fit on one shelf the major books and articles in English. Economics itself is relatively new, but theological reflection on it is even newer.

Part of the reason may go back to this antagonism toward capitalism. The word itself is really pejorative, negative. Where does that come from?

There are so many sources. In practically every language and every religious tradition, there is an anti-commercial attitude, finding commerce vulgar, materialistic, earthy.

But it makes sense. In an ancient world, wealth was a zero-sum game, and it seemed obvious that if someone gained, they had to take from someone else. How did Rome become wealthy? It conquered the

Barbarians. How did the Barbarians become wealthy? They sacked Rome and took the booty home.

And so your theory is this changed when capitalism came onto the scene, which began using intelligence to create greater abundance.

Adam Smith was the first person in history to ask the fruitful question, What is the cause of the wealth of nations? And in a single word, his answer is wit—that is, human discovery or invention. Calling the system by a name derived from the word *caput*, head, is exactly right. The cause of wealth is the head.

Adam Smith was writing two hundred years ago, but still today we have an active, vehement anger toward capitalism.

That's not quite true. Most of the world's poor flock to capitalist centers. They vote with their feet. The poor are the world's greatest capitalists. It's the only system that gives them opportunity, it does not oppress them.

You yourself are a former socialist. How did you come to make the switch?

If you were brought up with a good liberal arts education, as I was, you never read a poem or a play or a novel that was in favor of capitalism. From Blake's dark satanic mills to the novels of Dickens, to the protest novels of the 1920s, you were taught to think that capitalism was faintly evil.

But beginning in the 1970s, I couldn't help noticing that most of the programs of big government that I was in favor of weren't working very well. I looked around the world—I was forty at that point—and thought I should decide if I was a socialist or not. And I found there wasn't a single socialist country I wanted the United States to become more like. It occurred to me, maybe socialism is a beautiful idea and we just haven't got the hang of it yet. But if that's true of socialism, then maybe it's also true of capitalism. And finally, I got to thinking if capitalism is so bad why did my grandparents, all four of them in desperate poverty, come here? And why has our family flourished? I realized, for poor people the path is always toward the capitalist countries. The United States has been the first country in the world to prove that people do not stay poor forever.

So many people think of capitalism as mechanistic, a kind of daily grind, but they underestimate the sheer romance of business. It's much like the arts, really. There's the way a businessman may perceive opportunities long before anybody else does, and pursue them at great risk. Friends are saying you'll lose your shirt—and often he is the only one who believes in it. This is very much like the artist. Seeing a possibility of something that can be created, which others don't see.

And like art, sometimes it doesn't work, or doesn't come out as beautifully as you would have liked.

Other people focus so much on what's wrong with business, you focus on what's right.

You see, my approach is to sketch out the ideals of an enterprise, because that's more effective than setting up do's and don'ts. If we know the ideal, we can see clearly where we're falling short of it. But if you begin by stressing the negatives, you somehow engender the idea that, well, if we don't do those things we're OK. Moral action comes to be something like avoiding stepping on the cracks in the sidewalk. It's more than that. Moral living is essentially a creative enterprise.

There's the old legend of a bet between the sun and the wind about who could get a man on a horse to take his cloak off. The wind blew and blew, and the more fiercely it tried to blow the cloak off, the more the man grabbed it close. And then the sun came out and just smiled. And the more it smiled, the warmer it got, and pretty soon the man took his cloak off. It shows there are two ways to get someone to change.

One is by tugging, forcing. And the other is . . .

By creating an environment that encourages change.

21

THE FIVE STAGES OF CORPORATE MORAL DEVELOPMENT

by Linda Starke

Psychologists have been analyzing and evaluating the moral development of children for many years, having reached a consensus on age-appropriate steps from infancy to adulthood. But what about businesses?

The following article asks the question: Can companies have developmental ethical attitudes that are demonstrated both in their relationships to employees in the workplace and to customers and society at large?

Yes. Corporations can range in moral behavior from devilish to saintly, according to Eric Reidenbach of the University of Southern Mississippi and Donald Robin of Louisiana Tech. And they name some names, but only those approaching the side of the angels.

Linda Starke is a free-lance writer and educator based in Washington, D.C., specializing in environmental issues. She is the author of the book Signs of Hope: Working Toward Our Common Future.

Is there such a beast as an ethical U.S. corporation? Not at the moment, say Eric Reidenbach and Donald Robin, developers of a new model of corporate moral development. While they classify a growing number of organizations in the fourth stage, which they term "emergent ethical," they have found none in the fifth and highest stage, termed "ethical."

Reidenbach, from the University of Southern Mississippi, and Robin, from Louisiana Tech, were inspired by earlier theories of individual moral development to create a comparable corporate model. As with Elisabeth Kübler-Ross's five stages of grief, all stages are not necessarily reached, progression is by no means linear, and one can certainly slip from one stage back to an earlier one. The stages:

Stage One: The Amoral Corporation—Pursues winning at any cost; views employees merely as economic units of production.

Companies at this stage are often forced out of operation, because they violate societal values and rules. An example is Film Recovery Systems of Illinois, which extracted silver from old x-ray film through a process using cyanide—until the company was closed down in 1983, after the death of a worker from cyanide toxicity.

Stage Two: The Legalistic Corporation—Concerned with the letter of the law, but not its spirit; adopts codes of conduct that read like products of legal departments (which they are). Reidenbach and Robin identify this stage as the most common for corporations in the U.S. today. One example is the attitude of Ford in the Pinto case of 1973.

Stage Three: The Responsive Corporation—Interested in being a responsible corporate citizen, but primarily because it is expedient, not because it's right; has codes of conduct that begin to look more like codes of ethics.

Outside events often give companies a hard shove into the responsive stage. One example is Procter & Gamble's reaction to a 1980 government report about toxic shock syndrome. Without any indication their own tampon products were implicated, management pulled Rely off the market, bought back all unused products, and financed an educational campaign. An understanding that ethical decisions can be in the company's long-term economic interest even if they involve an immediate financial loss is the hallmark of the responsive corporation.

Stage Four: The Emergent Ethical Corporation—Recognizes the existence of a social contract between business and society, and seeks to instill that attitude throughout the corporation. Johnson & Johnson is an excellent example here, both for a corporate credo that balances ethical concerns and profitability, and for the company's handling of the Tylenol tampering situation—when the company did a massive national recall of Tylenol following local cases of poisoning.

Stage Five: The Ethical Corporation—Balances profits and ethics so completely that employees are rewarded for walking away from a compromising action; includes ethical issues in training; has mentors to give moral guidance to new employees. This idealized corporation, of which Reidenbach and Robin can find no examples, starts out with a founding moral stance that permeates the culture.

Perhaps the researchers can find no such beasts because they are looking in the wrong place. A growing number of entrepreneurial companies put social responsibility at the very center of their operations. The place to look may be among corporations like Ben & Jerry's, The Body Shop, or Smith & Hawken. Firms like these may have started out at stage five and never looked back.

22

THE CORPORATION AS A
JUST SOCIETY

by David W. Ewing

Corporations today are like governments or self-contained city states. Within them the issue of due process for internal dispute frequently emerges, particularly when employees require some mechanism for challenging managerial power.

Concerned that their governance be fair, more and more corporations are creating internal systems of justice. Only a minority of corporations have due process mechanisms so far, but their number is growing by leaps and bounds.

In the following essay, we see how corporate due process is approached at several major companies, including Federal Express, IBM, and Northrop. Panels, appeal boards, grievance committees, judges who are managers or elected from the ranks—a variety of systems and techniques are being applied depending on disparate needs of specific corporate cultures. Overall decisions average 70% against management. And it's predicted that this process is destined to become familiar on the corporate scene in the years ahead.

David W. Ewing is the former managing editor of the Harvard Business Review. *He is a consultant to numerous corporations on corporate justice, just dismissal, and employee rights. He is also the author of numerous articles and books, including* Do It My Way or You're Fired, Long Range Planning for Management, *and* Freedom Inside the Organization.

At too many companies today, untold thousands of employees silently endure shame and humiliation because they are afraid to challenge an unfair or neurotic supervisor, for fear of losing their livelihood. When a subordinate can go to an ombudsman or hearing panel and have an unjust decision overturned, it is a bracing tonic—not only for that employee, but for the morale of the entire system.

Today, a growing number of leading-edge companies recognize that justice in any large organization requires some mechanism for challenging managerial power. Companies like Federal Express, IBM, and

Northrop have created grievance procedures that ensure internal "due process," which can be defined as the fair, reasonable, and expeditious treatment of those who challenge the system.

Although corporate due process is a far more primitive set of standards than due process of law, it springs from the same notion of equity. In effect, the corporation says that no employee should be deprived of his or her job and well-being in the company without a fair hearing.

Corporate due process can take many forms. It might be a panel, board, or committee that considers both sides of a complaint and renders a decision. Or it might take the form of objective investigators who look into both sides of a dispute and resolve it. The form can be tailored to the style of your organization.

You can choose an approach that is low-profile and informal, or you can choose a two-tier hearing system, as at Federal Express, which is high-profile and carefully structured. You can have judges who are picked on a case-by-case basis, as at General Electric's Columbia, Maryland, plant, or who serve indefinite terms of office, as at John Hancock. You can have judges who are managers, as at Honeywell, or who are elected from the employee-at-large ranks, as at Donnelly. You can have the group's decisions be final, as at SmithKline Beecham, or you can cast the group in an advisory role, as at Control Data. Corporate due process works so well because its form is not cast in iron but can be adapted to the needs of each organization.

One of the greatest benefits of corporate due process procedures like these is that they make other, more adversarial approaches unnecessary. Due process won't eliminate lawsuits entirely, but it will cut off many before they start. In my own research, when I compared companies with and without due process, I found the former had fewer lawsuits by a factor of eleven to one.

Another key benefit is greater compliance with company policies. Ann Liebowitz, senior legal counsel for Polaroid, says that when line supervisors know their decision may be subject to open review, it has "an astonishingly strong tendency to keep them honest and prevent abuse of discretion." Grievance procedures also put pressure on managers to deal constructively with complaints. As one department head said, "You go before a bunch of managers to defend what you did. Hey, who needs that? It's embarrassing. So you try your damnedest to make a hearing unnecessary. You try to work out that guy's complaint before he takes it any further."

Corporate due process is that which is due a complaining employee in light of contemporary standards of fairness—and it includes the right to present evidence and rebut charges in a fair and impartial process, the right to be represented by another employee of the complainer's choice (though rarely an attorney), the right to confidentiality, and freedom from retaliation.

Codes of conduct are not enough, for ethical conduct cannot be legislated by management—it must be forged in the resolution of conflict over actual problems. Due process succeeds where a guidebook may fail, because it allows situations that cannot be anticipated to become part of the web of standards by which behavior is governed.

Some might ask whether better trained managers could make such systems unnecessary. The answer is no, because employees today have come to see justice as a *procedural* as well as a substantive matter. They believe justice can only be accomplished when both parties to a dispute have a voice in the resolution and agree on the outcome, or let a neutral party decide. This is another aspect of the rising trend toward participative management.

Representative of the many systems in place at companies today are those at Federal Express, IBM, and Northrop. Each has found due process an integral part of good employee relations, and each has built a process that fits the unique character of its corporate culture. These three systems might be considered among the best to be found anywhere.

GUARANTEED FAIR TREATMENT AT FEDERAL EXPRESS

Management at Federal Express supports its Guaranteed Fair Treatment Procedure (GFTP) in every way it can—with money, with time, with communication, with constant monitoring. Perhaps the most striking show of top management support comes from CEO Frederick W. Smith, who sits on the Appeals Board (one of two adjudicating groups) almost every Tuesday, where meetings sometimes last up to a full day. Board members say Smith has the best attendance record of anyone in the group.

Executives believe that GFTP, used by nineteen employees per thousand in 1986, has contributed to a higher and more uniform quality of management at Federal Express, and has given top executives a deepdown look at how policies are working and what changes might be useful.

The first three steps of the procedure involve appeals to higher levels within a division, and about half of all complaints are resolved there. What makes the system unique are the two higher levels of appeal: the five-member Board of Review (with three members who are peers to the complainant); and the Appeals Board, which is the "supreme court" of the company and is composed of the CEO and other top executives.

About half of all cases involve terminations, and a smaller proportion involve allegations of unfair treatment by a superior or other complaints. Hourly employees and lower-level managers file the majority of grievances, but from time to time a director will file a complaint, and one case was brought by a vice president.

The company makes no secret of the fact that managers' decisions are often reversed. This is considered normal and may not have a negative effect on the manager concerned. In 1986, the GFTP upheld management in only 61 percent of contested decisions.

THE OPEN DOOR AT IBM

IBM's Open Door procedure began with Thomas Watson, Sr., the company's first chairman, who made it his practice to visit plants and branch offices to talk to employees. "If you can't solve your problems with your manager, go to your plant or branch manager," he would say. "If you're still not satisfied, my door is always open." The open door became Watson's trademark, and many employees took him up on it.

As IBM's workforce expanded to more than 40,000 in the early 1950s, the procedure became more formalized, with Watson's administrative assistants—IBM calls them AAs—taking over. The AA would write up the complaint and initiate the investigation, with Watson making the final decision. This is the distinctive feature of IBM's due process system: the investigators work as advisors to the chairman.

The workforce today has grown to 400,000, but the Open Door policy is the same. Any employee is entitled to a review from any level of management, up to the chairman, if he or she isn't satisfied with a decision at a lower level. Dismissals, transfers, pay raises, performance evaluations—all these and many other issues are possible subjects for an Open Door complaint.

Let us assume an employee named Stone feels his manager has given him an unfair performance appraisal. Unable to change his manager's mind, he decides to "go Open Door," in IBM parlance. He contacts an

AA in the chairman's office, who assigns the case to the appropriate operating unit. There, an Open Door coordinator helps choose an executive to handle the investigation. That person serves as Stone's advocate during the investigation, and then renders a decision. The entire process is confidential, and no reference to Open Door is placed in any employee's file.

An important component of IBM's employee relations philosophy, the Open Door is brought to the attention of a new employee the first week on the job. High priority is given to the resolution of Open Door cases, and no excuse is acceptable for failure to cooperate in an investigation.

IBMers may be the first to say the Open Door doesn't always work perfectly, but its power and acceptance seem beyond question. "The Open Door has a mystique all its own," a onetime IBM employee told me. "It comes as close to being sacred as anything in the company."

FOUR DECADES OF DUE PROCESS AT NORTHROP

The only aerospace company listed in *The 100 Best Companies to Work For in America,* Northrop Corporation is regarded by industry analysts as the best-positioned defense contractor for the next decade. A great many factors are responsible for Northrop's success, and a key aspect is the company's enlightened personnel policies, including its grievance procedure.

The founder, John K. Northrop, liked to handle the day-to-day problems and complaints of employees, but as the company grew he found it increasingly difficult. To handle complaints more systematically—and to come closer to offering what a union plant could offer—the company developed a grievance procedure, with outside arbitration as the final step.

The idea was unprecedented and, to many people both inside and outside the company, appalling. Such well-known competitors as Douglas and Boeing did not share Northrop's convictions. It seemed madness, to let a neutral group in the company and possibly an outsider question a line manager's decision. But top management went along with the revolutionary proposal, and in 1946 the grievance system was established. Only one other company, Polaroid, has had a nonunion grievance system in place as long as Northrop.

The system is one of the key reasons Northrop remains the only firm among its aerospace competitors that is not unionized, which one expert calculates saves the company 25 percent in production costs.

And close to a quarter of Northrop's employees have been with the company for twenty years or more.

The first step in the process is informal hearings and negotiations with the employee relations staff. Employees are expected to go to the staff within five days of the event in question, and if the issue can't be resolved there, the next step is to file a written grievance with the administrative officer.

One example of a case heard by an administrative officer involves an employee named Martin, who had been given a final warning notice for threatening a co-worker. Because Martin had been given oral warnings for previous confrontations, and because he had a history of absenteeism, management felt strong action was in order. But after hearing the case, the administrative officer reduced the final notice to a second notice.

Had Martin been dissatisfied, he might have gone the next step, to the Management Appeals Committee, a group of three vice presidents. Cases at this level involve hearings that are likely to last all day, with witnesses being called and a decision often rendered on the spot. If the grievant is still dissatisfied, the case goes to outside arbitration.

How unbiased is the procedure? In 1984, not an atypical year, almost seven out of ten decisions went *against* management. Sixteen percent of the cases supported management, and an equal number resulted in compromise.

The benefits of due process systems like these are many, from improved employee morale and better execution of policy, to reduced litigation. But a more intangible benefit is the most intriguing: For decision-makers, due process makes people below the managerial level more real. I remember one day standing with an executive in his office, looking down on the street far below. "You know," he said to me, "as managers, our decisions don't always work out like we thought they would. But from up here, it's as hard to see the effects down the line as it is to make out the people on that street down there. Our complaint system brings those people to us full size."

EXEMPLAR:
Working Assets Funding Service

Laura Scher, CEO and co-founder of Working Assets Funding Service, represents an organization that is more important in socially responsible business than its own financial numbers would indicate. It is also exemplary in the way its internal operations mirror its external social focus.

When Scher joined Working Assets Money Fund, it was one of the first socially responsible money market funds in the U.S. and eventually became the largest. But her contribution was to develop the first donation-linked credit card. The Working Assets Visa card donates two dollars for the first use and five cents for every subsequent use to nonprofit organizations—with no extra charge to the user. Donations are made to nonprofit organizations working in four broad areas: peace, the environment, human rights, and economic justice. The appeal of the card was far beyond the company's original expectations. After five years of business, they had over one hundred and fifty thousand customers and the card was donating close to four hundred thousand dollars a year to a variety of organizations. In addition, Working Assets cardholders help in determining the organizations that receive the funds.

But this Working Assets innovation did more than just support nonprofits and give people a new way to make a contribution to the betterment of society. Their idea spread to other organizations sponsoring social causes to the point that there were approximately three thousand five hundred organizations offering donation-linked credit cards.

The same kind of growth seems to be happening to Working Assets' more recent donation-linked services: long-distance telephone calling (for which one percent of charges is donated) and travel service (2 percent of charges donated). Once again the growth was strong, and once again Working Assets was copied by other organizations, even large long-distance telephone service, thus spreading the social effect of their innovation.

It is all the more important that Working Assets' external social consciousness is mirrored by the way the company operates internally. The first time someone on the original small staff was pregnant, Scher developed a generous and compassionate parental leave policy rather than just a maternal one, taking into account the need for the male spouse to take a leave in the early months of a child's life. It even applies to adopted babies, and Scher says that it will be expanded to an elder-care policy if this becomes necessary.

The consistency in social responsibility extends to even small aspects around the office. At one point all the senior managers in the company were having frequent breakfast meetings. As Scher tells it: "So here we are, we are the highest paid people, and we're getting a free breakfast. And the lower paid people are going out and buying their own muffins. So whenever we have a breakfast meeting, we buy enough muffins so that everybody gets a muffin. It's sort of a trivial thing, but it's a way of treating people right."

This kind of care relates not only to the employees and customers of Working Assets but also to the stockholders (who get a somewhat lower financial return but a much greater social return than they get with other investments), and to the banks and telephone companies that provide service to the nonprofit organizations who receive funds. The consistency, empathy, compassion, and vision of Working Assets Funding Service drives a way of business that will thrive in the current times.

23

THE SHIFTING PARADIGM OF ENVIRONMENTAL MANAGEMENT

by Suzanne Gauntlett

Probably the most visible and dramatic shift from old to new paradigm thinking for corporations today has been in the area of environmental protection. Public outrage and governmental regulation have accelerated an increasing sense of social responsibility in the business community. Most policy has now changed from reactive (cleaning up after the fact) to preventive (preventing pollution from the beginning of the manufacturing process).

In the following article, the author first provides a brief history of the impact of environmentalism on business, then goes on to provide examples of companies that are taking progressive steps toward "proactive environmental management," including 3M and AT&T. Finally, they offer a comprehensive case history of the start-up of a new plastics manufacturing facility at a large petrochemical company. This long-term environmental management involved designing new technological systems, implementing new operational organizations, and overcoming technological and psychological resistance throughout.

Suzanne Gauntlett is President of the Gauntlett Group, a San Francisco Bay Area company specializing in organizational productivity and quality improvement.

Although slow and arduous in its process, a quantum leap is taking place in the relationship between corporations and the general public. We are witnessing a shift from an industry-driven market to a consumer-driven market. In the past, companies dictated to consumers what they should buy. Today, people are demanding that corporations behave in a socially responsible way and manufacture products that are environmentally sound.

Ethical values are becoming part of a company's track record. Social and environmental investors are now taking good corporate citizenship into account when evaluating a company's stock. Executives are starting to conduct business with a "win-win" mind-set, partnering with employees and customers to produce better-quality products that have a positive impact on people and the environment. Firms are slowly emerging from the old "we-them" paradigm.

A BRIEF HISTORY

One of the central causes of environmental degradation today lies in our intellectual heritage of the fifties, when Science and Technology were promoted as the all-powerful gods. In the postwar era, economic growth seemed limitless. Industrial development would provide wealth to everyone, science would end all diseases, and technology would ensure mankind's absolute control over nature.

It took us forty years to understand our mistake, and we are just now realizing what it will take to reverse the industrial and demographic processes that have caused ecological disasters on a planetary level.

The public became aware of environmental problems in the sixties when the "counterculture" created controversy about industrial practices: was "progress" worth polluting our communities and destroying our natural resources? Political activists and concerned citizens denounced companies for dumping chemicals into rivers and oceans, abandoning hazardous waste on landfills, spraying food crops with toxic pesticides, and organizing massive killings of whales and seals.

But the majority of the population did not truly understand the scope of the environmental devastation that was occurring. To many, the ecology movement was merely an extension of the peace-and-love movement. Biologist Rachel Carson's *Silent Spring*, first published in 1962 and a best-seller for many years, contributed to raising environmental consciousness. The book alerted the public about the harmful effects of herbicides and pesticides on human health. *Silent Spring* had a strong impact on people's perceptions, not only because of its content, but because of the author's scientific background. In the public's eye, the warning was to be taken seriously because it was blessed by the authority of science!

In 1970, the first Earthday was organized. The environmental movement was snowballing. Only two years later, in 1972, the United Nations put the environment on the global agenda by organizing the international "Human Environment Conference" in Stockholm.

Leaders from world governments convened to raise global consciousness about the escalating human impact on the earth's natural resources. But industries were lagging behind. They were alerted to the
severity of global pollution and were asked to adopt urgent conservation measures, but most corporations did not take the Stockholm alert
seriously and continued business as usual. This was mostly due to the
absence of governmental regulations and enforcement measures.

The Environmental Protection Agency (EPA) and the Occupational
Safety and Health Administration (OSHA) were created in 1970 to
respectively monitor the environmental performance of companies and
their attention to worker safety. It took these organizations several
years to develop their staff and structure adequately before they were
able to function as efficient enforcement agencies. By the end of the
seventies pressure from concerned citizens was such that the EPA was
starting to create strict regulations and fine companies that didn't
comply. Ongoing atrocities like Love Canal, Three Mile Island and
massive oil spills were continual reminders of the scope and severity of
environmental damage.

THE TURNING POINT

The major turning point occurred when eight thousand workers died
at a Union Carbide plant in Bhophal, India, in December 1984 from a
poisonous gas leak. This catastrophe shook industry at large and
especially the chemical companies. Bhophal became the symbol of
what could happen to any major multinational corporation dealing
with hazardous materials.

Another bridge was crossed when thirty-five nations signed an
international agreement at the Montreal conference for the Ozone
Layer Protection in 1987. They pledged to halve their production of
chlorofluorocarbons (CFCs) by 1998. CFCs are gases used mostly in
household and industrial refrigeration systems that are harmful to the
earth's protective ozone layer. The ozone layer protects us from being
burned by the sun. Satellites have photographed large holes above the
poles as well as above North America, and scientists have related these
to excessive evaporation of CFCs into the atmosphere. The "Montreal
Protocol" made a mark in history. It was the first public acknowledg-
ment that local pollution was affecting the planet as a whole.

Industry could no longer lag behind. At the end of the 1980s,
companies were finally starting to respond. In 1989, Dow Chemical
made environmental protection the central theme of its annual report.

Earthday 1990 saw the largest attendance ever and seemed to be the point at which critical mass had been attained. Understanding at last that a "green" image is good for business, companies were now advertising good corporate citizenship toward the environment.

THE QUANTUM LEAP

A quantum leap was achieved when executives in leading-edge companies started to think proactively: how can pollution be prevented at the beginning of the manufacturing process? How can harmful materials be eliminated? How can waste quantities be reduced? How can energy and water be conserved?

3M was the first company to apply the concept of preventing pollution rather than cleaning it up after the fact. It took an early start in 1975 with its "Pollution Prevention Pays" program. Two thousand five hundred changes were introduced in the manufacturing processes in order to eliminate toxic materials and bulk waste. As a result, the company saved 500 million dollars between 1975 and 1990.

By 1990 several companies were leading the effort toward "proactive environmental management," breaking loose from the race to catch up with new regulations. Being in compliance was becoming more and more expensive, and pioneering firms were researching how to prevent pollution so they could avoid regulations altogether. Like 3M, they were discovering that pollution prevention pays. Monsanto will have cut 70 percent of its toxic waste levels by 1992. Dow Chemical has already reduced its total emissions by 50 percent. Although these figures are impressive, it is important not to view them out of context. For example, Du Pont is phasing out its entire CFC manufacturing division, a 750-million-dollar business, but, at the same time, is the largest emitter of pollutants in the United States.

OVERCOMING THE OLD MIND-SET

Even at this stage, however, very few companies have demonstrated strong and unambiguous moral responsibility toward the environment. Part of the problem is that most firms still view environmental protection as a technical problem for engineers and regulation specialists. Compliance is merely a process to obtain permits. Environmental issues are not elevated to a strategic priority.

Xerox is one of the very few firms that gives environmental concerns priority over economic considerations and understand that conservation issues are not just a specialty for engineers and regulation experts. Conserving the environment is every employee's business. Xerox treated the environment responsibly long before regulations even existed. When its manufacturing facilities were growing in Webster, New York, in 1966, the company funded a state-of-the-art sewage system for the town. Now, in the 1990s, environmental responsibility has become a respected value in the company's culture and translates into the way people conduct their work at all levels of operations.

Looking at the human aspect of environmental management, Xerox created an Environmental Leadership Program that promotes employee responsibility and innovation. The program links all plant managers and all concerned employees world-wide through a computerized network, allowing them to exchange data and ideas for environmental improvements that are then institutionalized and spread out to the rest of the company.

The whole idea is to give plant managers accountability for their environmental health and safety performance and to encourage employees to conserve resources and eliminate waste before it is generated.

THE POWER OF CITIZEN ACTION

Since the sixties, environmentally aware consumers have demanded "green" products. The Procter and Gamble diaper scandal and the StarKist tuna boycott are two examples of citizen action that companies have responded to positively. In the eighties, Procter and Gamble marketed disposable diapers that were advertised as biodegradable. But, instead of decomposing and breaking down into fibers, used diapers were lying on top of landfills and staying perfectly intact.

When it was discovered that, given the current landfill situation, Procter and Gamble's diapers were not bio-degradable, the media denounced the company for false advertisement. In response to consumer demand, Procter and Gamble researchers have developed a composting method that decomposes used diapers into potting soil. They are presently working in collaboration with two communities that have created total waste management facilities to compost organic waste.

In 1989 consumers were boycotting StarKist because it was selling tuna caught with dolphins. Because schools of tuna usually travel with groups of dolphins, when the fisheries caught the tuna, they also caught the dolphins. They killed the dolphins and dumped them back into the sea. In addition, StarKist fishing boats used drift nets and pelagic nets, called "walls of death" by marine conservation groups. These nets kill not only tuna but all forms of marine life as they are laid over thousands of miles every night. The use of these nets is responsible for destroying millions of fish, whales, dolphins, seals, sea birds, and turtles every year.

In response to the consumer boycott, StarKist has promised to sell only "dolphin-free tuna" and, to prove its commitment, has signed a contract in 1991 with the marine conservation group Earthtrust. The group will monitor the company's fishing methods and will mark its "Flipper Seal of Approval" on every dolphin-free approved tuna can.

A NEW CORPORATE IDEOLOGY

Although profitability has been the most important force in driving businesses to adopt environmentally sound practices, another contributing factor has been slowly shaping a new corporate ideology.

Individuals who grew up in the sixties and seventies are now assuming leadership positions in businesses and corporations. These new leaders belong to the same generation that created the environmental movement. Former environmentalists have become directors of Environmental Health and Safety departments, and a few are chief executive officers. John Bryson, co-founder of the Natural Resources Defense Council, is CEO at Southern California Edison. William Ruckelshaus, former head of the EPA, is now CEO at Browning-Ferris, an enormous waste-management company.

This shift in corporate values is mirroring other shifts in the basic paradigms of management. In the seventies and eighties, businesses began adopting values of good corporate citizenship. Affirmative action efforts increased the work force diversity. Corporations provided funding for community-development projects. Management practices emphasizing employee involvement, shared decision-making, and self-management were developed and became commonplace. These activities, indicating stronger values around humanitarianism and moral responsibility, have set the stage for the "greening" of corporate culture.

Part of this paradigm shift is the new perception of global market forces: people in companies are starting to understand that local corporate activities have global implications. The opening of our home markets to international competition has been an eye-opener for many traditional American businessmen: the United States is part of the larger world! In the old context, we were accustomed to thinking that pollution could not affect us if it wasn't in our backyard. But when holes in the earth's protective ozone layer became apparent and the global warming effect could not be denied any longer, a new understanding was born.

SUSTAINABLE DEVELOPMENT

In April 1991 the first global movement for businesses and industries to adopt environmentally responsible practices was inaugurated. The World Industry Conference on Environmental Management (WICEM II) brought together senior executives from industry to review current environmental practices and develop strategies for protecting the earth's resources. Senior executives from companies such as Union Carbide, Du Pont, BASF, Browning-Ferris, Ciba-Geigy, and Kodak signed the Business Charter for Sustainable Development.

This Charter emphasizes that "environmental protection must be amongst the highest priorities of every business." Recognizing that economic growth and environmental preservation have, for too long, been regarded as separate agendas, the Charter proposes new rules of the game, based on a cooperative spirit between governments and industry; between corporations and their communities. A poll of the business leaders having signed the Charter found that they expected to spend 50 percent more money on pollution reduction in the next ten years and to cut their emissions by half during that time.

A new phrase, "sustainable development," is appearing with increasing frequency in discussions at all levels: international business forums, environmental-preservation conferences, and United Nations meetings. Everyone seems to agree that the idea is to form an alliance between economic development and natural-resource preservation, with the goal to meet the needs of the present population without compromising the ability of future generations to meet their own needs.

RESISTANCE TO CHANGE

Many companies are making significant improvements in their environmental management practices. The factors driving them, as we have seen, are increasing consumer preference for green products, changing organization values, greater responsiveness to community and global concerns, stronger internal leadership, et cetera. But, why aren't organizations moving more quickly toward developing environmentally responsible practices?

First, there is a general phenomenon of resistance to change. Individuals and corporations have developed successful methods for doing things. Over time, through experimentation and learning, we have created an effective way of producing a good or service. Introducing a new variable, in this case environmental responsibility, disrupts that well-established pattern and creates interferences in the process routine. People resist this disruption, and struggle to maintain the status quo.

There is also an element of risk in developing new processes and methods. The new methods may not be as quick, efficient, or profitable. It takes time to train people in the new methods, to develop new technology, and implement new procedures. During these transitions, there is reduction in efficiency and output. A company's competitors may seize the opportunity to capture market share or increase their profitability.

The second factor is the basic systems and structures that are found in most organizations. Managers and executives have traditionally been rewarded according to production and profitability criteria. Many organizations stress the importance of safety and environmental responsibility, but are not rewarding or punishing managers according to environmental performance. Environmental management, moreover, is not usually part of managers' or workers' job description. Instead, it is the responsibility of a separate department, called "environmental health and safety" and is the specialty of engineers and regulation specialists. Consequently there is not enough emphasis on training workers to monitor their own work and to be responsible for their work's impact on the environment. In the process of corporate evolution, the introduction of new operating values is usually perceived as a threat to the bottom line. For example, when unions started fighting for worker rights, management was convinced that the well-being of employees was in conflict with profits. One important turning point happened when leading companies adopted Total Quality Management in the 1980s. This eventually brought the realization that employee satisfaction actually contributed to productivity and to boosting profit margins.

The same thing has happened with environmental values. It is a total surprise to most companies that being "green" can turn out to be profitable. Although businesses are still struggling to become good corporate citizens and to reverse the manufacturing processes that are damaging our ecology, the environment has definitely achieved a spot on the priority list of corporate America.

The hardest battle to win remains preserving our natural resources in developing countries. The whole world is watching the massive destruction of our rain forests. The general public feels absolutely powerless to stop it. The large international aid organizations that have promoted industrial development in third world countries are just now realizing the need to take the environment into account. In the United States and Europe, we are recycling and eliminating toxic by-products from our industries. But, in the Southern Hemisphere and in Eastern Europe, hazardous waste is dumped everywhere without discrimination, forests are being logged, whole species of animals are destroyed forever.

Most often, our own companies are perpetrating these crimes. They do not understand the need for ethical practices abroad, when host countries don't have any environmental regulations. It's still difficult for the technical and financial people leading our industries to grasp the importance of preserving plants and animals in a faraway forest that they will never see. After all, didn't dinosaurs disappear? Technology is still god in many people's minds.

EXEMPLAR:
The Body Shop

Anita Roddick bases her international company on business ethics, environmental awareness, responsibility to the community, and respect for employees and customers who, she assumes, are discerning and wise. This policy has led to all the traditional signs of success, including rapid growth in sales and number of stores, in a field, cosmetics, that is known for its vicious competitiveness. But more important to her is service to the planet.

Each Body Shop store has a community project that employees do on company time. The company has a Third World trade department that, as she puts it, "goes into areas of the Third World creating trade in an ethical way, paying First World prices, making sure that the environment is protected, and making sure that the social fabric of that environment is protected." They raise large amounts of money for rain-forest peoples. When they had to open up a soap production plant, they put it in Glasgow, "the worst housing area in the whole of western Europe." In addition to cutting the unemployment rate drastically, the company gave 25 percent of the profits of that plant back to the Glasgow community to do with as they wished to improve the area.

This socially related purpose of the Body Shop is based on doing business with care in every aspect. Cosmetics are developed without animal testing. Natural ingredients and products from around the world are used, and everything is displayed with honesty, yet excitement. For instance, Roddick points out that almost no henna shampoos contain actual henna, because it smells like horse manure. The Body Shop henna shampoo contains actual henna, and the labeling very clearly explains the source of the bad odor. Instead of showing high-fashion models as in traditional cosmetic shops, the walls of Body Shops display pictures of people like Mother Teresa, inspirational quotes, explanations of the cultural background of the products, and beautiful pictures of the people and places representing the countries that supply the store's products and ingredients.

What is Roddick's "secret ingredient"? She says, "Euphoria. We have such a bloody good time doing it. And it's a wonderful feeling to be able to teach the Nepalese how to make paper from banana fiber. . . . Paper's coming out of Nepal that just makes your heart sing. We've also set up disabled women's associations making products for us. . . . Down in southern India, whole villages are working now on little things like footsie rollers for us, which reaps them profits of a hundred thousand, so they're setting up more roller craft shops."

The success of the Body Shop is so phenomenal that *Inc.* magazine ran a cover story on Roddick with the headline: "This Woman Is Changing Business Forever." One part of that change is a special attitude. She explains:

"I think The Body Shop has worked brilliantly well because it's very, very much female. A lot of feminine principles are endemic within it, like gut feelings, instincts. In terms of ethics, you know, the male is very much justice, proprietary behavior; for women, it's care. We have so many females in the organization that care becomes a very natural vocabulary."

This attitude comes through in the caring for employees. Roddick will not accept that executives can be seen as doing good for their companies by such "immoral" acts as corporate raiding and "firing five hundred people at the stroke of a pen." She has proven that her way is not only moral, but good for the company, everybody connected with it, and the world as well.

Part V

VISIONS OF
THE FUTURE

The crisis is in our consciousness, not in the world.

J. K. KRISHNAMURTI

To know is not to prove, nor to explain. It is to accede to vision. But if we are to have vision, we must learn to participate in the object of vision. The apprenticeship is hard.

ANTOINE DE SAINT-EXUPÉRY
Flight to Arras

The economics of abundance is a direct reflection of the prolifigacy of Life that is at the heart of the female principle. It will produce businesses in which the equality of the male and female principles is fundamental. As more and more individuals begin the journey toward authentic empowerment, . . . the antagonisms between men and women and between business and the environment will be replaced with new, harmonious and mutually reinforcing relationships between men and women, business and men and women, and business and the environment.

GARY ZUKAV

If you see in any given situation only what everybody else can see, you can be said to be so much a representative of your culture that you are a victim of it.

S. I. HAYAKAWA

INTRODUCTION

The guiding new paradigm principles of wholeness, inner wisdom, and authority lead to new ways of doing business that nurture society and, ultimately, all parts of the world.

However, it is difficult, if not impossible, to determine what the new paradigm is when one is in the midst of a paradigm shift. In this section, six authors present their own visions of the present transition in business and what it might mean to all of us.

It is most important for us to remain open to possibilities. A change such as we are now experiencing can potentially lead to behavior that foments into history's political revolutions. People harden their positions, take sides, and become fundamentalists. As Jagdish Parikh, managing director of the Lemuir Group of Companies in India, points out, he dislikes the term "new paradigm business" because it suggests that some people or businesses are "new paradigm" while others are not.

While labeling businesses in this way falls somewhat short of an inquisition, it misses the point that there are business practices that are appropriate for certain situations and not for others. It polarizes people instead of moving us to a higher synthesis of all the ways we might work in the current transition. By making lists of new paradigm business characteristics, we can fall into the trap of closing our options and closing our minds as to what might be possible.

Curiously, we cultivate the kind of open-mindedness and vision necessary when we are willing to look without flinching at the situation, no matter how painful that might be. Like the medieval knights who went on quests, we must have faith in our inner resources. We need to avoid the blame and criticism that come from fear of the unknown. We need precise observation, with the objectivity of a scientist and the curiosity and wonder of a child. We need to address the penetrating questions that come naturally from these observations.

Systems theorist and social activist Joanna Macy provides an example of a modern knight on a quest into the new paradigm. Her primary concern is with the problem of nuclear wastes. At one point, she realized that the half-life of some of those wastes was two hundred and fifty thousand years. That means these buried wastes have the potential to destroy all life on the planet at any time over ten thousand generations. This seemed to be such a hopeless situation as she contemplated it that she went into a deep state of despair. Her condition was so extreme that she felt paralyzed.

But, as she "maintained the gaze," as she puts it, as she stayed with the power of her observation, she began to see things that she could do. She experienced strong motivation as a result of considering the issue and going deeply into the source of her despair. The experience was so profound that she wrote a book about it called *Despair and Personal Power in the Nuclear Age*. She continues to develop activities that decrease the accumulation of nuclear wastes and at the same time warn future generations. Macy's main contribution is in raising consciousness and helping people to build their vision of the future on the basis of clear attention to the present and a tapping of their own wholeness, inner wisdom, and authority.

Macy developed, for instance, something called the Parsifal Exercise. This is based on the myth of Parsifal and the Holy Grail, which has been told and celebrated in many cultures, including the English, French, and German. The knight Parsifal enters the Fisher King's kingdom and finds it dry and barren. Nothing seems to grow or thrive there. The king is wounded so that he is impotent and barely able to move. Yet people in the court seem to be operating in a business-as-usual mode.

Periodically, the young knight Parsifal would see the Holy Grail carried from room to room in the castle. But he didn't ask any questions about all this. Earlier his mother and one of his teachers urged him not to ask questions, and so he blindly followed their advice and asked no questions—even though this asking of questions turned out to be his life's purpose. Later, he is banished from the Fisher King's realm, presumably never to return and never to fulfill his life's purpose of asking the questions.

In some versions of the story, however, he returns to the Fisher King's land and castle after great hardship and with help from some key allies. This time he asks two questions: What aileth thee? and Whom does the Grail serve? As soon as he asks these questions, the kingdom comes alive. The king regains his health. Trees and fields begin to blossom and grow with the issue of nature. Birds start singing and the sun seems to warm and energize everyone. Just asking the questions was the cure.

In Macy's Parsifal Exercise, people go out door to door or wherever people gather. They ask questions that are similar to the ones asked by

Parsifal but put into a modern context: What do you feel is the greatest danger facing us today? Is it getting worse or better? Do you talk to anyone about it? If so, where do you talk about it—at home, at work or school, with friends? What do people say about this danger(s)? What, if anything, can be done about it? What gives you hope?

Macy reports that when people do this exercise, there is an awakening similar to that experienced in the Fisher King's kingdom. Both those who ask and those who answer begin to come alive, even though the consideration of the issues may be painful. They discover that there is hope, and that just in going on the quest with faith, with no negative inner judgment, with precise observation, and with penetrating questions, they gain an energy that makes them alive in a new way, ready to confront life positively.

The visionaries whose writing is represented in this section all have confronted the world situation and are encouraging others to do the same. All of them are Fellows of the World Business Academy with the exception of Willis Harman, who is a Founding Trustee. They bring to us a vision of the future that already exists in many ways, if we pay attention and ask the right questions.

24

A SYSTEMS APPROACH TO THE EMERGING PARADIGM

by Fritjof Capra

The state of the world's environmental health, as annually surveyed by the Worldwatch Institute, is steadily declining. Our social and political problems, at the same time, are escalating throughout the globe at an alarming rate. Meanwhile, most of these essential issues are completely absent from the American political dialogue. Why? And what is to be done?

In the following essay, Fritjof Capra, internationally known physicist, systems theorist, and best-selling author, offers his view of the "old paradigm," which has dominated our world for the past several hundred years. He then analyzes the emerging paradigm as a more "holistic" world view based on "deep" ecological awareness.

Capra contrasts the old, fragmented, parochial way of operating in the world with a bold new paradigm application of systems theory that deals with the interconnectedness of environmentalism and economic growth within the context of new values that are both practical, cooperative, and spiritual.

Fritjof Capra is author of The Tao of Physics, The Turning Point, *and* Uncommon Wisdom. *He developed the film "Mindwalk" and wrote* Green Politics *with Charlene Spretnak, and* Belonging to the Universe *with Brother David Steindl-Rast.*

Today we are faced with a whole series of global problems which are harming the biosphere and human life in alarming ways that may soon become irreversible. We have ample documentation about the extent and significance of these problems. One of the best sources is the series of annual reports, *State of the World,* published by the Worldwatch Institute.

In assessing the "environmental health" of the planet, these reports have observed the same alarming trends year after year. The Earth's forests are receding, while its deserts are expanding. Topsoil on our croplands is diminishing, and the ozone layer, which protects us from harmful ultraviolet radiation, is being depleted. Concentrations of heat-trapping gases in the atmosphere are rising, while the numbers of plant and animal species are shrinking. World population continues to grow, and the gap between the rich and the poor continues to widen.

CRISIS OF PERCEPTION

And yet, while public awareness of all these problems is rising dramatically everywhere, they are strikingly absent from the American political dialogue. It is strange that today the general public and the media have become much more aware of the critical issues of our time than our political leaders. In fact, those so-called "leaders" do not lead at all. They reluctantly *follow* society's increasing ecological and global awareness instead of providing vision and leadership.

I believe that there are two reasons why these issues have been excluded from the political dialogue. One concerns concepts, the other concerns values; and both of them are closely interconnected.

The more we study the major problems of our time, the more we come to realize that they cannot be understood in isolation. They are systemic problems—interconnected and interdependent. Stabilizing world population will only be possible when poverty is reduced worldwide. The extinction of animal and plant species on a massive scale will continue so long as the Third World is burdened by massive debts. Only if we stop the international arms race will we have the resources to prevent the many destructive impacts on the biosphere and on human life.

In fact, the more you study the situation, the more you realize that, ultimately, these problems are just different facets of one single crisis, which is essentially a crisis of perception. It derives from the fact that most of us, and especially our large social institutions, subscribe to the concepts of an outdated world view, a perception of reality inadequate for dealing with our overpopulated, globally interconnected world.

At the same time, researchers at the leading edge of science, various social movements, and numerous alternative networks are developing a new vision of reality that will form the basis of our future technologies, economic systems, and social institutions.

So we are at the beginning of a fundamental change of world view in science and society, a change of paradigms as radical as the Copernican Revolution. But this realization has not yet dawned on our political leaders. The recognition that a profound change of perception and thinking is needed if we are to survive has not yet reached most of our corporate leaders either, nor the representatives of our large universities.

The technologies and practices of the corporate community, most of which have been unhealthy if not outright destructive, are firmly supported by the scientific establishment. However, the reason for the unmitigated support of dangerous and harmful activities is not a conspiracy. It comes from the fact that our corporate, academic and political leaders, as well as the scientific advisors to our governments, the grant-giving foundations, the established political parties, and the majority of the corporate community are captives of the same outdated perceptions that have brought about our global crisis.

THE OLD PARADIGM

These perceptions form the so-called "old paradigm," which has dominated our culture for several hundred years, during which it has shaped Western society and has significantly influenced the rest of the world. This paradigm consists of a number of ideas, among them the view of the universe as a mechanical system composed of elementary building blocks (the influence of Cartesian philosophy and Newtonian physics); correspondingly, the view of the human body as a machine, which is still the conceptual basis of the theory and practice of our medical science; the view of life in society as a competitive struggle for existence (inherited from the Social Darwinists); and the belief in unlimited material progress to be achieved through economic and technological growth. All of these assumptions have been fatefully challenged by recent events. And, indeed, a radical revision of them is now occurring.

THE NEW PARADIGM

The emerging new paradigm may be called a "holistic" world view, seeing the world as an integrated whole rather than a dissociated collection of parts. It may also be called an "ecological" view, using the term in the sense of deep ecology. The distinction between "shallow" and "deep" ecology was made in the early seventies by the philosopher Arne Naess and is now widely accepted as a very useful terminology for referring to the major division within contemporary environmental thought.

Shallow ecology is anthropocentric. It views humans as above or outside of nature, as the source of all value, and ascribes only instrumental, or use value, to nature. Deep ecology does not separate humans from the natural environment, nor does it separate anything else from it. It does not see the world as a collection of isolated objects but rather as a network of phenomena that are fundamentally interconnected and interdependent. Deep ecology recognizes the intrinsic values of all living beings and views humans as just one particular strand in the web of life.

Ultimately, deep ecological awareness is spiritual, or religious awareness. When the concept of the human spirit is understood as the mode of consciousness in which the individual feels connected to the cosmos as a whole, it becomes clear that ecological awareness is spiritual in its deepest essence. It is therefore not surprising that the emerging new vision of reality, based on deep ecological awareness, is consistent with the so-called "perennial philosophy" of spiritual traditions, the spirituality of Christian mystics or with the philosophy and cosmology underlying the Native American traditions.

LIVING SYSTEMS

In science, the theory of living systems, which originated in cybernetics in the 1940s but emerged fully only during the last ten years or so, provides the most appropriate scientific formulation of the new ecological paradigm.

The systemic approach, or systems approach, looks at the world in terms of relationships and integration. Systems are integrated wholes whose properties cannot be reduced to those of smaller units. Examples of systems abound in nature. Every organism—from the smallest bacterium through the wide range of plants and animals to humans—is an integrated whole and thus a living system. Cells are living systems, and so are the various tissues and organs of the body, the human brain being the most complex example. But systems are not confined to individual organisms and their parts. The same aspects of wholeness are exhibited by social systems—such as family or a community—and by ecosystems that consist of a variety of organisms and inanimate matter in mutual interaction.

All these natural systems are wholes whose specific structures arise from the interactions and interdependences of their parts. Systemic properties are destroyed when a system is dissected, either physically or theoretically, into isolated elements. Although we can discern individual parts in any system, the nature of the whole is always different from the mere sum of its parts. Accordingly, the systems approach does not concentrate on basic building blocks but rather on basic principles of organization.

The systemic, or ecological way of thinking has many important implications not only for science and philosophy, but also for society and our daily lives. Because living systems span such a wide range of phenomena, involving individual organisms, social systems, and eco-systems, systems theory provides the ideal language for unifying many fields of study that have become isolated and fragmented.

SUSTAINABLE SOLUTIONS

Let me now return to the question of why the critical issues of our time have been excluded from the political dialogue. The point I have tried to make is that these issues—the major problems of today—are global, systemic problems that require a systemic approach to be understood and solved. They are excluded from the political dialogue because most of our political leaders are not yet capable of this kind of global, systemic thinking.

Confined by the narrow framework of the old paradigm, they continue the fragmented approach that has become so characteristic of our academic disciplines and government agencies. Such an approach can never solve any of the problems, but merely shifts them around erratically. One year it's inflation, then it's drugs and crime, then the greenhouse effect—but it's really the same problem in different guises; the same crisis of perception.

Not only do our leaders fail to see how different problems are interrelated; they also refuse to recognize how their so-called solutions affect future generations. From the systemic, ecological point of view, the only viable solutions are those that are "sustainable." This concept of sustainability has become a key concept in the environmental move-ment and is indeed crucial. What does it mean? Lester Brown of the Worldwatch Institute has given a simple, clear, and beautiful defini-tion: "A sustainable society is one that satisfies its needs without dimin-ishing the prospects of future generations."

This, then, in a nutshell, is the challenge of our time: to create sustainable societies—social and cultural environments in which we can satisfy our needs without diminishing the chances of future gener-ations. What will such a sustainable society look like? There are as yet no models, but some basic criteria have merged over the past decade.

The basic shape of a sustainable society is sketched out in the World-watch report *State of the World*.

The decisive characteristic of a sustainable economy will be the rejection of the current blind pursuit of unqualified growth. The purpose of economic activity will not be to increase the GNP but to increase human welfare.

Now, economic growth may well increase human welfare, but only under certain conditions. The first question we have to ask is: growth of what? The goods and services produced must be valuable and beneficial. The second question is: growth for whom? Only when goods and services are distributed widely enough through society will the general welfare increase. And, finally, we have to ask: growth at what cost? The benefits of economic growth must outweigh the social and environmental costs of production.

In other words, economic growth will not be defined purely quantitatively as increase of production, but qualitatively as increase of human welfare. Such a new concept of growth represents a shift from quantity to quality that is typical of new paradigm thinking in general. At the same time it is fully consistent with the systems view of life. In the living world, growth has not only a quantitative but also a qualitative meaning. For a human being, for example, to grow means to develop to maturity, not only by getting bigger but also qualitatively through inner growth. The same is true for all living systems. The systems concept of growth is qualitative and multi-dimensional.

NEW VALUES

Since many aspects of such qualitative economic growth cannot be given monetary values, they will have to be implemented through the political process. The non-monetary choices to be made are political choices based on values. And this brings us to a most important aspect of the current paradigm shift, the question of values.

So far I have emphasized perceptions and thinking. If that were the whole problem, the paradigm shift would be much easier. There are enough brilliant thinkers among the proponents of the new paradigm who could convince our political and corporate leaders of the merits of systemic thinking. But that's only part of the story. The shift of paradigms requires not only an expansion of our perceptions and ways of thinking, but also of our values.

And here it is interesting to note a striking connection between these changes of thinking and of values. Both of them may be seen as shifts from self-assertion to integration. These two tendencies—the self-assertive and the integrative—are both essential aspects of all living systems. Neither of them is intrinsically good or bad. What is good, or healthy, is a dynamic balance; what is bad, or unhealthy, is imbalance—overemphasis of one tendency and neglect of the other. In the old paradigm, we have been overemphasizing the self-assertive values and ways of thinking and have neglected their integrative counterparts. So what I'm suggesting is not to replace one mode by the other, but rather to establish a better balance between the two.

With that in mind, let's look at the various manifestations of the shift from self-assertion to integration. As far as thinking is concerned, we are talking about a shift from the rational to the intuitive, from analysis to synthesis, from reductionism to holism, from linear to nonlinear thinking.

As far as values are concerned, we are observing a corresponding shift from competition to cooperation, from expansion to conservation, from quantity to quality, from domination to partnership.

THE PATRIARCHAL ORDER

You may have noticed that the self-assertive values—competition, expansion, domination—are generally associated with men. Indeed, in patriarchal society they are not only favored but given economic rewards and political power. And this is one of the reasons why the shift to a more balanced value system is so difficult for most people, and especially for most men.

Power, in the sense of domination over others, is excessive self-assertion. The social structure in which it is exerted most effectively is the hierarchy. Indeed, our political, military, and corporate structures are hierarchically ordered, with men occupying the upper levels and women the lower levels. Most of these men, and also quite a few women, have come to see their position in the hierarchy as part of their identity, and thus the shift to a different system of values generates existential fear in them.

However, there is also another kind of power, which is more appropriate for the new paradigm—power as influence of others. The ideal structure for exerting this kind of power is not the hierarchy but the network, which is also one of the central metaphors of systemic thinking. Thus the paradigm shift includes a shift in social organization from hierarchies to networks.

ALLIES IN THE RISING CULTURE

The new values, together with new attitudes and lifestyles, are now being promoted by widespread grassroots movements: the ecology movement, the peace movement, the women's movement, the holistic-health and human-potential movements, various spiritual movements, numerous citizens' movements and initiatives, Third-World and ethnic liberation movements, and many others. During the sixties and seventies these movements operated largely separately without realizing how their purposes interrelate. But since the beginning of the eighties they have begun to coalesce, recognizing that they represent different facets of the same new vision of reality. The political success of the European Green movement is the most impressive example of that new powerful force of social transformation.

During the past several years, this new global force, which I called the "rising culture" in my book, *The Turning Point,* has found an ally in Mikhail Gorbachev. To show you to what extent Gorbachev's "new thinking" is of the kind I have presented to you, let me quote a few passages from his speech to the United Nations. About the paradigm shift itself Gorbachev said: "It would be naive to think that the problems plaguing mankind today can be solved with the means and methods which were applied or seemed to work in the past. . . . [New] realities are changing the entire world situation. . . . Some of the past differences and disputes are losing their importance. . . . Life is making us abandon outdated world views. . . . This is one of the signs of the crucial nature of the current phase in history."

Here is how he showed himself a global, systemic thinker: "[We are witnessing] the process of the emergence of a mutually interrelated and integral world. . . . Efforts to solve global problems require a new scope and quality of interaction of states. . . . The world's economy is becoming a single organism. . . . International economic security is inconceivable unless related not only to disarmament but also to the elimination of the threat to the world's environment. . . . The bell of every regional conflict tolls for all of us."

And finally, here is what Gorbachev had to say about the shift of values from domination to partnership: "The use or threat of force can no longer and must no longer be an instrument of foreign policy. This is the first and most important component of a non-violent world as an ideal. . . . We are speaking of cooperation, which could be more accurately termed co-creation and co-development. . . . We must build a new world—and we must do it together."

EXEMPLAR:
GE Plastics

Leaders of one of the fastest-growing divisions of General Electric, GE Plastics, were constantly looking for ways to increase team building. This became even more crucial when they acquired one of their greatest competitors, Borg-Warner. The typical competitive games would not do. Instead, they asked how these old adversaries could work together.

The answer to that question represents a breakthrough in both team-building and creative business social responsibility. Instead of playing games and having wilderness experiences, the teams from the two companies did something constructive and of lasting value. In San Diego they worked on renovating a boys' club, a shelter for the homeless, and three YMCAs—all greatly in need of repair.

Participants were moved when they realized that people outside of GE would benefit, especially children. One of the YMCA directors talked about the energy that he witnessed when ten buses with a total of 400 people pulled up to his building and teams charged to their projects. In one day they used 3,200 gallons of paint, installed 200 windows, and laid more than 40,000 square feet of flooring. They built teams by working together toward a common goal, rather than competing with each other. One former Borg-Warner employee said that all his fears about the lack of family or community feeling within GE were dispelled almost as soon as the projects began.

This model has now spread to other parts of GE. In Miami, NBC employees renovated a day care center. In Minneapolis, a GE customer organization built a community playground. And GE has produced a booklet that can be used by other organizations to do similar projects.

25

EVOLUTION AND BUSINESS

by Gary Zukav

In the following visionary article, the award-winning author Gary Zukav draws a striking parallel between the evolution of the human species and what he perceives to be the inevitable development of contemporary commerce.

Just as humanity is now evolving beyond the limited perception of the five senses, so will the world of new paradigm business reflect the values and behaviors of an emerging consciousness and sensibility. Whereas humanity is now evolving toward nonphysical aspects of reality and perception, so will business, he says, begin to reflect a new sense of power, values, ownership, productivity, and profit.

Gary Zukav won the American Book Award in Science for the international best-seller The Dancing Wu Li Masters: An Overview of the New Physics. *A graduate of Harvard University who lives in Northern California, he is also the author of* The Seat of the Soul. *This article is the first half of a chapter from a forthcoming book.*

The challenges facing the business community today are far beyond those that are ordinarily thought to be the most fundamental. No analysis of business within the commercial framework that has been in place for the last two centuries will bring to light the underlying dynamics that are starting to shake the business world, and will soon transform it beyond the recognition of contemporary businessmen and -women.

The long history of interhuman commerce from primitive barter through intercontinental trade through global multinational corporations has unfolded in a context that no longer characterizes the evolutionary modality of humankind.

In order to understand the next step in the development of the entire system of mutual support and assistance that has metamorphosized into contemporary commerce it is necessary to understand the changes that are occurring in the evolutionary development of the human species. Commerce as we currently experience it is a product of an evolutionary mode that is now obsolete. Commerce as future generations of humans will experience it will reflect the values and behaviors of a new humanity that is in the process of being born.

Since the origin of the human species, it has evolved through the exploration of physical reality—through exploring that which can be tasted, heard, smelled, touched, or seen. In this process, it has acquired the ability to manipulate and control those things that can be detected by the five senses. This is external power. The pursuit of external power and evolution through the exploration of physical reality are the same thing.

During this period, humanity has been limited to the perception of the five senses.

The human species is now leaving behind the exploration of physical reality as its mode of evolution, and, simultaneously, the limitations of the five senses. Five-sensory humans are becoming multisensory humans—humans that are not limited to the perception of the five senses.

The magnitude of this transition has no historical precedent. Therefore, it is not possible to predict what commerce will look like once this transition has been accomplished. Nonetheless, it is possible to see the outlines of the economic system that the emerging humanity will construct by understanding the nature of the changes that are underway within humanity.

AUTHENTIC POWER

Humanity is now evolving through responsible choice with the assistance and guidance of nonphysical guides and Teachers. It is beginning the process of moving consciously into partnership with nonphysical aspects of reality that are not accessible to five-sensory perception, and taking its place consciously in a larger fabric of Life than five-sensory perception is able to detect.

In place of the pursuit of external power—the ability to manipulate and control—humanity is now evolving through the pursuit of authentic power—the alignment of the personality with the soul.

Prior to the emergence of multisensory humanity, which is now underway, the distinction between personality and soul remained a theoretical, religious concept. As more and more humans develop the ability to acquire data beyond those that the five senses can provide, the distinction between personality and soul is becoming a more and more recognizable reality.

The personality is that part of an individual that is born into time, develops in time, and dies in time. The soul of an individual is that part of the individual that is immortal. Increasing awareness of the existence of the soul is emerging in many individuals as a thirst for meaning that cannot be filled with ordinary activities and accomplishments. Old victories no longer satisfy. Old goals no longer fulfill.

INTUITION

Others acquire this awareness through different or more direct means. In all cases, intuition becomes centrally important, or begins the process of moving in that direction. To the five-sensory human, intuition is a curiosity. It is not taken seriously. To the multisensory human, intuition is fundamentally important.

Intuition is the voice of the nonphysical world. Since the nonphysical world does not exist for the five-sensory human, the five-sensory human does not take intuition seriously. The multisensory human depends more upon intuition than any other human faculty. The multisensory human does not deny the data of the five senses— multisensory humans do not walk in front of moving trucks—but the multisensory human acts on hunches about where trucks are more likely to be and where they are less likely to be.

In terms of commerce, this means that intuition will replace rationalization as the primary source of data in the development of long-term strategies, the means of implementing those strategies, and in the resolution of everyday challenges. The underlying requirements of efficiency, productivity, and profitability will not disappear, but the means of attaining them will no longer be the sole product of the intellect.

The intellect and its offspring—such as cost effectiveness analysis and statistical quality control—will be at the service of a higher directorate. They will have been demoted, in other words, from their current position at the top of the decision making hierarchy. They will no longer command, but instead will serve.

VALUES

Alignment of the personality with the soul automatically brings with it a set of values and behaviors that are different from those that are based upon the perception of power as external. The soul always strives for harmony, cooperation, sharing, and reverence for Life. As the deep and sometimes difficult inner work of aligning the personality with the soul through the mechanism of responsible choice begins to produce authentically empowered individuals within the business community, the values and behaviors that these individuals bring to the community will both strengthen and foretell the major shift that is underway, and attract others in whom this process is becoming conscious.

These individuals will find themselves—and are finding themselves—in an arena of activity that is no longer satisfying or challenging: the sole pursuit of return on investment for stockholders. Stockholders also are undergoing the same evolutionary transition, of which socially responsible investing is a manifestation. Natural alliances will form between those organizations that begin to move toward values and programs that reflect the goals of authentically empowered entrepreneurs and employees on the one hand, and similarly empowered investors on the other.

As entrepreneurs, employees, and investors move toward their own authentic empowerment, they will create commercial structures which reflect an economic reality that is strikingly different from our present experience.

The current economy is based upon scarcity and oriented toward exploitation. Its underlying assumption is that the Universe does not provide adequately for all, and that deprivation, therefore, is a natural part of the human experience for parts of the human population. It is oriented toward the extraction of gain in all circumstances—either from other humans, from the Earth, or from both.

Success in an economy that is based upon the assumption of scarcity is the accumulation of surplus. This is called "profit." The same assumption that drives the entrepreneur to generate profit drives the investors that invest in the enterprise. The accumulated surplus is divided between the stockholders and the entrepreneur, or enterprise.

Within the enterprise, individuals also strive to maximize accumulation of surplus. They maneuver for ever-increasing salaries, bonuses, and options. Likewise, investors strive for ever-increasing returns on their investments. The result is competition within enterprises between employees, and between enterprises for investors.

The individual, or enterprise, that acquires the most surplus is most able to influence and control the market—the environment and others—through domination via economy of scale, threat of dismissal, threat of relocation, threat of hostile takeover, manipulation of resources, manipulation of product availability, and so on.

This economy and the activities that it generates reflect the perception of power as external—the ability to manipulate and control—

which has been a part of our evolution through the exploration of physical reality.

So long as our species evolved in that mode, this economy and its activities served the evolution of humanity, although they were not necessary. Humanity could have chosen to explore five-sensory reality in a spirit of cooperation and reverence, as Native cultures around the world chose. Instead, we chose to explore physical reality with a sense of conquest and domination. This produced the painful and destructive consequences that fill our world today and shape our institutions, including our economic institutions.

That mode of evolution has come to an end, and, therefore, so has the utility of the economics of scarcity and exploitation. Further pursuit of external power in the field of economics, and every other area of human endeavor, now produces only violence and destruction.

The economy that is emerging will be based on abundance and oriented toward contribution. The characteristics of this economy, therefore, are directly opposed to those of the present economy. This means that as the new economy begins to emerge, it will redefine all of the basic concepts that underlie the economy of today—ownership, productivity, and profit—in the process of replacing them with their successors.

OWNERSHIP

"Ownership" is a concept that is meaningful only within the domain of the five senses. Until now, the evolution of humanity has been confined to this domain. Beyond the domain of the five senses there is nothing to own except who and what a soul is. As humanity undergoes the transition from five-sensory perception to multisensory perception, the concept of "ownership" will at first become confusing, then questionable, and finally meaningless.

Ownership is a means of exerting external power. To own property—a mule, a wife, a piece of land, a house, a Mercedes—everything that is felt to enhance one's sense of security—is an attempt to influence or control others and the environment. Every "No Trespassing" sign is an attempt to exert external power over another being. Every violation of such a sign is the same thing. By the number of slaves a person owns, or animals, or vacation homes, humans throughout their history have proclaimed the amount of external power that they have acquired.

External power can be gained, stolen, lost, and inherited. The lack of external power is a cause of anxiety to those who do not have it, because they fear abuse by those who do, and a cause of anxiety to those who have it, because they fear to lose it.

"Ownership" is the reflection of this dynamic.

With the development of contemporary commerce, ownership has become abstract. Ownership now extends to market share on the part of enterprises—wherein the transitory nature of external power is demonstrated daily—to stock holding on the part of investors— wherein individuals and groups challenge one another for board seats. Intangibles such as portfolio size and bank balance have replaced numbers of pigs or olive trees, but the dynamic beneath the drive for ownership of both concrete and abstract assets in excess of what is needed to support a comfortable life is identical—the pursuit of external power.

As individuals within the business community come to recognize themselves as immortal souls, and experience within themselves the shift from pursuit of external power—the ability to manipulate and control—to pursuit of authentic power—alignment of the personality with the soul—their understanding of the dynamic that lies beneath the concept of ownership will cause them to question the utility of this concept.

This is a natural development in the system of human values as the arena of human evolution expands beyond the material to include awareness of nonphysical dimensions of Life. This development will affect businesses as well as individuals. "Ownership" is a means of preventing cooperation, hoarding resources, and obstructing the aspirations of others as well as developing one's own visions, surrounding one's self in the environment of one's choosing, and protecting one's self from the unwanted intrusions of others.

As humanity moves toward authentic empowerment and harmony, cooperation, sharing, and reverence for Life replace competition, hoarding, focus on one's own needs, and exploitation of Life, the necessity for "ownership" will disappear. What was once a requirement for the acquisition of external power will become an obstacle in the acquisition of authentic power. Like an old technology that has been replaced with a new, it will lose its value naturally through obsolescence.

From the point of view of contemporary commerce, business cannot exist without ownership. All relationships between businesses are defined in terms of what is owned and what is not, what is controlled and what is not, and the desire to increase what is owned and what is controlled in every instance.

From the point of view of the emerging commerce, all relationships between businesses will be defined by the ability of each enterprise to contribute to Life, and to assist other enterprises to contribute to Life. Negotiations will center not over extending control, but over providing resources. Conferences will be held not to exploit the weaknesses of competitors, but to augment the strengths of friends. Assessments will be made to determine which enterprise is most able to provide the need of society that is under consideration, and how it can best be supported by others.

As cooperation replaces competition and mutual support replaces conquest, "ownership" of resources, access to markets, raw materials, and marketing potential will come to be thought of as "common," and then the concept will drop away for lack of use and meaning.

PRODUCTIVITY

"Productivity" within the domain of the five senses has come to be identified with the ability to transform material resources into products. As the economy has shifted from one that rests upon a manufacturing base to one that is primarily service oriented, "productivity" continues to mean the ability to transform raw materials—in this case human creativity and abilities—into profitable products. This shift reflects within the domain of the five senses the larger shift in the evolutionary path of humankind away from its original focus on the physical world toward increasingly conscious participation in the nonmaterial aspects of its reality.

"Productivity" is another expression of the idea of "product." While humanity was limited in its perception to the five senses, the only products possible were those that are discernible to the five senses. We understand that the "product" of love, trust, good will, and the intention to grow together can be a healthy relationship, but in economic contexts the term "product" refers to the material result of a conscious application of human will and material resources that, when produced, can be marketed.

Productivity is closely related to efficiency. As the products of a service-oriented economy become increasingly labor intensive, and as the price of the educated labor that is necessary to these businesses increases, the ability to extract the maximum amount of product—service—from the labor force in the least amount of time is prerequisite to competitiveness and profitability.

Time is a concern of the personality. It is not a concern of the soul.

The personality completes its life within a period of time. The soul is immortal. The personality sees its lifetime as the entirety of its existence. The soul views the same lifetime as one learning opportunity among many to gain the experiences that it seeks to experience, and to contribute the gifts that it seeks to give.

As humankind leaves behind the limitations of the five senses and multisensory perception becomes as central to the human experience as physical vision, hearing, taste, touch, and smell, the "productivity" of human enterprises will be appraised not on the basis of the material product or service that each produces, but on their contributions to the spirit.

Beyond the physical needs of a comfortable life are needs that are as vital to human growth and development as food and shelter. These are the needs of the soul. Productivity until now has been measured in terms of the ability to fill physical needs. In the emerging economy "productivity" will encompass also the ability of enterprises to fill spiritual needs.

Spiritual productivity is measured by the heart, and only the heart can create a spiritually productive enterprise. We live in a Universe of maximal spiritual productivity. Each encounter, experience, and circumstance of each human life, including those that are painful and traumatic, serve equally the needs of each soul involved. The pain in each human life is a measure of the distance between the desires of its personality and the needs of its soul.

The spiritual productivity of the Universe flows not from the exquisite appropriateness of each experience to the needs of the experiencer, but from the compassionate essence of the Universe that at every moment and in every way serves the needs of each soul as it moves toward increasing awareness, responsibility, and freedom.

In the same way, the spiritual productivity of a commercial enterprise springs from the compassion for Life in all its forms that lies at the heart of the enterprise. Currently, this is extremely rare. Therefore, spiritual productivity measured in terms of the authentic empowerment of the individuals that participate in commercial activities is virtually nonexistent.

It is not possible for an enterprise to produce authentic empowerment. Each individual is responsible for moving into his or her own authentic power—the alignment of his or her personality with his or her soul. The alternative is pain. Pain results not because the Universe is cruel or vindictive, but because it compassionately provides for each soul the experience of what that soul has chosen to create through its own choices. Eventually, every soul will learn, through its own experiences, to create with wisdom and love a world without violence and conflict—a world without pain.

As more and more humans begin to see themselves and others as immortal souls involved in a learning process that entails the experiencing of consequences that each has chosen, they begin to choose their actions and responses to the actions of others more carefully, and, hopefully, more wisely. This is responsible choice. Striving to understand the circumstances of one's life and to live one's life from the point of view of the soul accelerates spiritual growth. This is spiritual productivity.

A spiritually productive enterprise, therefore, is one that reflects the same compassion and generosity of the Universe in which we souls evolve. It is one that honors the choices that individuals make, that allows the freedom to choose. It is one that celebrates the contributions of each individual and, therefore, enjoys the fruits of collaborative efforts made on the basis of conscious individual choices to allow others the same freedom. It is one in which freedom to choose and responsibility for the consequences of the choices that are made are not limited to the upper levels of a hierarchy, since, in the practice of Life, no soul is exempted from experiencing the consequences that it has created.

Individuals working together, each with the realization that authentic empowerment is an individual responsibility, and, therefore, each taking responsibility for his or her actions and interactions, creates an environment from which both material and spiritual productivity can spring in an abundance that is now only glimpsed by the emerging multisensory humanity.

PROFIT

As five-sensory humanity evolving through the exploration of physical reality becomes a multisensory humanity evolving through responsible choice with the assistance and guidance of nonphysical guides and Teachers, and the economics of scarcity and exploitation is replaced with the economics of abundance and contribution, the concept of profit as surplus will become meaningless. "Profit," or a term that replaces it, will still refer to benefit, to the successful accomplishment of consciously created goals, but the goals and benefits of the emerging business community will be those that enhance the soul.

The measure of success will not be growth of net revenue, but the spiritual development and physical well-being of all those whom the business touches. The bottom line for each individual involved will be the yield of fulfillment and gratification that cannot be threatened, versus the yield of dollars, marks, or yen that must be surpassed the next quarter to remain a viable competitor.

As the goal of economic activity shifts from maximal extraction from the environment—human and nonhuman—to maximal contribution, the perception of humanity, the Earth and Life will shift from that of "resource" to "symbol of Divinity." All that now appears as grist for the mills, ore for the smelters, and workers for the plants will appear as gifts of Life from Life to Life. As the objective of maximal contribution to Life—already emerging within the world's businesspeople as it is in the rest of the human family—becomes the magnet around which consciousness orients itself, the relationships between businesses and employees, vendors, customers, stockholders, host communities, the environment, and the world will change dramatically.

As the goal of maximal contribution is applied to each of these categories of partnership, the world of commerce will come to reflect the values of the soul just as it now reflects the values of the personality. As individuals undergo the task of aligning their personalities with their souls, businesses will undergo a transformation from the pursuit of external power—competition for market share and investors—to the pursuit of authentic power—ability to empower the individual and better Life on the Earth.

EXEMPLAR:
Des Moines Water Works

The power of people in groups to be creative, particularly beyond the efforts of management, is illustrated most poignantly by Randy Theis, an employee of the Des Moines Water Works, as reported in James Autry's book *Love and Profit*. Theis contracted cancer and, because of a series of operations and recoveries, used up all of his sick leave. Since he has five children under the age of fourteen, this was a particularly difficult situation. What could the company do? Costs for health insurance are skyrocketing. Could they make an exception? Probably not.

Then a group of employees came up with an idea. They would start a program whereby individuals would donate sick leave days to Theis. The company changed their regulations to allow this. Twenty-five fellow workers signed up to transfer their sick-leave time. In addition they organized a food drive to help the family and collected money to help Theis' children at Christmastime. Autry points out that "we managers have the opportunity to lead and direct people in that evermore powerful bond of common enterprise, and at the same time to create a place of friendship, deep personal connections, and neighborhood. How about this for a new management bumper sticker: IF YOU'RE NOT CREATING COMMUNITY, YOU'RE NOT MANAGING."

MOVING BEYOND BREAKPOINT

by George Land and Beth Jarman

Breakpoint changes occur when an organization or company moves from one monumentally different phase to another. For example, the move from an entrepreneurial first phase to a managerial, standardized, and efficient second phase requires a breakpoint, a severe shift in structure, style, and corporate culture.

Similarly, another crucial breakpoint occurs when an established second phase corporation must again reinvent itself—to succeed in difficult economic times, to react to changing environmental and global conditions, to reform its organizational style and effectiveness. This breakpoint shift to the third phase can be extremely difficult because it requires profound changes in internal controls, a new sense of creative innovation, and a cycle of rebirth.

In the following essay, George Land and Beth Jarman illustrate how to overcome breakpoint obstacles, and also offer an inspiring vision of the future beyond breakpoint, as organizations encounter a third phase environment that will need to be challenged and integrated if they are to survive.

George Land has taught interdisciplinary science and creative process to the faculties of some three dozen universities. Over two hundred corporations and other institutions have employed his techniques of problem solving, innovation, and strategic thinking. He is the author of Grow or Die: The Unifying Principle of Transformation.

Beth Jarman serves as president of Leadership 2000, an International Leadership Development Corporation based in Phoenix. She is the author of You Can Change Your Life by Changing Your Mind *and, with George Land,* Breakpoint and Beyond.

Breakpoint changes are sweeping us *not* toward doing things better, but forward to a monumental revolution that will redefine the way work is organized and performed—and the very nature of organizations themselves. An astonishingly new system of human endeavor will send shock waves throughout organizations that will eclipse the impact of the industrial revolution.

The familiar S curve will be used quite differently from the usual exposition of birth, growth, maturity, and decline of an enterprise. Our exploration of this growth and change process will show how natural growth leads to extraordinary Breakpoint shifts in the way organizations must operate for initial success to occur, how this is followed by different forms of quantitative growth, and how the usual decline and demise of a successful organization can be replaced by renewal and reinvention of the enterprise. (Horizontal movement shows the passage of time, the vertical motion indicates growth of the organization.)

Let us follow the growth and change of an organization to reveal exactly how the hidden drama of Breakpoint change unfolds.

PHASE ONE—ORGANIZATIONAL FORMING

The first phase of an organization is the entrepreneurial stage. Entrepreneurs believe, for any of a diverse number of reasons, that they have an idea for a product or service that will solve someone's problem. They are convinced, with a deep fervor and obsession, that their idea will be *needed* and wanted in the marketplace; it could make a real contribution.

The entrepreneur:

- Imaginatively probes and explores the environment in extremely creative and dynamic ways to learn everything possible,
- Experiments by attempting all manner of things to find what succeeds and what fails,
- Rebounds between the terror of survival and having fun, bouncing ideas around and trying things out, and
- Brings together an essential blueprint of success, with the desirable resources that marries the product or service with the market.

This period is very ingenious and unpredictable, a time of trial and error, of success and failure, of untold frustration and great triumphs. Yet, it certainly isn't a period to merely survive, but to find, in the most creative and inventive way, how to operate and structure their enterprise in order to connect with the larger environment. The successful

Organizational Growth - Phase One

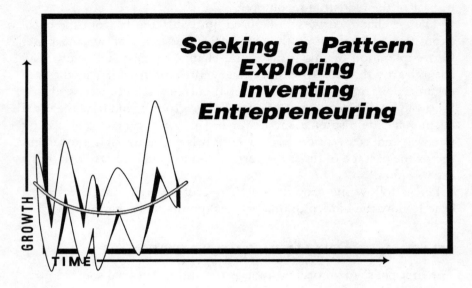

Seeking a Pattern
Exploring
Inventing
Entrepreneuring

GROWTH

TIME

entrepreneur is, in the words of Peters and Waterman, "a Maniac with a Mission."

Edwin Land, of Polaroid fame, personifies the entrepreneur. He had such tenacity that he wouldn't be stopped from realizing success with instant photography. Many people, observing his inventive style, concluded that he could never succeed. He worked in a laboratory atmosphere of chaos and confusion. He and his associates weren't "manageable." When Tom Watson of IBM wanted to replace punch cards with invisible electronic signals, the experts regarded him the same way. Lillian Vernon, Chairman and CEO of her own company, started out with $2,000 and an ad in *Seventeen* magazine forty years ago. Today she runs an incredibly successful mail order catalog business.

The type of creativity in phase one is *invention*. At its most elementary level, behind the process of imagination and exploration, is the basic drive to find a repeatable pattern of success.

Because of the tremendous difficulties in creating a new pattern, if the entrepreneur does not have a clear goal, exceptional determination, and commitment, along with ideas, resources, and an ability to cultivate good market contacts, success is unlikely. The entrepreneur must explore the environment relentlessly, almost obsessively, to discover that special pattern and then go out and win acceptance for it. This period requires great flexibility and adaptability to meet the unpredictable circumstances that inevitably appear.

Most first phase organizations, whether for profit or not for profit, fail to find a pattern of success. In nature, new cell mutations typically fail well over 99 percent of the time. One acorn out of thousands will grow into a healthy tree. In business organizations, 84 percent of those that make it past the critical first year fail within five years. They don't find or invent the successful product or service, or they don't discover a real need. Some entrepreneurs just give up too soon. Business is totally "natural" in that most small businesses fail to find that critical pattern of success.

The start-up period has little or nothing to do with the classic idea of management. It has everything to do with inventiveness, decisiveness, commitment, and flexibility. We characterize the most successful entrepreneur in phase one as a sort of benevolent Genghis Khan. Quick decisions, bold initiatives, and resourceful ways of solving problems are the only standards. To the entrepreneur, none of this is risky; it is necessary! The underlying success factor in phase one is the willingness to fall down, pick oneself up, start all over again. The rules—do it, try it, fix it—totally agree with what happens in the beginning for everything in nature.

PHASE TWO—ORGANIZATIONAL NORMING

The trap that can ensnare organizations as they attempt to grow is that each phase in this cyclical pattern is extraordinarily different from the others. Movement from one phase to another brings about an all-out shift in the rules that govern how the system connects internally and with its external environment.

Once an organization finds a workable pattern, the first Breakpoint occurs—with a 180 degree shift in the rules. In order to grow in the most efficient and effective way, the dynamic disorder so characteristic of the entrepreneur is replaced by focusing on a pattern. Henry Ford standardized the manufacturing of automobiles, moving the auto industry into its second phase. Scores of first phase automobile manufacturers soon disappeared.

Organizational Growth - Phase Two

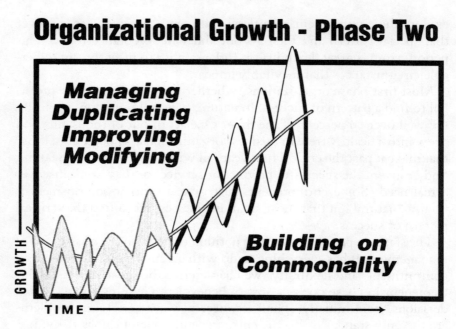

Managing Duplicating Improving Modifying

Building on Commonality

GROWTH

TIME

TRANSITION PROBLEMS

At this Breakpoint, if the entrepreneur keeps inventing and introducing new products into the environment, it can be disastrous. A number of recent corporate examples of entrepreneurs not making the shift from phase one to phase two have become legends. Steve Jobs and Steve Woycniak, the creative founders of Apple Computer, were successful entrepreneurs. Woycniak left Apple after the adventuresome entrepreneurial phase. Adjusting to a phase two management system with rules and regulations was not conducive to his creativity or propensity for invention. Steve Jobs stayed on and ultimately ran into trouble because he continued inventing when Apple needed replication. John Sculley, the Chairman of Apple Computer, suggested that if he were writing a want-ad for an entrepreneur like Steve Jobs, it would read, "Wanted: Impresario to orchestrate a workshop of wizards."

SECOND PHASE RULES FOR SUCCESS

The rules governing success in the second phase change totally. The primary objective at this point is to set up methods to repeat, extend, and improve those things that work and to discard those things that don't fit the pattern. Managers at this point talk about the "best surprise is no surprise," "solid bottom line," "running a tight ship," with "clear lines of authority." The opportunities for growth are now very different from the entrepreneurial situation. The wasted energy of trial and error in phase one must be replaced by policies, practices, and procedures that guarantee the repetition of the successful second phase pattern. The rule becomes "When you find something that works, stick with it."

A thriving phase two business regulates its internal processes, supplies, manufacturing, product lines, and selling methods and continually seeks to extend and improve its particular group of activities. During this stage, organizations strive to achieve uniform methods, efficiency, and effectiveness; a system that will support pattern repetition and extension. Clear direction from the top—policies, procedures, and measurements—is established to limit activities to those already proven successful in the past. It is a period of *growth through limitation*. Because the energy in the system can be focused on replicating the success pattern, growth in the second phase is usually very rapid.

One of the most fascinating things that happens once phase two begins is that walls are erected to exclude anything that does not fit the basic pattern. The ruling method of growth in phase two builds on *similarity and likeness*. Anything that might disturb the basic pattern is eliminated or discarded.

Fast food chains specialize in limited types of food and service with standard quality and low price. Domino's Pizza and McDonald's, for example, focused on particular products, services, and market segments. UPS and Federal Express didn't try to compete with the postal service in all areas. They selected very restricted market niches, excluding anything that didn't fit their particular pattern. The system works because of well-established limits.

Creativity does not disappear in phase two; it is focused on incremental improvements in the system. Speeding and scaling up production, reducing waste, maximizing investment in inventory, eliminating bottlenecks, and lowering defects make up a few of the areas on which second phase organizations focus. Trends such as *Management by Objectives, Just in Time* and *Total Quality* dominate organizations. Breaking original patterns or innovating by introducing the *new and different* are not appropriate or welcome. The natural fact in the second phase is that thinking too differently is actually dangerous to continuing success and sometimes even threatens the survival of the enterprise. It is unsuitable. Good managers know this and far-ranging creativity is discouraged, if not completely killed. One primary purpose of management in the second phase is *to limit and control the creative potential of the people in the organization*.

SECOND PHASE RULES AND TRAPS

Consider the ideal working rules of successful second phase systems:

- Management procedures, processes, and controls are geared to maintain order and predictability.
- Reward systems motivate the preservation and expansion of past investments and routines. Compensation is standardized and competitive.
- Quantitative measurements are used to judge the health of the system.
- People connections are narrow and specialized. People know little about what is happening outside their own area, and problems are seen as not relevant if they are outside one's own department.
- Internal organizational priorities, resource allocation, and political problems have precedence.
- The organization maintains an atmosphere of agreement. A "don't rock the boat" mentality prevails, thus reinforcing past practices. Solutions to many problems and experiments or innovations are viewed as disturbances.
- New, incompatible, and unexpected customer and competitive changes are not noticed or investigated; reality is what is communicated within the system's regular reporting processes, and malfunctions and misdirections may not be detected for long periods, particularly if they are not in the area of such normal quantitative indicators as costs, sales, or production figures.

As a consequence, although these rules work well in a predictable, stable second phase environment, when organizations encounter a third phase environment, they naturally resist change that involves doing things differently. They will resist change *regardless of obvious need or changed conditions*. The result is that unpredictable modes of failure regularly occur, often where least expected. The organization will not be able to make the vital changes needed for survival and growth.

SHIFTING TO PHASE THREE

The Breakpoint shift from second phase management to third phase Breakpoint Leadership is even more difficult than the previous leap from the entrepreneurial to management phase. Tremendous resistance can arise to make forces within the organization gear up to fight—and defeat—the change. Organizations must develop early warning signals as to when standard management will begin to produce diminishing returns. Then, it must reenter the divergent part of the creative process—in a totally new way!

The organization must open up to permit what was never allowed in to become a part of the system, not only by doing things differently, but by *doing different things*. This de-structuring the old and restructuring to integrate the new is the natural creative process at work.

The de-structuring process at Breakpoint in the business environment seems, at first glance, very disorderly. We find common symptoms that indicate that a business organization has reached the second to third phase Breakpoint:

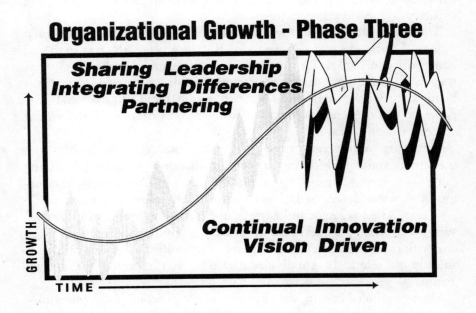

Organizational Growth - Phase Three

Sharing Leadership
Integrating Differences
Partnering

Continual Innovation
Vision Driven

GROWTH

TIME

• Rapidly Increasing Internal and Market Place Complexity in Such Areas as Product Proliferation and Market Divisions

- Internal Competition for Resources
- Increasing Costs of Manufacturing and Sales
- Diminishing Returns
- Declining Share of Market
- Decreasing Productivity Gains
- Growing External Pressures from Regulators and Influence Groups
- Increasing Impact of New Technologies
- New and Unexpected Competitors

Today's organizations in the United States and other postindustrial nations face a new kind of change. Never before has America's posture in world trade, health care, education, and production been challenged with such vigor on so many levels. The strategies that were so successful in the past are no longer working. And because today's forecasts are based on past performance, many businesses are finding that continuing growth and expansion no longer ensure profitability. The uncertainty of current trends and projections, as well as the frequency of economic and political surprises, clearly indicates that change is an irrevocable necessity, that organizations have depleted the carrying capacity of second phase patterns.

The winds of change blow from unpredictable quarters. We must now deal with a new two-tiered global marketplace: the transnational competitive organization and individual consumers who buy what they want regardless of where it comes from. Today, in order for a business to work, there must be both national and international purposes as well as extreme sensitivity to the rapid variations in individual customer needs.

Versatility and target marketing now has vast potential. The breakup of standardized markets and production is occurring throughout a wide range of products, rapidly replacing mass-produced commodities with diversified, high value-added, almost custom-made products. The magazine industry is an excellent example of this trend away from mass production. Rather than a few magazines with huge circulations, the industry is now based on literally thousands of magazines with relatively small circulations, each targeted for special groups.

Mass-produced commodity businesses are a second phase phenomenon and rest on outmoded notions of large-scale production, standard management, and mass marketing. The third phase shift to many small, special markets integrates ideas and material that were neglected in the second phase pattern. These changes include specialized consumer needs, market niches, vendor and consumer partnerships, quality over quantity, and products that are almost custom made.

REINVENTION OF THE ORGANIZATION

In phase three, *two activities occur simultaneously.* While the mainline or core business grows around creative innovations, a simultaneous renewal phase is completely reinventing the enterprise. This is technically called a *bifurcation.* The result will be the beginning of a new first phase. The renewal line is based on new *inventions.* The mainline or core business is based on *innovations.*

Even though the two processes are occurring in tandem, they require completely different kinds of creativity, leadership, and ways of doing business. They must be kept away from one another or the resulting confusion will be extreme. Entrepreneurs and core managers operate differently. The two enterprises can and will powerfully interfere with one another. The invention process is very "noisy." It looks alien. In the beginning, since there is no detectable pattern, it cannot even be recognized as relevant. In fact, *if an effort does look relevant to the core business, it probably is not part of the invention process.*

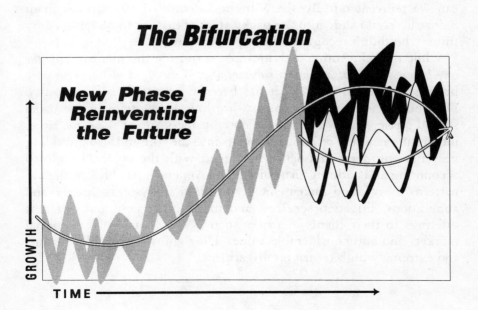

The Bifurcation

New Phase 1
Reinventing
the Future

GROWTH

TIME

In practice, a useful approach is to keep the two efforts geograph-ically and physically separated from each other with a well-organized information-sharing process. In many cases, each undertaking can incorporate discoveries made by the other. What can't be shared is the type of creativity that will assure success. Innovation doesn't mix with invention. The initial success of IBM's Entry Level Division in Boca Raton, Florida, and its creation of the business personal computer industry far away from corporate influences in Armonk, New York, shows how well such separation can work. Their integration back into the main business also demonstrates how creativity based on invention can quickly be squashed in a traditional second phase environment.

The group reinventing the enterprise, operating away from the mainline or core business, is given the mandate to re-create the organization—in a totally new way. The central question guiding this group is, "How can we put ourselves (the core enterprise) out of business?" This is done by exploration, invention, repatterning, and trial and error. The ultimate objective is that the core business and the reinvented enterprise merge in late phase three into a re-created com-pany with the same organizational purpose, but doing it in an entirely different way from what anyone expected.

Today, the public schools, large mature businesses, the transporta-tion industry, the energy industry, medicine, and the legal system, to name just a few, need groups totally dedicated to the question, "How can we reinvent ourselves?" Without a dedicated effort, even giant industries could slide into the backwaters of history to be replaced by those who didn't recognize the impossible.

While the reinvention activities go on outside the mainstream, *the core business itself also changes substantially in the third phase.* The core business continues with what has become essentially a commodity. Distribution is large and margins are low, lower than in the usual second phase. Other parts of the core business are, at the same time, integrating new and different elements into the core and also providing very new products and services aligned with the core. The global accounting and auditing firm of Arthur Andersen has broken the old patterns by offering management consultation, systems designs and applications, litigation services, and many other new and different offerings to their clients. Services such as these are aimed at special markets and add considerable value. They enjoy very high margins and extremely high return on investment.

AVOIDING THE PROBLEM

Most organizations think improving on their past successes will solve their problems. They begin recentralizing control, cutting out the fat, reducing costs, eliminating unnecessary people and programs, trimming management down to a lean, mean team. Numbers are watched with magnifying glasses. Accountability dominates. Departments compete ruthlessly for scarce resources, salespeople wheel and deal in the marketplace to make their quotas, and supervisors push workers to the wall to get production. The entire organization moves into a siege mentality to defend itself from any threats, real or imagined. This is what we have come to call the *Back to Basics Bump*. It is seen as the ultimate solution for getting out of the temporary downturn.

Unfortunately, normal accounting and auditing practices support the illusion that going Back to Basics is a solid strategy. If management's major attention is focused just on the bottom line, going Back to Basics in late phase two appears to pay off. Sales and profits rise over the short term. The audits look good. At the same time, everything not directly related to making the numbers is set aside. *Any innovation or change that might not produce immediate and certain results is squashed.* Even competition edging into market segments with new products and services is ignored. No one wants to rock an already unsteady boat by asking for significant changes in products or procedures. Everyone knows what happens to messengers carrying bad news.

What never appears on audit sheets are the absolutely critical elements like:

- Fostering creativity
- Amount and rate of product and process innovation
- Knowledge about customers' and prospects' needs
- Employee morale and turnover
- Developing leadership skills
- Competitive information
- People's commitment to a common vision

Because of the shortage of information in these essential areas, following the Back to Basics cure ultimately kills the patient.

Alternatively, some businesses try to solve their economic problems by aggressive acquisition and diversification. The results of this strategy have produced a litany of failures. Instead of avoiding the problem, as Back to Basics does, this is an effort to *change the problem* by entering another business. The vast majority of these undertakings by big companies to diversify their business lines since 1950 have ended in failure.

According to Michael Porter, a management expert at Harvard Business School, companies that fail in diversification typically chose the wrong businesses, spend too much for them, or ignore whether the linkages truly add anything to either side. In a study of thirty-three of the largest United States companies, Porter looked at 3,788 entries into new businesses through acquisitions, joint ventures, or start-ups from 1950 to 1986. The results showed that diversification succeeds *only* when the old and new units transfer skills back and forth or share activities.

Without question, all organizations that resist the Breakpoint leap from phase two to three will eventually go out of business. In nature, this results in the extinction of a species. In political terms, it results in the collapse of parties or governments. The big question is how to make that great leap from the past to the future.

MAKING THE BREAKPOINT SHIFT TO THE THIRD PHASE

When we consider the changes that must occur in the usual organization to succeed in a highly competitive, fast, and unpredictably changing third phase world, solutions include such shifts as:

- From mechanical technology to electronic technologies
- From uneducated, unskilled, replaceable workers doing simple physical tasks to educated, skilled, career workers performing complex mental tasks
- From mass production to specialized and global markets
- From a "factory-out" product focus to a customer-focused system
- From functionally organized systems to integrated, multifunctional, multicultural teams organized around markets
- From clear and sharp divisions between controlling managers and directed workers to managers as supportive, resource finders and workers as self-managers
- From making incremental improvements to adding significant value through innovations
- From price competition with vendors to long-term, value-added relationships

The Breakpoint shift to the third phase is difficult because it requires:

- Valuing and trusting employees and others who have an interest in the organization
- Shifting from repeating and improving to creative innovation
- Committing to and being guided by an inspiring and compelling vision
- Recognizing the interdependence of the organization, its employees, the community, constituents, and customers in a global setting

In that process the organization unearths and asks completely new questions, it lets go of the limits of management control and understands that those within the organization are no longer the preeminent experts, that customers, employees, owners, community members, and vendors must truly become valued partners in creating the organization's future.

Unfortunately, many leading management theorists, consulting firms, and colleges of business continue to focus on how to become successful second phase managers. The traditional business cycle shows an enterprise going from birth through robust growth to maturation and decline without either a phase of innovation or a cycle of rebirth. They show no third phase. It is accepted that innovation and replacement traditionally come from outside the industry, not inside it. Motels were not created by the hotel industry, softcover publishing wasn't the brainchild of the hardcover publishers, desktop publishing did not grow out of the printing establishment, air travel was not invented by the railroad industry. Re-creating the enterprise is as difficult, in fact probably more difficult, than the shift from phase one to phase two.

MOVING BEYOND BREAKPOINT (ALMOST)

The new reality at this turning point in history is a great opportunity to go beyond Breakpoint. Once we recognize that solutions from our past second phase simply won't work anymore, we can move to the unequaled challenges before us and apply totally new rules for success.

Today, as organizations abruptly encounter a third phase environment they have begun to undergo the processes of third phase integration. They realize it makes good sense to organize to meet a new set of needs. Those needs could be stated as:

- Unleashing the creative capacity of employees
- Responding rapidly to customer changes
- Innovating to meet competition
- Adding new and different value to products and services
- Partnering relationships with customers
- Manufacturing and selling to new, different and smaller market segments around the world
- Planning geared to anticipate emerging problems and opportunities
- Understanding and working with outside pressure groups
- Producing quality within a work environment where managers and workers trust and value one another
- Integrating new technologies
- Integrating diverse cultures in the organization

In order to meet these new needs, organizations have employed a variety of contemporary techniques. The methods range from participative management, global marketing, and quality circles to employee involvement and innovation teams. Organizations enter upon programs to change the culture and replace the management hierarchy with a horizontal structure. They practice strategic planning, segmented marketing, and "management by walking around."

All of these solutions have value. *Most have failed to bring about the desired results.* In fact in the hundreds of organizations we have worked with and studied, we observed that implementing these changes has usually created more problems than it has solved. Introducing the new and different has so interfered with the way the organization has always worked that natural resistance to change rears its head and either openly or unconsciously sabotages the solutions.

The great challenge facing organizations today goes far beyond what can be accomplished by introducing a new program or using cookbook techniques. Organizations defeat their best intentions by continuing to operate with essential beliefs that automatically perpetuate the second phase.

The most obvious sign of these basic obstacles is that of the continuity of a management system. In normal second phase organizations, management exists in a tightly controlled hierarchy in which managers are unquestioned emblems of authority. The manager's function—to control, organize, and predict—is critical and necessary in any second phase organization. Otherwise the processes of replication, improvement, exclusion of differences, incremental increases, and standardization could not work. *Yet, the fact is that management's primary role is to limit the potential of the organization!*

One of the few things you can predict about the third phase is that many of the things an organization said it would never do while it was in the second phase, are exactly what it will be doing in the third. Barriers crumble, values shift, rules change, and they do it very dramatically—more dramatically than we can easily imagine.

We are entering a period that demands that we operate in such a way as to empower the incalculable assets of human intelligence and creativity. The major distinction, for example, between old and new methods lies not in the methods themselves, but in the ability to integrate human beings into meaningful work. The new world requires humans to function as essential information and idea resources, creating solutions we have never seen before. In this kind of situation, human labor is no longer a disposable commodity, but a unique creative resource, in which an *individual's development is as valuable as the organization's growth.*

The main current of creative change in the third phase is the fulfillment of the organization's potential. In human and organizational terms, it is characterized not just by accepting and bringing in the previously excluded, the new, and the different, but by the people in the system functioning in trusting and interdependent relationships, by committing to a vision and long-term purpose, by acknowledging the unlimited creative potential of its people and by connecting with those outside the organization in creative and mutually benefiting partnerships. This kind of behavior violates the basic principles of logic, control, predictable order, and results that worked so well in management for so very long.

Just as when cells shifted from copying themselves to exchanging DNA in hybrids, the shift from phase two to phase three in organizations is revolutionary; growth no longer occurs through the limited extension of likeness or similarities but in sharing, exchanging differences, creating what has never before existed, and fulfilling the unrealized and unknown potential of the system.

Many nonprofit organizations and foundations are making the third phase shift far more successfully than entrenched government bureaucracies, the education establishment, or mature businesses. The Girl Scouts, founded in 1912, has continued its dedication "to inspiring girls with the highest ideals of character, conduct, patriotism, and service." Committed to innovative ways to reach young girls, the Girl Scouts today extends its programs to homeless girls in inner cities and has expanded its volunteer program at a time when volunteers in nonprofit organizations have fallen precipitously. The rapid changes in family structure have had a dramatic impact on the lives of young girls, causing the organization to extend its programs to girls who are five years old rather than the customary age of seven. The Girl Scouts continually shifts its programs to meet special conditions, whether it be nutrition counseling, working with children of divorce, or offering a stable hand in time of crisis.

Strikingly few examples of successful phase three businesses exist and, for the most part, they are relatively small and nonmainstream organizations such as Herman Miller in Michigan, Johnsonville Foods in Wisconsin, North American Tool and Die in California, Branch Bank in North Carolina, The Body Shop in England or company divisions such as the Business Systems Consulting group at Arthur Andersen, the Palo Alto Group at Xerox, and the Saturn Plant of General Motors in Tennessee. This is understandable because the massive cultural forces surrounding organizations have reinforced second phase rules and beliefs. Today's emerging culture makes shifting to the third phase both necessary and possible.

27

THE AGE OF LIGHT

by Hazel Henderson

Light—rather than matter, energy, or time—is fundamental to the universe. Consequently, the author has chosen this metaphor to take us beyond the Information Age into the dawning of the Age of Light.

Light as an organizing principle for the future demands a shift from the old paradigm "inert" classical physics view of the world to the organic living system perspectives of biology and ecology. Light implies energy and demands action. Light both illuminates and inspires. Light is the essence of nature's technological genius.

In the Age of Light, "economic development" will be described as a more ecological "sustainable development." And the Age will herald a new synthesis of scientific, religious, and spiritual traditions.

These and other visions are presented here by Hazel Henderson, who served on the Advisory Council of the United States Congress Office of Technology Assessment from 1974 to 1980. She is the author of Politics of the Solar Age *and* Paradigms in Progress: Life Beyond Economics. *She is currently an international consultant on alternative development, a Limited Partner of the Global Environment Fund, a board member of the Calvert Social Investment Fund, and serves on the Editorial Board of* Technological Forecasting and Social Change *in New York.*

The "Information Age" has become a ubiquitous image among futurists seeking fruitful metaphors for the ongoing restructuring of industrial societies. New images of post-industrial society proliferated in the 1970s as the restructuring of industrial societies accelerated. Alvin Toffler's *The Third Wave* (1980) depicted a globalizing human culture based on information, more appropriate use of technology, and more productive, proactive individuals outgrowing consumerism. In *Alternative Futures for America* (1970) and several other books, Robert Theobald[1] outlined what he called "the Communications Era," describing a shift toward community empowerment, automation, and greater dissemination of information.

My own view is that information disseminated more broadly could facilitate the rise of networks of citizens that could cross-cut old power structures, facilitate learning, and initiate a widespread politics of reconceptualization, transforming our fragmented world view into an new paradigm based on planetary awareness: an Age of Light, auguring planetary cultures sustainably based on renewable resources and a deeper understanding of Nature. At a more basic level, we know from quantum physics and Planck's constant that it is *Light* (rather than matter, energy or time) that is fundamental to the Universe. Planck's equation holds that quanta of light are also quanta of *action*. The Age of Light has been augured in most religious literature, most notably in the Bible. In Genesis, God's first command was, "Let there be Light."

The Age of Light lies beyond the Information Age. The Information Age is no longer an adequate image for the present, let alone a guide to the future. It still focuses on hardware technologies, mass production, narrow economic models of efficiency and competition, and is more an extension of industrial ideas and methods than a new stage in human development. Information is an abundant resource rather than a scarce commodity (as in economic theory) and demands new cooperative rules from local to global levels.

Information itself does not enlighten. We cannot clarify what is *mis*-information, *dis*-information, or propaganda in this media dominated, "spin-doctored" environment. Focusing on mere information has led to an overload of ever-less-meaningful billions of bits of fragmented raw data and sound bites rather than the search for meaningful new patterns of knowledge.

My view of the dawning Age of Light involves a repatterning of the exploding Information Age. This requires nothing less than a paradigm shift to a holistic view of the entire human family, now inextricably linked by our globe-girdling technologies. The Earth is re-perceived as a living Planet, and the most appropriate view is organic, based on the self-organizing models of the life sciences. Biological sciences become more useful spectacles, and it is no accident that biotechnologies are becoming our most morally-ambiguous tools.

The Age of Light will follow from the Solar Age as humans gradually learn that it is light and action that are fundamental in the universe. The technologies of the Age of Light are already appearing. Beyond electronics, these phototronic technologies are miracles of speed and miniaturization, such as the new 0.25 micron "superchip" (400 times thinner than a human hair). These superchips now on the drawing board can pack hundreds of millions of transistors—ten times today's record. In the year 2000, 0.1 micron widths will be the cutting edge, small enough to cram billions of transistors on a single chip. Even today's advance optical printing methods will have to give way to higher frequencies in the spectrum, using x-ray lithography.

The Age of Light is an image that reminds us that it is the light from the sun that drives the earth's processes and powers its cycles of carbon, nitrogen, hydrogen, and water and the climate "machine." It is these light-driven processes—which are then mediated by the photosynthesis of plants—that maintain conditions for us to continue our evolution beyond the Information Age. Our present technologies are already maturing from their basis in electronics and are shifting to phototronics. These new lightwave technologies include fiber optics, lasers, optical scanning, optical computing, photovoltaics, and other photoconversion processes.

As we progress in these areas we will notice how each one leads us into a deeper appreciation of Nature's technological genius; we have modeled our earlier breakthroughs, such as flight, on that of birds. Nature's light-conversion technologies, the basis of which is photosynthesis, still serve as design criteria and marvels of miniaturization, such as the chloroplast cells all green plants use to convert photons into usable glycogen, hydrocarbons and cellulose. This is still the basic production process on which all humans rely and when our photovoltaic cells can match the performance of the chloroplast, we will be on the right track. Thus the Age of Light is more than the new lightwave technologies emerging from the computer, robotics and artificial intelligence labs. The Age of Light will be characterized by our growing abilities to cooperate with and learn from Nature. The Age of Light will build on today's biotechnology, still in its exploratory, often exploitative, moral infancy.

The Age of Light will bring a new awareness and reverence for living systems and the exquisite information technology of DNA, the wisdom and coding of all living experience on this Planet. The Age of Light will go far beyond industrial, manipulative modes toward deeper interconnecting, co-creative designing with and learning from Nature, as we become a species consciously co-evolving with all life forms on this unique water Planet.

The Age of Light will also be one of a time compression, as we include our holistic, intuitive, right-brain hemisphere cognition with our more analytical, left-brain functioning, and as our computers catch up in their abilities for parallel processing with the simultaneity of our own brains' synapses. The peerless design of the human brain still presents the ultimate challenge to computer designers, despite the much-vaunted progress in so-called "artificial intelligence" systems.

At the same time we are learning much more about our own bodies' responses to light, and how humans deprived of full-spectrum, natural light in indoor living and working conditions can suffer weakening of their endocrine and immune systems. Thus the wisest of us recognize that our Earth still has much to teach us—if we can humble ourselves and quiet our egos long enough to really listen and see, hear, smell and feel all her wonders. When we can feel this kind of attunement to the whole creation, we are transported with natural delight to the "high" that psychologist Abraham Maslow called "peak experiences." As we reintegrate our awareness in this way, we no longer crave endless consumption of goods beyond those needed for a healthy life, but seek new challenges in our societies for order, peace and justice, and to develop our spirituality.

It is in this way that humans can overcome the dismal Second Law of Thermodynamics in the continual striving for learning and wisdom. We no longer blind our imagination with the dismal deterministic view of a universe winding down like a closed system. Since Prigogine, we know that the universe is full of surprises, innovation and evolutionary potential.[2] In fact, Cartesian science's search for certainty, equilibrium, predictability and control is a good definition of death. We should happily embrace the new view that uncertainty is fundamental, since it also implies that everything can change—for the better—in a twinkling of an eye! As we move on to post-Cartesian science, we can acknowledge the earlier period of the Scientific Enlightenment of Descartes and Newton, Liebniz and Galileo. Its instrumental rationality and manipulation of Nature did lead to that greatest outpouring of technological hardware and managerial virtuosity which we call the Industrial Revolution.

The whole process of human development is teleological and evolutionary, and therefore cannot be explained or predicted by existing reductionistic scientific paradigms. This great purposeful unfolding of human potentialities toward goals—bettering human societies, perfecting the means of production and fostering conditions of people's lives so that they might fulfill themselves—is essentially a spiritual, as well as an instrumental and materialistic endeavor.

Binding such a transcendent set of human goals and visions for the future within the so-called "laws of economics" was and is a travesty.

With new perspectives and new paradigms in the 1990s we can move beyond old conceptual prisons, whether the reductionist view of the Information Age or the, so far, literal interpretations of the Solar Age.

Human development and social organization are processes that, by definition, have goals, purposes and values—and move toward them. Thus any discipline still based on classical physics and Newton's celestial mechanics, particularly economics, cannot be overhauled or expanded enough to map the dynamics of such unfolding processes. In fact, Western science has many specific *prohibitions* against any hypothesizing about values and purpose, and most often denies the existence of teleological aspects in Nature. Thus, its methods are based on the search for certainty, fundamental laws and exactitude (what I have termed "micro-rationality" to distinguish these endeavors from the mapping of larger contexts and more holistic enquiries, which I term "macro-rationality"). A hopeful sign of today's shift to broader paradigms is the fact that the process of human development is being referred to less and less often as "economic development." The word "economic" has been dropped altogether in the new ecological definition: "sustainable development."

Meanwhile, classical science still has no theory of *process,* and development is a multi-dimensional process. Arthur M. Young in *The Reflexive Universe*[3] presents a sweeping synthesis of science and human development in his Theory of Process, based on quantum, as well as classical physics. Young, the developer of the Bell helicopter, assumes that the universe is based on freedom and that the fundamental laws that humans have discovered are constraints on this freedom, but they are secondary. As any artist or designer knows, constraints actually serve the creative process—providing the medium, conditions and context for the play of creativity. Young believes that the problem with the main body of Western science is that it limits itself to focus on the material plane, dealing with "inert" matter, i.e., molar objects, such as rocks. (These appear "inert" because the random motions of their molecules cancel each other out.) Young's Process Theory starts not from matter as fundamental, but with light, or action as fundamental (i.e., Planck's constant, as mentioned, views light as quanta of action, also as quanta of uncertainty). From this beginning point, Young assumes that processes are, by definition, purposeful and involve *individual* actions of atoms, molecules and organisms with inherent goals (rather than the statistical probabilities or averages of the classical view).

Thus, the Age of Light is metaphoric to many levels:

First, it is based on the re-membering and re-wholing of human perceptions and paradigms. Nowhere is this now more evident than in the wide understanding of the First Law of Ecology: Everything is connected to everything else.

Secondly, this new paradigm and worldview also represents a new synthesis between Western science and religious and spiritual traditions, since it embraces purpose and meaning as fundamental to life processes. Furthermore purpose implies cognition, consciousness, heuristics, goal-seeking and visioning as central to all life, at various levels, and most pronounced in humans.

Thirdly, the dawning of the Age of Light augurs the current reintegration of ourselves into a new level of awareness of the needs of the gene pool, as we engender ever greater risks to future generations with our technologies. Thus there is also a reawakening of the values of the Great Mother and a concern to rebalance gender roles and responsibilities in a new partnership society, with cooperation and peaceful conflict resolution now clearly the *sine qua non* of our survival. Gregory Bateson's *Mind and Nature* provides a valuable synthesis.[4] Naturally, such a vast cultural change has also ushered in a new search for more comprehensive meaning to decode all of our accumulated cultural DNA in finding a new place for humans in the cosmos and new significance for the human journey on this Earth.

The Solar Age and its politics have also arrived—a decade later than I had predicted—given ghastly impetus by the 1991 Gulf War. This tragic, unnecessary conflict, which could have been avoided, will be viewed as the inflection point of fossil fueled industrialism. The politics of the shift to the Solar Age is fundamentally different from that of the industrial period. In *The Politics of the Solar Age,* I credited the insights of English chemist Frederick Soddy (1877-1956) who shared the Nobel Peace Prize with Rutherford. Soddy's *Cartesian Economics* (1922) could have corrected economic theory for the Solar Age,[5] but he was ridiculed by the economists of the time and had to self-publish his book. The Solar Age will be more decentralized and the transition to more democratic processes will be necessary. Hierarchical mega-governments and mega-corporations, continent-wide transport and distribution of food and goods were all predicated on cheap oil. The underlying dynamic of the Solar Age, as Soddy predicted, will be how to control energy flows in human societies most efficiently and implies a top to bottom design revolution in all societies, which is at last beginning.

The forces and lobbies of the past—nuclear and fossil energy companies, interstate highway builders, concrete pourers, automakers and all the other industrial sectors built on waste, maximum energy use and rapidly increasing levels of entropy—are now, all over the world, locked in legislative and market combat with the emerging sectors. The new industries which minimize entropy are based on refined, miniaturized, and more "intelligent" technologies which pinpoint end-use energy needs, re-use and recycle all resources and tackle the job of cleaning up the devastating effects of industrialism. The newest enterprises must address environmental restoration and enhancing where possible the performance of eco-systems.

In 1991, one of the first "trade shows" of this budding sector of 21st century economies was convened in Florida by the Society for Ecological Restoration. Here biologists replanting sea grasses rubbed shoulders with ecologists from power companies in charge of remediation of spoiled lands and specialists in restoring ruined soils with specially designed crops or micro-organisms. Bio-remediation and desert-greening will be big business in the 21st century, a point I have been emphasizing since the 1970s. Of course, this whole scenario will depend on capturing more elegantly and efficiently some of the planet's abundant daily photon shower from the Sun. As Soddy put it in 1922, "How does man, or anything live—BY SUNSHINE!"

This will require that economics be demoted from a macro-policy tool to a micro role in keeping books between firms, based on full-cost pricing. But the *data* on externalities and social costs will have to be developed by more realistic disciplines: thermodynamics, biology, systems and chaos models and ecology. For example, as economic growth models disordered and destroyed ever larger ecological and biospherical systems, the analysis of this damage was taken over by such interdisciplinary teams of scientists as the U.S. National Committee on Man and the Biosphere (MAB) and its program for evaluation of Human Dominated Systems (i.e., those significantly affected by human activities). MAB's programs, started in 1989, include in its 1991 agenda a U.S. Action Plan for Biosphere Reserves. Economists are *not* included in most of its scientific committees, since its central concerns are for ecological sustainability.[6]

As I have emphasized for the past 20 years, *these* are the criteria that must form the context for all human activities and "development" goals—rather than *any* of the unscientific formulas of economic theory, still based on the outmoded "welfare" theory, Pareto Optimality (which ignores income distribution and asks absurd questions, about how much people are "willing to pay" to preserve a wilderness area from developers who can always outbid citizens, because the "development" will reward them rich profits).

The dire consequences when ignorant humans trespass into "managing" natural systems is now clear, for example, adding some seven billion tons of carbon to the Earth's atmosphere each year—contributing to global warming—while at the same time cutting down between 30-50 million acres of carbon-absorbing forests. World Resources Institute of Washington, DC, offers some strategies to check this looming disaster. Tree planting is a primary strategy—one adopted all over the world by ordinary citizens. At the same time I pointed this out while serving as a member of the Advisory Council of the U.S. Congress Office of Technology Assessment in 1975, scientific committees were still arguing about whether there was a problem. In 1989, the experts and politicians caught up with citizens' movements such as Chipko and Africa's Greenbelt tree-planters, when environmental ministers from 68 countries signed the Noordwijk Declaration (in the largely below-sea level Netherlands) which called for the goal of an annual 30 million acre net increase in forest cover by the year 2000, to reduce net human carbon emissions.[7] Thus economists are learning that investments in the 1990s will have to be directed into ecological restoration and social programs—health care, education and population control—a far cry from their current investment priorities to hype GNP growth.

The Age of Light will also be a time of re-weaving the world's cultures, most of which down through history have understood our planet's total dependence on the sun. They understood and worshipped our Mother Star in myths and traditions, as well as the primal light of the universe, whether from stars or distant galaxies. As physicist David Peat notes in *The Philosophers Stone,* synchronicity is the bridge between mind and matter, and he lovingly describes the new sciences of "chaos" now inching toward mapping some parts of this wonderful universe where light, action and surprise rule, all within the constraints so well mapped by classical physics.[8] Peat envisions an era of "gentle action," where millions of more aware people in more democratic societies can act more intelligently together. As Arthur Young adds, "science is humanity's map, but myth is its compass."

The Age of Enlightenment, some 300 years ago in Europe, expressed some of these hopes and visionary designs for human potential and development. As we move beyond the Information Age to greater wisdom, we may steer through today's crises and clouds into the sunshine of the Age of Light.

NOTES

1. See for example *The Rapids of Change,* Robert Theobald, Knowledge Systems, Inc., Indianapolis, 1987.
2. Ilya Prigogine, *From Being to Becoming,* H.H. Freeman, San Francisco, 1980.
3. Arthur M. Young, *The Reflexive Universe,* Delacorte, New York, 1976.
4. Gregory Bateson, *Mind and Nature: A Necessary Unity,* Bantam Books, New York, 1980.
5. Hazel Henderson, *The Politics of the Solar Age,* current edition from Knowledge Systems, Indianapolis, 1988, p. 225 on Frederick Soddy.
6. *U.S. MAB Bulletin,* Vol. 15, #3, August 1991, U.S. Department of State, Washington, DC 20522-3706.
7. World Resources Institute, "Minding the Carbon Store: Weighing U.S. Forestry Strategies to Slow Global Warming" Mark C. Trexler, January 1991.
8. Another classic resource for further exploration of these understandings is the four volume *Dynamics: the Geometry of Behavior* by Ralph H. Abraham and Christopher D. Shaw, Aerial Press, Santa Cruz, 1982-1988.

28

FOUNDATION FOR A NEW WORLD ORDER

by Riane Eisler

Here is a global call to action, proposing a systems approach focusing on three interrelated, long-range, strategic objectives: changing the foundations for human relations; values, beliefs, and myths; and economics.

Riane Eisler is the author of the international best-seller The Chalice and the Blade: Our History, Our Future. *She is co-author with David Loye of* The Partnership Way: New Tools for Living and Learning, *and co-founder of the Center for Partnership Studies, in Pacific Grove, California.*

A growing number of nations have or will soon have the chemical and/or nuclear capacity to terrorize and even destroy our planet. At the same time, our planetary habitat is being decimated by "man's conquest of nature." To effectively deal with these problems, we must immediately begin to concentrate our creative and financial resources on fundamentals: a worldwide shift from domination to partnership in human relations, in values, and in economics.

I. A GLOBAL CAMPAIGN AGAINST VIOLENCE AND ABUSE IN INTIMATE RELATIONS

Terror in the home, terror in an authoritarian state, and international terror are inextricably intertwined. It is through our intimate relations that we learn habits of feeling, thinking, and behavior in all human relations be they personal or political. This is why this first strategic objective focuses on interpersonal relations (specifically between parents and children) as well as between women and men (both inside and outside the family).

Although this is rarely articulated, women and men *are* the two halves of humanity. Consequently, the way the relationship between them is structured is a fundamental model which, along with parent-child relations, profoundly affects whether all other relationships will be modeled on partnership or domination.

Yet in many parts of the world, systematic and severe violence against children is still not recognized as child abuse. Nor is wife beating recognized as a violent way of one individual dominating and terrorizing another.

An important sign of hope is that there is in our world today a strong movement toward what I call a partnership rather than a dominator family. Millions now recognize that a family based on control rather than trust is dysfunctional. There is also a strong movement toward real partnership in all spheres of life between women and men. But this movement is still localized and its growth far too slow at a time when a dominator model of society and high technology are an increasingly lethal mix.

The urgent task at hand is to accelerate this process everywhere. An effective, achievable tactic is a Global Campaign Against Violence and Abuse in the Family. The United Nation's Year of the Family in 1994 offers a ready-made opportunity for international networking to support such a campaign.

II. A GLOBAL CAMPAIGN FOR PARTNERSHIP— EDUCATION AND ENTERTAINMENT

We must question basic assumptions embedded within our values and myths if we are going to survive. Unfortunately, not only through the mass media but through many of our religious and secular classics, the message handed down from generation to generation is not only that domination and violence are inevitable, but also that there is something wonderful about them. In story after story, men who kill are considered truly manly or heroic, and women who are self-sacrificing and servile are considered truly feminine. Violence is presented to us as entertaining and fun. Abusive relationships are the stuff TV sitcoms are made of.

To counteract these messages which maintain dominator relations, we must quickly and effectively replace them with different cultural messages, different archetypes, heroines, and heroes suitable for a partnership world.

It is essential that we effectively use both our educational system and mass media to accelerate these shifts in consciousness rather than continuing to export dominator myths and values all over the world, thus seeding our own destruction. One key tactic is to launch a Global Campaign for Partnership Education and Entertainment and to organize a Media Consortium committed to prioritizing resources and focusing creative energy on a media partnership blitz. Another key tactic, relating to the next strategic objective, is a Global Campaign for the Equal Education of Women initially focusing on women's literacy, which will provide an essential missing component for successful economic and social development worldwide.

III. A GLOBAL CAMPAIGN FOR PARTNERSHIP— ECONOMICS

Thousands of books have been written about the links between economics and warfare, between poverty and violent crime. These are real links, but their larger context needs to be better understood and addressed.

A good starting point is the additional correlation between overpopulation and warfare, and the fact that, not coincidentally, the poorest and most warlike regions of our world are those where women have little access to education, remunerative employment, and/or family planning. Also, not coincidentally, these are generally regions characterized by "machismo" (the equation of masculinity with domination and conquest) and thus areas where chronic violence and counter-violence (and with this, the destruction of economic and ecological resources) is a major contributor to chronic poverty.

Once we begin to recognize the connections between the personal and the political, it also becomes evident that our economic systems—whether capitalist or socialist—rest on fundamentally imbalanced foundations. The basic model for habits of economic thinking and acting are internalized in our childhoods. And globally, to a large extent, this still takes place in families where caring and nurturing, and the work of maintenance and cleaning (essential for our ecological survival), is given lip service, but, in fact, is considered inferior, and often not even classified as "real work."

Even more specifically, our learning of economic attitudes and behaviors by and large takes place in families where women (who do most of the caring and cleaning) in fact work much longer hours than men (according to UN statistics, twice as long) and have little if any economic decision-making power or control over how resources are distributed. The result, according to UN statistics, is that women earn globally one-tenth of what men do and own only one-hundredth as much property. With such a model, why would funding for caring and nurturing work (social services, education, health, etc.), and ecologically responsible ways of cleaning up our environment be top policy priorities?

It is evident that unless we shift to a partnership economics, beyond both capitalism and communism, caring and cleaning will inevitably take second place to the "important" things, such as ever-improved ways of dominating and controlling—even though the enormous expenditures on weaponry rather than human services today threaten to bankrupt, and, ultimately, destroy our planet.

A sign of hope is the growing recognition among corporate managers and individual entrepreneurs of both the greater productivity and creativity of partnership (as in teamwork and in nurturing leadership styles) and the urgent need for a new, more humane, socially and ecologically responsible business ethos. However, these partnership trends need to be supported and strengthened—with particular attention to the still largely ignored dynamics of how so-called "women's issues" such as comparable worth and intrafamily economic relations impact both politics and economics worldwide.

A Global Campaign for Partnership Economics would include more realistic measures of productivity that include women's unpaid services, as well as policies promoting the entry of women into economic decision-making positions. It would include lobbying governments to link foreign aid to respect for human rights in both the family and the state, which will help destabilize familial and social dominator structures of violence, abuse, and exploitation. This will help stabilize the world by constructing a basis for international, social, and economic cooperation, rather than international terrorism.

CONCLUSION

I am convinced this three-pronged strategy can be achieved. It will require the commitment of substantial time and money. It will require the effective networking of organizations and individuals all over this country and the world. It will require the innovative and organizational skills of entrepreneurs who understand that the most essential and thus most *profitable* enterprise in the world today is fundamental social, economic, and ideological transformation. Most important, it will require massive education as the basis for more realistic long-range policy priorities.

If we begin to address the fundamentals quickly, we and our children have a chance. If we do not, regardless of all our good intentions and good works, we will only be stirring the surface, with inevitably disastrous results.

29

APPROACHING THE MILLENNIUM: BUSINESS AS VEHICLE FOR GLOBAL TRANSFORMATION

by Willis Harman

In this essay, Willis Harman looks beyond the current first steps of new paradigm thinking to address the necessity for a broader, revolutionary pattern of global transformation. He identifies both the forces for change and the obstacles to it, particularly identifying the crucial role of business, as the dominant social institution on the planet, in achieving this radical transition.

Harman presents a realistic view of our ability to emerge from these difficult times, proposing such systematic new paradigm goals as greater ecological awareness, peace and common security, decentralization, trans-materialist beliefs, social responsibility, cultural pluralism, empowerment of people, and nonviolent change.

Few doubt that major changes are taking place in the business corporation. John Naisbitt and Patricia Aburdene write of "re-inventing the corporation" and observe that *"The new corporation differs from the old in both goals and basic assumptions.* In the information era . . . the strategic resource is information, knowledge, creativity. There is only one way a corporation can gain access to these valuable commodities. . . . People—human capital—are its most important resource. . . . The word will get around about which companies have nourishing environments for personal growth, and those will attract our very best and brightest."

Perry Pascarella, executive editor of *Industry Week,* writes: *"A quiet revolution is taking place . . . in the business corporation.* . . . Individuals are awakening to the possibility of personal growth and finding ways to attain it. . . . More and more managers are coming to believe that they have to refashion organizational structure and procedures to establish a culture that makes use of workers' quest for self-development and commitment to something outside themselves."

Alvin Toffler notes these cultural changes and finds us facing "the deepest upheaval and creative restructuring of all time. . . . The transformation of the corporation is part of the larger transformation of the socio-sphere as a whole. . . . Taken together, they add up to a massive historical shift."

The "new paradigm" as it is often termed—the new pattern of business in society—is coming about partly because of this awakening on the part of managers and workers. But it is also coming about partly of a widening perception that industrial society has been following a path that in the end doesn't work.

To understand this better, and to see what kinds of response are called for, we propose discussions along the lines indicated by the following five questions:

1. What is meant by "global transformation"?
2. Is it realistic to think of such a profound change in a period of a few decades?
3. What leads us to believe that business has such a special role?
4. What needs to be done?
5. Can we do it?

1. WHAT IS MEANT BY "GLOBAL TRANSFORMATION"?

Every society on Earth has been influenced by the Western industrial paradigm, most of them profoundly so. This has brought undeniable benefits, but also problems. The hazards of modern weapons of mass destruction, environmental deterioration, man-made climate change, and toxic wastes are well known. The Western paradigm appears to have contributed to the world population problem in that it has contributed to reduced mortality rates and also, in ways less understood, increased fertility rates. It has impacted traditional societies in many regions in such a way as to contribute to chronic hunger and poverty. These problems, taken together, present such a powerful challenge that some people feel they can only be resolved through a fundamental transformation of the prevailing values and dominant institutions of modern society.

There are indications, too, of significant cultural changes around the globe. People everywhere are less willing to put up with despotic regimes, and challenge their legitimacy using the watchwords "liberty" and "democracy." In the South, those who had, for so long, accepted the role of privation, inferiority and servility are less and less willing to do so. In the rich countries of the North a major cultural shift seems to be underway, spearheaded by such movements as "Green" thinking, "deep ecology," new concepts of management and leadership, and the recent emphasis in the women's movement on reassessing basic values. Perhaps the two chief components of this shift could be identified as *holism* (understanding in terms of whole systems and organisms rather than fragments; non-separateness; appreciation of "everything connected to everything" in a single unity), and reliance on the *inner authority and inner resources* (intuition, deep spiritual center; "we create our reality").

Together, these two forces—the "push" of the global dilemmas and the "pull" of a vision of what could be—define and actuate the incipient global transformation.

2. IS IT REALISTIC TO THINK OF SUCH A PROFOUND CHANGE IN A PERIOD OF A FEW DECADES?

Would it have been realistic, in the mid-1980s, to think of the profound changes that have actually taken place in Eastern Europe and Russia? When masses of people change from perceiving the locus of *authority* to be external, and make it internal; when masses of people recognize that they can challenge the *legitimacy* of whatever oppresses them—then the balance of power between institutions and people shifts. What then can limit change?

This is not to suggest that a profound transformation can be manipulated into being. But when the inner changes have quietly taken place over time, the consequent outer change can take place with remarkable rapidity. Are we at such a point in history?

Item: Evidence of Fundamental "Change of Consciousness" or "Awakening" in the Business World and in Society

• Indications of a redefinition of management, away from using the power of position to direct the resources of the corporation, toward the development and encouragement of the creativity of others.

• Indications of a redefinition of the corporation, toward considering product and profit more as *means,* and human growth and development, and achievement of truly fulfilling lives, as the real goals of corporations. Related to this is a tendency to delegitimate the idea that investors (stockholders) call the shots, and a tendency toward enhancing the influence of employees (who invest their *lives*)—through employee ownership and in other ways.

• Clues from the nature of recent executive development seminars and workshops, which emphasize topics like intuition, creative imagination, power of vision, working on purpose, learning to trust, developing an attitude of "all experience is feedback."

Item: Indications That Fundamental Change Is Needed to Resolve Societal and Global Dilemmas:

There was a time when the most serious problems of humankind had to do with satisfying basic needs and dealing with the hazards of the natural environment. However, is it not true that the most serious problems of modern society stem from the *successes* of the industrial-society paradigm? The horrors of modern warfare, worldwide environmental spoliation, progressive resource depletion, interference with life-supporting ecological systems, widespread poverty and hunger, prevalence of hazardous substances, stress-related disease, the possibility of detrimental man-caused climate changes, are interconnected world dilemmas which are all directly rooted in the belief-and-value system of modern industrial society. Is it not likely that their satisfactory resolution will not be accomplished by problem-solving approaches of the types we have been attempting (technological, managerial, creating new institutions), but rather, will be achieved only through fundamental change in that paradigm?

Other Questions to Bother You

• Is it really a good idea to measure the performance of our society by economic indicators, such as the GNP, which are essentially measures of how rapidly the Earth's resources are being used up, converted to economic product?

• Is it really good to put such emphasis on economic growth, as though it were unreservedly a good thing? (It is necessary to create jobs, we hear, and to create purchasing power so that there will be a market for all that economic product. And these jobs—will they be devoted to ennobling activities such as fostering wholesome human development, beautifying the environment, caring for the natural world, promoting virtue? Well, no, we are told, that sort of thing tends to be a drain on the economy, because those things are performed in the public sector and supported by taxes. The created jobs will produce goods and services for the marketplace—products like computer games, and anti-aircraft missiles, and services to financial speculators, and adult toys for the "leisure industry," and . . . Does that really make sense?)

• Economic production is taken to be the primary basis for the individual's relating to society. The overwhelming portion of recognized social roles involve having a job in the production economy, being married to someone who has a job, or training to get a job. With modern means of industrial production, many jobs have ceased to be meaningful and satisfying. Furthermore, as planetary limits to further material growth are approached, and as economic rationality pushes for further automation and robotization of production, the number of jobs will increasingly fall short of the number who want them. Does it really make sense at this point to engage in frenzied activities to *increase consumption*? Is it really necessary to keep economic production and consumption at such levels as to assure that practically everyone can have a job in the mainstream economy? Or is it possible to think of other ways in which people can have meaningful lives and satisfying roles in society?

• Regrettable as it may seem, U.S. society, we are told, can no longer afford really good education for every child. It can no longer afford to protect citizens on city streets at night, nor to ensure that every citizen has access to some kind of decent shelter from the elements, nor to provide needed health care. On the other hand, extravagant packaging and advertising, wasteful consumption, unnecessary transportation all add to the GNP—that is, they are "good" for the economy. The tendencies in Europe and Japan may be less pronounced, but they are similar. Does that all really make sense?

• Is it really true that nothing can be done about the recent tendency of business to take a very short-term view, essentially discounting the future and focusing on the near-term financial performance? (Many years ago, before the ethic changed, there was a tradition that the farmer should leave the land to the next generation *better* than he found it. Such sentimental notions fly in the face of "sound" financial management, which puts the emphasis on next quarter's bottom line.) To what extent is this tendency rooted in the concepts of absentee ownership and equity holding as speculation?

• In the days of the Holy Roman Empire the Church, as the dominant institution in society, took major responsibility for the well-being of the whole. Business is the dominant institution in modern society; does it need to accept a similar responsibility?

• What is the future of the populous and impoverished countries of the South, or Third World? Is it to become a mass-consumption society like the United States? Is it to remain poor, hungry, and politically marginal? Is it to adopt some socialist form of government because capitalism isn't working for them?

• It has been calculated that with modern food production and distribution systems the food on your table ends up representing many times more fossil fuel energy (in the form of fertilizer, tractor fuel, packaging, freezing and thawing, long-distance hauling, etc.) than solar energy. In the long run this is certainly ecologically foolish; is it really true that it is nevertheless "economically sound"?

• The dwellers in this society are proud of its being a society of "abundance." Yet we can't help noticing that this abundance and affluence have brought about new forms of *scarcity*—scarcity of natural resources, of fresh air and water, of arable land, of the waste-absorbing capacities of the natural environment, of resilience of the planet's life-support systems, of spirit-renewing wilderness. These are partly a consequence of consumption levels and the kinds of technology used. The "new scarcities" are of course also related to population growth, especially in the South, which in ways less obvious and more subtle is also related to the impact of the spread of "modern" Western culture. Doesn't this paradox suggest a need for a fundamental shift in direction?

• Is it true that national and global security cannot be assured through military strength, as they may have been in the past? If so, what are the implications for business?

• The prevailing knowledge system in modern society, namely reductionistic science, emphasizes the ability to "control" nature. Does this not seem to be confused thinking, since human beings are so obviously an intrinsic part of nature? Is it not an even more serious matter that this powerful knowledge system which has such a powerful influence on policy and action totally ignores such matters as altruism, courage, virtue, eternal values?

Item: Clues to the Nature of the New Paradigm

Some clues as to the new *societal paradigm* come from examining the goals of social movements (environmental, peace, Green, women's, etc.) and analyses such as Fritjof Capra's, Robert Theobald's, and others. From such sources, a tentative list of characteristics follows:

• *Wholeness.* Resolution of the world's dilemmas will come only from a whole-system view. People do not behave like "economic man," and the economic system cannot be adequately considered apart from the greater society.

• *Ecological awareness.* The holistic view includes awareness of the finiteness and multiple-connectedness of the planetary ecosystem, and the inextricable interdependence of all human communities and dependence on the planetary life-support system.

• *Peace and common security.* Present "national security" policies diminish both security and well-being. The psychological climate of insecurity stemming from the nuclear arms race affects all, especially children. Resources going to the world arms races, nuclear and "conventional," are in effect stolen from the world's poor. Arms spending reduces the capability of the state to provide programs that would increase the well-being of its citizens. Thus achievement of sustainable global peace and nuclear disarmament is imperative.

• *Decentralization; human scale.* Bigness and concentration of power contribute to the feelings of alienation and depersonalization in modern society. The desire for high quality of life will require decentralization of much social and political activity, rebuilding of community, an appropriate technology (i.e., human scale, ecologically compatible, "kind" to human beings and the planet).

• *Postpatriarchal perspectives.* Sensitivity is needed to the destructive aspects of patriarchal society and masculine competitive, aggressive, exploitative values. There must be a counterbalancing of these values with feminine nurturing, cherishing, conserving, cooperative values and appreciation of the feminine perspective.

• *Trans-materialist beliefs.* The new emphasis includes self-realization, transcendent meaning, and inner growth leading to wisdom and compassion.

• *Social responsibility.* It is imperative that appropriate measures be taken to ensure that the poor and working classes will not get hurt by programs to restructure the economy and consumer society along lines that are more ecologically sound.

• *Solidarity with the Third World.* The future of the Third World is of intimate concern to the industrialized countries. As economic growth is not an adequate goal for the developed countries, so economic growth alone is not an appropriate goal for the developing world. An emerging redefinition of growth and development includes emphasis on human development and well-being, social and cultural goals, and self-reliance.

• *Steady-state population and economy.* Finiteness of the globe dictates both that world population should approach steady-state conditions and that the interaction between the total world economic activity and the earth-system should approach some kind of equilibrium. The latter will require new concepts of work and of the healthy economy, since the creation of jobs through boundless economic growth and consumption is not in the end a viable strategy.

• *Cultural pluralism.* The richness of cultural diversity is a planetary resource just as is the richness of diversity of plant and animal life. The tendency of the world industrial economy to stamp out competing cultures must be corrected.

• *Nonviolent change.* Necessary and fundamental societal change must come about through a spreading awakening. The political manifestations of this must involve nonviolent change if the change process is to be compatible with the ends desired.

• *Empowerment of people.* For the other conditions to be met, the emphasis must be not on goals but on process—on people becoming empowered to take responsibility for their own lives and for changing society as necessary. The process is an evolutionary one, and the goals are emergent. To repeat, one of the most powerful tools for change is the power of the people to withdraw legitimacy from the existing order.

3. WHAT LEADS US TO BELIEVE THAT BUSINESS HAS SUCH A SPECIAL ROLE?

As the dominant social institution on the planet, business and industry will play a key role in shaping the future of the globe, whether for good or ill. Business corporations are far more flexible and adaptive than government bureaucracies, education systems, or other institutions; the ability to respond quickly to changes in the environment is part of their very nature. Furthermore, business has attracted into its leadership positions some of the brightest and most competent persons in society.

For these three reasons, the role of business is crucial in addressing the extremely difficult times ahead. Furthermore, the dominant institution in a society needs to take a responsibility for the whole—as the Church did in the days of the Holy Roman Empire. But business has not had a tradition of taking responsibility for the whole. Thus this is a new role, not yet well understood and accepted.

It is important to grasp that this new role will not be a matter of applying old forms of hierarchical management, fiscal administration, and technological problem solving. It is genuinely new, and will require genuinely new ways of thinking, feeling, and behaving.

4. WHAT NEEDS TO BE DONE?

The nature of the transformative force is such that there is little business could do either to incite it or to quell it. The crucial issue is, if the transformative force is large and growing, what can be done to help the transition to be relatively smooth, socially nondisruptive, and non-violent? It is here that business is in a pivotal spot. The business leader is recognized as having competence to deal with such a practical matter as how to change course without running the ship aground. If he/she speaks from integrity, reflecting a sense of moral authority, and also demonstrates an understanding of whole-system aspects of the situation, the positive influence will be considerable.

The force for change will be coming both from within and from outside the organization. The business leader knows "where the lever arms are in the system," and that is knowledge that will be essential to a smooth restructuring.

If there is anything at all to the above arguments that the basic patterns of society and business are changing, the transition years just ahead are likely to be turbulent, and the "causes" given in the public press will not be the most fundamental causes.

Businesses that try to be in alignment with the emerging paradigm will be in one kind of trouble if they shift too soon; another kind of trouble if they delay too long. It will be crucial to make decisions on the basis of an accurate assessment of what is going on.

5. CAN WE DO IT?

In the emerging paradigm there is inherent a faith that the wisdom for finding the new path and following it resides within the deep inner resources of people. It involves mainly people getting in touch with their own deep sense of purpose, and following that. Taking that individual responsibility is the first step in anyone's positive contribution.

As to whether we, the people, can re-create the system—why not? People built it in the first place.

EPILOGUE:
Rebuilding the Spaceship
While It Is Still in Flight

by Michael Ray

During the last great paradigm shift, in the sixteenth and seventeenth centuries, observers characterized seemingly great undertakings in terms of the sea—the vast oceans of this planet and the ways we knew to get across them at that time. Even today, probably because the same paradigm has been dominant for the last three and a half centuries or so, we use the same imagery. For instance, people still say "rebuilding the ship while it's still at sea" to describe a change that has to occur within a government, economic system, business, or other organization while it still has to keep functioning.

But now, as a result of the worldwide transition that this book reflects, we need new metaphors—beyond ships and even beyond jet trains, supersonic airplanes and space shuttles. We are participating in a process of rebuilding this spaceship, as Buckminster Fuller called the earth, and it is moving through a change so discontinuous that it is like the acceleration of some futuristic outerspace vehicle—the jolt of hyperspace.

What is our role in rebuilding in hyperspace? What can individuals in business do? We have learned that as the dominant institution on the planet, certainly the one most responsive to change, business must take responsibility for the whole. How is this responsibility to be implemented? How can there be a continuous rebuilding that also sustains the flight? How does business interact with institutions, with other life-forms and with the ecology in which it finds itself? How can we rebuild the spaceship in hyperspace?

We can't. At least not by ourselves. And not merely by the actions of business. To believe that is possible is to participate in an ignorant arrogance. Some observers, such as Theodore Roszak, warn us about this arrogance by saying that the question is not what we are going to do for the earth, but what the earth is going to do to us. They point out that the earth has done housecleaning before—many millennia ago when the dinosaurs were eliminated from their position as the dominant species and again in the Middle Ages with the Black Plague.

Of course, it isn't as simple as this. Roszak and others point out that it is a great interaction of human actions and nature that is operating. In this context we have to live with faith in the wholeness and interconnectedness of every creature and everything on this planet. We have to both recognize our greatness and the enormous resources of creativity we have within us and, at the same time, be humbled by the power of the universal forces of nature. We have to begin to recognize the immanent spirit within us and within others, while also recognizing the transcendent spirit of the universe.

With these principles we can begin to live our own individual lives in a way that will utilize our intuition, will, joy, strength and compassion to rebuild our relationships and organizations and thus contribute to the rebuilding of our nation and the world into a new form.

Business in the new paradigm seems to be evolving as a spiritual discipline. This isn't religion. Rather, it means that each individual has a responsibility, supported by their business and economic system, to develop as fully as possible in order to serve the needs of this world in transition.

We have to act with all our business acumen with a frame of mind like that of the young woman in the following story. She was walking on a long beach that was littered with thousands of starfish, which had been left there to die by the receding tide. As she walked along, she was saving their lives by picking them up one by one and depositing them back in the ocean. An older man came along and was puzzled by what she was doing. He told her that she was wasting her time because there were so many starfish on the beach that what she was doing couldn't possibly matter. She picked up a starfish to be put back in the water and turned to the man saying, "It matters to *this* starfish."

Individuals and organizations in business acting like this woman are multiplying with a speed that matches the rapidity of the transition itself. The exemplars in this book show just that—ways of doing business that are helpful in the short run and the long run. A few years ago, we couldn't have found more than a handful of examples. Now they are becoming less the exception than the rule.

Business already has become involved collectively in reducing society's reliance on military solutions to problems, in helping to improve educational systems and in dealing with problems of poverty, conflict, and the environment.

But business is always going to be the root of the problems until the underlying fundamental assumptions and systems for doing it are totally changed. This book has indicated that much of this work already has started. We have begun to rebuild our spaceship while it is in flight, but we must continue to fly our organizations while moving them and our economic systems toward more humane, sustainable and systematically integrated forms.

The emerging paradigm is going to include some synergistic combination of ancient spiritual wisdom and modern science. Just as scientific discoveries mirror what ancient wisdom has told us for millennia, ancient wisdom is becoming something of a context for our actions. The Native American call for decisions to be based on their effects on seven generations in the future is only one example.

Another is implied by the graphs in the scientifically based Chapter 26 by George Land and Beth Jarman. If you look at these graphs casually, you'll see just the smooth S-shape constituting the three phases of their model. But if you look closer, you'll see that this curve is merely the result of smoothing some very erratic up and down squiggles. These sharp waves reach something of a crescendo during the breakpoint period, while phase three is being supplanted by a new curve and a new first phase.

This shows graphically what we all experience in this time of transition. What works one day doesn't work the next. Something that seems to be a success turns out to be a failure. People and markets shift wildly in the short term. With the spaceship moving so quickly, it is hard to stay with any strategy unless you have faith in what you are doing. You need to see things from a wider perspective so that the contradictions can be understood. This is where discipline must prevail; this is where the persistence in action of business people really can be of value.

Even the new phase at breakpoint goes down at first before it begins to pay dividends and turn up. Many business people find that new approaches, like a new golf grip or dance step, take a little while to begin to work. The same is true as we begin to recreate our way of doing business and serving the world. Unless we have a faith that springs from a deep inner understanding for our actions, we will find it difficult to persist through these challenging times.

We must practice integrity in everything we do. In India a story is told about a couple whose young son was obsessed with sugar. His parents tried all the modern medical and psychological approaches to help him cut down on his consumption of sugar, but there seemed to be nothing they could do. No matter how much they tried to keep him away from sugar-based food and sugarcane, he still got to it. His health was deteriorating.

Now this couple was very modern, they thought, in their outlook on life. They always wanted to avail themselves of the best scientific methods, rather than the traditional Indian approaches. But none of the scientific methods had worked. So when they were told that a wise man who lived near their town might be able to help, they reluctantly brought the boy to him to seek advice.

They approached the sage with all the respect they could muster, told him of their problem and asked for whatever help he could give them. He listened intently and asked that they bring the boy back to him in exactly two weeks.

When they returned to the sage after two more weeks of the boy's overconsumption of sugar, the wise man asked them to bring the boy up to him. The sage held the youngster firmly by the shoulders and shook him as he repeated, "Don't eat too much sugar!" over and over again.

After that the boy miraculously stopped eating too much sugar. This both delighted and puzzled the parents. If the sage could have this dramatic effect, why did he wait two weeks? Why didn't he give his magical treatment right away?

When they asked him, his answer was simple. "First," he said, "*I* had to stop eating too much sugar."

Such can be the power of integrity in business and service in this time of transition toward the new paradigm.

PERMISSIONS

I. The Roots of Present Change

1. "The Breakdown of the Old Paradigm" by Willis Harman and John Hormann. From their book *Creative Work*, an Institute of Noetic Sciences Publication, published by Knowledge Systems, Inc., Indianapolis, IN. Copyright © 1990 by the Schweisfurth Foundation. Used by permission.

2. "The Transformation of Values and Vocation" by Marilyn Ferguson. From her book *The Aquarian Conspiracy*, published by Jeremy P. Tarcher, Inc., Los Angeles. Copyright © 1980 by Marilyn Ferguson. Used by permission.

3. "Redefinitions of Corporate Wealth" by Herman Bryant Maynard, Jr., and Susan E. Mehrtens. Adapted from a chapter in the book *The Fourth Wave: Business in the Twenty-first Century*, published by Berrett-Koehler Publishers, San Francisco. Copyright © 1993 by Herman B. Maynard Jr. and Susan E. Mehrtens. Used by Permission.

4. "Escaping the Career Culture" by Susan Albert. From her book *Work of Her Own*, published by Jeremy P. Tarcher, Inc., Los Angeles. Copyright © 1992 by Susan Albert. Used by permission.

5. "Competition, Cooperation and Co-creation: Insights from the World Business Academy" by Cynthia Joba, Herman Maynard, Jr., and Michael Ray. Copyright © 1992 by the World Business Academy. Used by permission.

6. "Labor as Trash" by Michael Phillips. From his book *Mental Snacks*, published by Clear Glass Publishing, San Francisco. Copyright © 1987 by Michael Phillips. Used by permission.

II. The Beginning of New Leadership

7. "A New Kind of Company with a New Kind of Thinking" by Rolf Osterberg. Reprinted from *Perspectives*, September 1987. Copyright © 1987 by the World Business Academy. Used by permission.

III. Organizational Transformation

18. "The Question of Employee Ownership," including "Employee Ownership, A Personal View" by Rolf V. Osterberg, reprinted from *Perspectives*, March 1989, copyright © 1989 by the World Business Academy, used by permission; "Lessons from an Employee Owned Business" by Tamas Makray, reprinted from *Perspectives*, July 1989, copyright © 1989 by the World Business Academy, used by permission; and "How to Make the Psychological Shift Necessary for Employee Ownership to Be Successful" by Terry Mollner, reprinted from *Perspectives*, Winter 1991, copyright © 1991 by the World Business Academy. Used by permission.

IV. Social and Environmental Responsibility

19. "Capitalism at Its Best" by Marjorie Kelly. Reprinted from *Business Ethics* Magazine, July/August 1990. Copyright © 1990 by *Business Ethics* Magazine, Chaska MN. Used by permission.
20. "Michael Novak: The Theologian of Capitalism" by Marjorie Kelly. Reprinted from *Business Ethics* Magazine, Summer 1989. Copyright © 1989 by *Business Ethics* Magazine, Chaska, MN. Used by permission.
21. "The Five Stages of Corporate Moral Development" by Linda Starke. Reprinted from *Business Ethics* Magazine, November/December 1989. Copyright © 1989 by *Business Ethics* Magazine, Chaska MN. Used by permission.
22. "The Corporation as a Just Society" by David W. Ewing. Reprinted from *Business Ethics* Magazine, March/April 1990. Adopted with permission from "Justice on the Job: Resolving Grievances in the Nonunion Workplace" by David W. Ewing. Published by Harvard Business School Press, Boston. Copyright © 1989 by the President and Fellows of Harvard College. Used by permission.
23. "The Shifting Paradigm of Environmental Management" by Suzanne Gauntlett. Copyright © 1992 by Suzanne Gauntlett. Used by permission.

V. Visions of the Future

24. "A Systems Approach to the Emerging Paradigm" by Fritjof Capra. Reprinted from *Perspectives*, Winter 1991. Copyright © 1990 by Fritjof Capra. Used by permission.

25. "Evolution and Business" by Gary Zukav. Copyright © 1992 by Gary Zukav. Used by permission.

26. "Moving Beyond Breakpoint" by George Land and Beth Jarman. From their book *Breakpoint and Beyond*, published by Harper-Collins Publishers, New York. Copyright © 1992 by George Land and Beth Jarman. Used by permission.

27. "The Age of Light" by Hazel Henderson. From her book *Paradigms in Progress*, published by Knowledge Systems, Inc., Indianapolis IN. Copyright © 1991 by Hazel Henderson. Used by permission.

28. "Foundation for a New World Order" by Riane Eisler. Reprinted from *Perspectives*, Summer 1991. Copyright © 1991 by the World Business Academy. Used by permission.

29. "Approaching the Millennium: Business as Vehicle for Global Transformation" by Willis Harman. Copyright © by the World Business Academy. Used by permission.

ABOUT THE EDITORS

Michael Ray, Ph.D., is the first John G. McCoy–Banc One Corporation Professor of Creativity and Innovation and of Marketing at Stanford University, where he developed the course New Paradigm Business. His co-authored books *Creativity in Business* and *The Path of the Everyday Hero* are based on his Stanford creativity course. He co-authored the companion book for the PBS series "The Creative Spirit." Michael Ray is a Fellow of the World Business Academy and lives in Santa Cruz, California.

Alan Rinzler has been an editor and publisher at Bantam Books, Simon & Schuster, and *Rolling Stone* magazine. His own published work includes *Youth Manifesto*, *Bob Dylan: The Musical Record*, and *Without Force or Lies*. He lives in Berkeley, California, where he is also a practicing psychotherapist.

THE WORLD BUSINESS ACADEMY

The World Business Academy emerged in 1987 from a series of private meetings held among a small group of business leaders and futurists over an eighteen-month period at SRI International (formerly Stanford Research Institute). The sessions were catalyzed by an awareness that a tidal wave of change was forecasted to wash over the international business community, and the entire globe, with unprecedented force. The goal of those meetings was to examine the essential nature of those changes and to begin the ongoing process of internal dialogue exploring the force of the change and how it could be shaped so as to maximize the possibility that a positive, sustainable society could evolve with a minimum of transition difficulty. That dialogue continues to this day at the international, regional and local meetings, conferences and retreats the Academy holds in various locales around the world.

For further information, please contact:
World Business Academy
433 Airport Boulevard
Suite 416
Burlingame, CA 94010
(415) 342-2387